GERMAINE DE STAËL

GERMAINE DE STAËL

Crossing the Borders

Edited by
MADELYN GUTWIRTH,
AVRIEL GOLDBERGER,
and
KARYNA SZMURLO

RUTGERS UNIVERSITY PRESS
New Brunswick, New Jersey

Library of Congress Cataloging-in-Publication Data

Germaine de Staël : crossing the borders / edited by Madelyn Gutwirth,
Avriel Goldberger, Karyna Szmurlo.
     p.   cm.
   Includes bibliographical references and index.
   ISBN 0-8135-1636-6
   1. Staël, Madame de (Anne-Louise-Germaine), 1766–1817—Criticism
and interpretation. I. Gutwirth, Madelyn. II. Goldberger, Avriel
H. III. Szmurlo, Karyna.
   PQ2431.Z5G47   1991
   848'.609—dc20

                                                      90-42141
                                                         CIP

British Cataloging-in-Publication available

CONTENTS

ARTICULATIONS OF INWARDNESS

TRANSGRESSING GENDER AND GENRE

TOPOGRAPHICAL SURVEYS

CONTENTS

PREFACE

Germaine de Staël interests us, now that we have mastered the arts of
ambiguity, in that she disquiets us. But there has never been a time,
since she came to public attention as the wonder child of her mother
Suzanne Necker, when she was not disquieting to those around her, or
to posterity, either. Born to the most eminent *nouveau riche* couple in
France, the bourgeois Genevan-born Protestants Jacques Necker and
Suzanne Curchod, she was already potentially disturbing, in the latter
days of Louis XVI's reign, by virtue of her unwonted social prominence and wealth. Her father had used the leverage provided by the
large fortune he had amassed in banking to achieve high station, ending up as chief minister to Louis on the eve of Revolution. Money
propelled the Neckers into the center of events. Indeed, it was Jacques
Necker's dismissal by the king in July of 1789 that occasioned the
storming of the Bastille. Simply the fact of being Necker's only child
would have made her the object of public curiosity: but this derived
status was hugely augmented by Suzanne Necker's decision to raise
Germaine "like Emile, not like Sophie." This meant that she intended
to develop the independence of judgment Rousseau in his *Emile* had
prescribed be cultivated in boy children, rather than the compliance of
character he had recommended to girls. By taking her daughter into
the literary salon to sit alongside her from childhood, Germaine's mother
fostered the girl's ability to learn and speak in a public forum among

an august company of highly intelligent adults, who were pleased to grant her own wit recognition and praise. This, then, is the first disquieting picture: the spoiled female brat of a pair of rich *parvenus*.

Instead of modulating this maturing, already none-too-welcome voice of hers, Staël went on insisting that it be heard: she married the Swedish ambassador, Eric-Magnus de Staël-Holstein, chiefly so that she could remain in Paris where her language and activity had meaning for her. And despite the vicissitudes of Revolution and exile, children and lovers, she continued to fight to be heard, if not in the Paris salon she strove endlessly to recreate (and did create against her will in gilded exile in the Swiss lakeside retreat of Coppet), then in her writings. "L'art d'écrire est aussi une arme," she wrote ("The art of writing too is a weapon"). And so she disquieted then, disquiets even now as a woman with an insistent voice. She has always been "noisy," for a woman: an interferer in politics; an interloper in art.

What is more, her choice of partners, of romantic attachments, was anything but discreet. A nobleman reputed to be Louis XV's illegitimate son (Narbonne), a Swedish regicide (Ribbing), and a brilliant but impecunious Swiss (Constant) played the main roles, but there were other attachments, some deep, some fleeting. Staël disquieted through her exercise of sexual mobility and affective freedom in a period progressively closing against it, especially as lived by women: that era of deep moral reproof of women's sexuality decreed that a woman such as she could be viewed only with distaste.

Finally, Staël disquieted in challenging power—not just any power, but that of the Emperor Napoleon himself, who had seen fit to maintain her in exile. As a woman challenging power, she created disturbance at both ends of the political spectrum. Idolized by elated opponents of Bonaparte, like the young Lamartine, she was detested by the emperor, by his entourage, by all the toadies of the time, and by the Napoleonic fellowship of cult followers that survived his lifetime. A woman challenging power, for like-minded Bonapartists, was a being counter-natural, even obscene, as Napoleon's own allegation that Staël had unnaturally formed male genitals attests. Female brat, clamorous sexual woman prancing about unseemly on her steed of principle: "Who did she think she was?" This was the question blocking the way to her texts.

Writing against the repressive tide—such was Staël's career. Now, after nearly two centuries of reading her, not always unfavorably, but nearly always through a screen of moralism, we suddenly seem able to read her with infinitely greater nuance. We perceive her person and her work as a site of conflict, neither static nor revolutionary in any facile sense, but full of edifying contradictions that able hermeneuts such as Charlotte Hogsett, Marie-Claire Vallois, Nancy Miller, and Carla Peterson have unearthed. An unreconstructed exponent of Enlightenment, she might serve afresh as butt for the Enlightenment-bashing of modern philosophers, if they but knew her. Instead her historical work and political theory have been renewed by the revival in France of interst in that generous liberalism of hers that posits an ecological purview (asking, for instance, that experimental science embrace a global perspective as it pursues avenues of research), as well as in her fervently sustained opposition to tyranny and devotion to representative government in a time that mocked it.

Even more, Staël speaks to the still unresolved conundrum of women's aspiration. Fictions from her pen plot the degree of entrapment of will and heart subduing women's powers. Her own "foreignness" to the political, social, and personal order in which she found herself forced her to traverse geographic frontiers, at first unwillingly, finally triumphantly. As to the received ideas concerning the borders framing female personhood, even as at moments she self-castigatingly verbalizes their propriety, she either presses insistently against them or, in her fictional personae, simply ignores them as she searches for other, more adequate contours of female being. The disquiet Staël now creates no longer produces a predetermined reaction, numbing all commentary; rather it impels us to the spirited, dynamic response her texts have always awaited. We seek clues to the disturbing riddle of her extremes of submissiveness—her filial piety, her slavishness in love—on the one side, her megalomanias on the other. Both now take on the appearance of tactics of survival rather than blemishes. Looking elsewhere in her eighteen volumes of writing in all the genres, we grasp her importance as a woman writing her way into fuller meaning, in historical terms as well as personal ones. Aware, but admitting it only intermittently in an era that forbade such discourse, that women suffered from irrational hatred like that so lavishly directed against the queen she defended, that women were as pariahs in society, and that the Revolution she had espoused had meant only loss for women, her own discourse in a sense went underground. It lies there for us now to disinter and mine as part of our own ground, the ground of women's seizure of their share of the terrain of culture. Wresting for herself the universal voice men thought they alone had warrant to use, Staël sought to speak for humankind; yet, in doing so, she never doubted that hers was a woman's voice. With its new listeners, better attuned, that voice is in exile no longer.

Madelyn Gutwirth

GERMAINE DE STAËL

INTRODUCTION

The dynamics of the will to transcedence in Staël's writings and the phenomenon of spacialization that characterizes them are the specific concerns giving rise to this volume. Geo-graphics infiltrate the titles and tables of contents of her work, illustrating how deeply her thought organized itself around ideas of wanderings, passages, crossings, and transgressions. This corpus of the voyage, governed by a metonymic logic of spatial contiguity, also functions as a metaphoric index: that is, the "denoted space" engenders the "connoted space" of desire.[1] The landscape in *On Germany* projects the mind of the "poetic and philosophical traveler" slowly progressing toward the mystery of a nation's creativity, and *Ten Years of Exile* subverts a melancholic journey of flight across the plains of Poland and Russia into victory.[2] As for the great novels, they can be classified as fictions of transgressed boundaries par excellence. *Delphine* is picaresque in its proliferation of milieux accessible to the heroine; whereas in *Corinne, or Italy*, a desire for expansiveness builds—as an architekton—a defense against failure and fatality, a sublimated maternal sphere of regeneration, wherein horizontal expansion parallels a descent into archetypal depths. The literature of "spatial constrictions" that Gilbert and Gubar find so typical of women is thus replaced in the Staëlian context by a persistent pursuit of openness. "From Ann Radcliffe's melodramatic dungeons to Jane Austen's mirrored parlors, from Charlotte Brontë's haunted garrets to Emily Brontë's coffin-shaped beds, imagery of enclosure reflects the woman writer's own discomfort, her sense of powerlessness, her fear that she inhabits alien and incomprehensible places."[3] Staël's work, on the contrary, abounds in what Gaston Bachelard calls "the reverie of the Earth," and in elements of a phenomenology of the "ex–." A literally cosmic vertigo results from the need "to wander freely through the spheres without belonging to any country," and "to exist beyond oneself to such a degree that one may entertain illusions about life's limits in time and space, and to see in the self metaphysical attributes of the infinite."[4]

In short, Staëlian difference is articulated in terms of a topos of distance and divergence. Canonical criticism has experienced this phenomenon as the disturbing decentralization and nonconformity of an "undisciplined *métèque*."[5] Those newer critical analyses which emphasize that the coming into writing may be effected through acts of "crossing over" have viewed it, however, as the generative moment of feminine inscription. Whatever their diversity, all of Staël's textual displacements are characterized by the process of "working through," by which a feminine counter-discourse breaks free from another discourse and strives to define its own sphere against a felt resistance. According to Lucia Omacini, Staël's theoretical texts are constructed on the basis of an "evicted" literature which "evolves by fits and starts, seeking an impossible harmony, [torn between] a desire for self-affirmation and an act of submission to the Norm."[6] From the same perspective, the elaboration of fiction seems to be a perpetual temptation by the forbidden, and is achieved, as Marie-Claire Vallois has convincingly demonstrated, in vacillation between desire and denial.[7] If one considers Nancy Miller's recent analysis of *Corinne* as a battle of gazes, or the concurrence of the "productive" mimesis and the mimesis of adequation which constantly threatens and absorbs it, Staël's writing becomes an exceptional locus of tension. Quoting Cixous's feminist manifesto in a Staëlian context, Miller insists that in *Corinne* "the very possibility of change" may be detected, "the space that can serve as a springboard for subversive thought, the precursory movement of a transformation of social and cultural structure."[8]

Seen in the work as a whole, this figure of emancipation takes on even more powerful resonances. Yet to understand it solely as a refusal of feminine incarceration would be to limit Staël's quest for the potential of the human mind and her contribution to the history of progress.

A pragmatist of movement, she formulates an entire ethics of confrontation as a driving and constructive force. Furthermore, she theorizes a dialectics "of resignation and will," finitude and expansion, as the universal principle upon which all accomplishments are based (*On Germany* 5:76).[9] Physical laws reappear in moral life, where the unending action-reaction "of internal power against outside circumstances, and of external circumstances against this power is the measure of man's true grandeur" (*Complete Works* 3:347). The same horizontal/vertical movement gains in dynamics in the concept of cosmopolitanism, for according to this definition, emancipation is possible within the multinational context through an interdependence of diversities which are best illustrated in the practices of the Group of Coppet. A fluctuating conglomerate of emigrants, an apparently exclusive and isolated group, actively fought oppressive government and influenced all of Europe. "This international salon, symbol of the desire to transcend space, fanned the flame of love to such an extent that this fire seemed to reappear in all its emanations in the guise of courage ready to brave the impossible."[10] After two hundred years of rethinking, this ideology, built not upon coercion but on mutually supportive yet antagonistic principles, remains an inspiration for us; we still recognize in its philosophical tone—bearing irrevocably the marks of the Revolution—the reality of our own modernity.

The essays brought together in this volume reflect various interpretive styles of three generations of European and American Staëlians: from historical and thematic to psychoanalytic, from semiotic to political and feminist, from textual to willingly interdisciplinary. Despite their methodological diversity, these texts have a common denominator in their pursuit of Staël's energy of assertion, which reveals itself most clearly in the interplay between never-fulfilled structures and in all sorts of "spaces" wherein hope is inscribed. The opening section, "History and the Imaginary," takes as its framework the Revolution of 1789, and uses the paradigm of simultaneous acceptance and refusal of the past to show the Staëlian reinvention of time. Michel Delon locates this process in the intertwining of the factual and the fictional in the *Considerations*, where hypotheses and variations of desire are superimposed upon faits accomplis. First Staël attempts "to hold together a philosophy of history and the management of the everyday, to bring a human spirit into accord with mankind as it is." She patiently demonstrates the paradoxical aspect of the Revolution: logical in relation to overall progress, yet contradictory of all logic in compromising itself through bloody instances of irrationality. In her next move, she frees herself from despondency over the atrocities of the Revolution by progressively distancing herself from them, going beyond the events. In the process of "consideration," a sign of anticipatory displacement appears: the proliferation of the conditional tense. This metaphoric mode of desire facilitates exploration of a temporality in which the Revolution would have been only a mutation without carnage, in which Louis XVI, Napoleon, or even Necker—their portraits redrawn and sublimated—would not have missed their rendezvous with history. It is in the provisional production of meaning, or in what Paul de Man and Jean Starobinski have spoken of as the contamination of the non-rhetorical by the rhetorical in Rousseau's work which destroys its claims to historicity, that Delon locates the modernity of Staël as a historian.[11] The interplay between what was irrevocable in reality and what was possible brings into question both the permanence of patriarchal constructions and the naturalization of monolithic institutions; furthermore it "opens space for militant action for work of signification that escapes both the absurd and all established dogmas of meaning." On the other hand, the illusory dimension of reality, created by the eruption of theatrical metaphors in the transcription of historical events, as Delon insists in his earlier work, suggests that the frontiers between history and fiction constantly challenge each other; their notorious complementarity reveals an activist thought that counters the finite and dilates the monumentality of History, which becomes less tragically determined.[12]

The same phenomenon of infiltration, presented this time in the context of a paternal/maternal discourse, is the subject of the diptych of essays by Charlotte Hogsett and Eve Sourian. Both in *Delphine* and in the *Considerations*, a linguistic/ideological intrusion is achieved literally through the conquest of textual space in the parental discourse, since, as Hogsett justly points out, Staël "had to find ways of moving it aside in order to make way for her own writing." The writer enters that discourse as a "thief of language," to use Claudine Herrmann's terms, not to appropriate the words of the other, but rather to exist there in a dialogical relationship. By placing as epigraph to *Delphine* a statement on the submission of women borrowed directly from Mme Necker, Staël implicitly questions its validity. In a remarkable reconstruction of maternal ideology, this novel of social confrontation takes up her mother Suzanne Curchod's conservative admonitions in order to impregnate them with liberal ideas on divorce, morals, religion, or the role of women, disseminated in revolutionary circles. Whereas Sourian reads the novel as a literary act of matricide (ideological and formal) freeing the daughter from "the anxiety of influence," Hogsett emphasizes her seizure of power within the father's theoretical discourse. Staël may begin the *Considerations* with the apologetic intention of transcribing Necker's work; however, she concludes by inscribing herself and establishing her own reputation as a writer. Paternal discourse shades off, refracted and fragmented in the daughter's interpretations as she exposes her own political competence. In the light of Foucault's view of power and knowledge as mutually guaranteeing and validating, Staël's writings would aim to remedy the inadequacy of this relation and to restore a balance not achieved in real life. From this point of view, the use of the conditional, already discussed by Delon, takes on a new dimension in Hogsett's interpretation, where it is seen as a manifestation of the desire for concrete action blocked in the past, but which is projected into the future: "Staël seems to move into still another conditional tense—what would have happened if *she* had had the opportunities afforded her father." While indicating a change of pronominal rather than verbal order, in which the he/I, him/me relationship is modified, this grammatical mode indicates a direct hold on life, the insertion of the self into the evolution of linear Time.

Feminine expansiveness courts repression. The second section of this volume, "Articulations of Inwardness," demonstrates the close relationship between silence and self-referentiality, but with a twist. Symptoms of weakness (aphasia, philters, suicide, or ruins) in their reversible connotations become organized into a strategy of assertion, into discursive means of aesthetic and political affirmation.

In this context, we recall how dramatically the disparity between the desire to "realize oneself" through speech and the failure of communication is felt by Staël. A disciple of Humboldt, she believed that words/ signatures *ergon*, make *energeia* burst forth: that is the vital intensity of all speaking subjects. This "myth of veracity," whereby speech is identified with its object, where "I speak" means "I am," implies specific semantic regroupings. Transparency functions here as a synonym for freedom, whereas the invisibility inseparable from the vertigo of insecurity is identified with a loss of *maîtrise* in the Hegelian sense of the term.[13] This is why Staël always longed for Rousseau's lyrical outpourings, whose intimacy was forbidden to her; in addition to the gender difference, they lived in two different moments of history, and Staël experienced the Terror and the threat of silence under Napoleonic despotic censorship. Frank Bowman's essay registers this throbbing fear. Repeatedly, the effort to communicate aborts on three levels: first because of repressive consequences, second for lack of signs adequate to the real intensity of the felt emotions; and finally, and paradoxically, through its very effectiveness, since once attained, transparency can only accelerate tragedy. The abundance and diversity of the examples chosen simply accentuate the homogeneity of the trauma. Bowman's enumeration of aphasic situations in which protagonists suffering from pulmonary complications lose their voices, or die before avowing their desires, is followed by a catalogue of discursive obstacles that degrade the natural power of words: among them irony, sophism, public opinion, calumny, lies, and excesses of power. The obsessive return, emphasized by the practice of indexing and *accumulatio*, seems to anticipate the effectiveness of figures of indirectness progressively acquiring the *pharmakon*'s reversibility. Even as it dramatizes Staël's fear of submersion, this methodological approach announces the active presence of the desire that seeks oblique paths of transcendence that eliminate the voice.

In the essays of Margaret Higonnet and Marie-Claire Vallois, allegories of absence—suicide and ruins—bear the imprint of the invading feminine. From an aesthetic perspective, suffering can be retraced in the imagery of the body as a funerary monument inscribing itself through a synecdoche of death and the mutilated space of ruins. What is more, visualization of the feminine drama acquires, from an ideological point of view, the force of a revolutionary exclamation point reactualizing life and creating a temporal perspective. Higonnet, reinterpreting Jean Starobinski's thesis on suicide as the lovers' manipulation, gives this act the new meaning of a "self-construction." Voluntary death, the consequence of social dissatisfaction, retains the symbolic structure of a violation/dismemberment of the past: "Fragmentation by breaking an order that is illusory forces us to look elsewhere and permits creative reinterpretation." The same anticipatory element can be found in the parable of ruins in *Corinne, or Italy* in which the Woman-Country-Legend relationship is a pivotal element. Comparing this romanesque travelogue to Chateaubriand's lofty prose, Vallois detects a remarkable visionary anthropomorphism rather than

6

an apologia of the past and alterity. The Staëlian ruins take on a dynamic charge, becoming palpable, literally resonant monuments, "the place of a renascence, of a re-birth of the self to the self, through the mediation of the voice." A defensive construction par excellence, this broken-up space is the locus of transmission for voice-power and for coming to creativity.

This entire novel, however, may be read as a palimpsest where another text, one that is indirect, in ruins, half-effaced, waits to be brought to light. *Corinne, or Italy*, published just as the authority of female writers went into decline, was attacked by critics as the ultimate example of the weakness of a genre "poised between the Scylla and Charybdis of impropriety and implausibility."[14] Condemned to marginality because of its de-concentrating and de-concerting of masculine models, it seemed a void in the history of the genre. Through recent feminist rereadings which strive to make the lack signify, to "see meaning in what has previously been empty space," the text of *Corinne*, revolutionary in its very inadequacies, has become a "mise-en-abyme of the 150 years of the French novel's history."[15] Whether one cites the absorption of linear intrigue by voluminous touristic descriptions, or the descriptive weakness in general, or the failure of voice in "spontaneous" improvisations, the accusative modes of the travelogue reveal in each instance the dispersion of the feminine subject exiled from the patriarchal order and genre. The abortive outcome of the inscription project proves the impossibility of the transition from "coming to voice" to "coming to writing," to actually legitimizing the authority of female authorship. In other words, old structures open up to what was formerly compressed, reincorporating the uncontrollable and invasive new-and-different, coded as feminine.

The essays in the section "Transgressing Gender and Genre" pursue the exfoliation of submerged meanings, this time concentrating on the eruption of transforming energies within fictional structures, on the subversive mechanisms of displacement from the "inside," which bursts open old moulds with new contents. Ellen Peel's essay stresses the ambivalence of the writing process within and against male tradition, calling into question the oblique means employed in *Corinne*, previously valorized by Higonnet and Vallois. Peel argues that an excess of indirect maneuvers symptomatic of patriarchal transcendence (delegated voice, "ventriloquism," letters, or absence) invades and nullifies the spontaneous forms of feminine affirmation; however, it is in this apparent turning from improvisation to silence, in this descent toward mutism (or plausibility), that the novel takes on all the brilliance of its accusation, because Staël "is using mediated, patriarchal means to reach feminist goals." In this process, similar to *"pèrodie,"* adaptation is linked to parricide, and borrowing to destruction.[16] The mediating means not only help seduce, manipulate, and obsess in order to assure the heroine's metaphorical survival, but they also function as effective catalysts for the "hostile substance," for the feminine rage that is compared to the sorceress' laughter, to the volcano's subterranean power, and "the pain of the witches' struggle to help the terrifying female powers of the night, moon, and earth express themselves."

The threatening power of feminine authority is further amplified in the two readings of the novel which take it to be a provocative challenge to Napoleonic imperialism. Making use of an interpretative fusion of Marxist criticism and neoclassical allegorism, Doris Y. Kadish reveals in the binary nature of the sentimental plot the fate of the Republic torn between two opposite forces: that of the Revolution in its most positive light and that of reaction. Simultaneously, Corinne—goddess of liberty, surrounded by an excessive allegorical apparatus—is perceived in a series of equivalents as the Republic, Italia-Matria, and the pacifist feminine counterpart of the King-Father. In response to the actual coronation, all these figures of feminine power in aesthetic ascension reinforce each other to dethrone and replace the authority of the Emperor.

Through the reading of both texts and iconography of the time, Joan DeJean continues the analysis of revisionism in *Corinne* by studying its reworking of the earlier Sapphic tradition. Even though the Ovidian model had been enriched by conjunction with political elements from the French tradition (Barthélemy) and the Italian tradition in which masculinity is deified (Verri), Staël energetically corrects her male precursors. Verri's work, put to great use by the Emperor's propagandists, was a "proto-fascist iconography of the male body . . . as a well-oiled machine for the domination of all forces that threaten, in Verri's terms, 'the peace of the soul.'" Joined with the representation of feminine suicide in Baron Gros's painting *Sapho au cap Leucade*, it provoked violent resistance from *Corinne*'s author. Responding to the order to remain silent, Staël "reinstates, literally with a vengeance, the writer in the Sapphic plot," first by putting the female generator of literary posterity into the center of the novel, and then by politicizing Sapphic inspiration and language. Through the intensity of songs/improvisations that seduce, divert, or put conquerors to sleep, the novel indicates the origin and permanence of the "hostile substance" that Peel in her essay on indirectness has also seen. According to DeJean, the somber ecstasy of Gérard's painting *Corinne au cap Misène* curiously intersects with the conclusion of the novel in which the ghost of *phobeitai* reappears in the song of the bard returning each year to (en)chant beside the patriarchal tomb.

Staël's metaphorical concepts of the feminine as political constructions, despite being inseparable from the fictional framework, did not remain inevitably discursive. Going far beyond symbolic and aesthetic valorization, they became stimuli to transformative action for the next generation of women: Margaret Fuller, Elizabeth Barrett Browning, Anna Jameson, Princess Belgioioso, and a number of others. In an analogous development, Staël's theoretical discourse underwent transformation on an international scale. The section of this volume called "Topographical Surveys" reveals this process of textual and ideological engendering. In his discussion of the reception of *On Germany* in America and its impact on the formation of an American identity and national literature, Kurt Mueller-Vollmer is specifically interested in demonstrating the reciprocal relations between doctrinal and rhetorical (internal to the text) transmutations. First of all, the Staëlian text mediates European romanticism and awakens the Transcendentalists' curiosity through its affinities with their own interests. Second, it serves as a practical model for a critical discourse. The genesis of this discourse in Staël and Emerson, juxtaposed with the gestation of a national literature, demonstrates the same dynamic of "coming-to-the-fore," the same element of "de-constitution and re-constitution." Using several examples of Staëlian intertextuality, Mueller-Vollmer retraces the patient translation/naturalization of Novalis that serves as a basis for Staël's Urtext. This alchemical method, together with a distinctive "reworking" pattern, influences the formative process of Emerson's prose to such an extent that his *Nature* "must be treated as forming part of a literary province within the discourse of European romanticism." In a broader perspective, *On Germany* provides the hermetic basis for the Transcendentalists, who will go on to create their own aesthetic program using the conceptual framework of Staël's discourse.

This creative pattern has the same qualifying value as do the revisionist displacements in the tradition of genres or strategies of intrusion into parental discourse, or even self-insertion into the "nonrhetorical" text of history. Yet, in a multinational context, it carries its real effectiveness even further to become an exemplum of emancipation and a verification of power. Staël's immense contribution in this realm has never been properly documented by positivist criticism, which, restricted by its own normative standards, allowed the extraordinary nourishing potential of *On Germany* to pass unnoticed. Mueller-Vollmer's essay corrects this oversight by demonstrating the phases of the work's reception, the ways in which it was disseminated, and especially the imposing orbit of intellectuals influenced by this "new cultural program and ideology that was aimed at developing a distinctively American identity while at the same time absorbing from and critically distancing themselves from European models."

Each of the shorter essays in this section, grouped under the rubric of "Frontiers," scrutinizes a boundary: Staël as pioneer exemplar of the liberal political woman; Staël as historian of Revolution; Staël and the frontier of self-destruction; Staël as a romantic recalcitrant to definition; Corinne's paradoxes of heroism; Corinne for and against patriarchy. This plurality of approaches scans Staël's problematic of allegiance—to genres, to literary movements, to literary structures, to history. They plot her strategies for crossing borders, for managing to belong in spite of exile and of border guards, or as she used to say herself, "not by following the rules, but in any way possible."

This entire volume boldly invites expanded reconceptualization of a body of texts charting a terrain that contemporary modes of interpretation have revealed to provide rich grounds for future readings.

Karyna Szmurlo

HISTORY AND THE IMAGINARY

STAËL AND LIBERTY: AN OVERVIEW

Simone Balayé

Liberty is a central theme in the life and works of Staël: liberty of nations, individuals, women, and slaves; liberty of thought and religion. She took an active interest in the dramas bred by political high-handedness, by society, by all manner of persecution, and she constantly sought paths to a more promising future. Thus the following passage from *Delphine* may serve as a fitting epigraph to a study of her thinking on liberty: "It is a great misfortune, I know, to live in times of political dissension: a reasonable man cannot be satisfied with the actions or principles of any party. Yet whenever a nation strives to achieve liberty, I may blame the means taken, but I would find it impossible not to sympathize with its goal."

She is fully aware of the tragic paradox of that conquest, and none of us can fail to see the appropriateness of her remarks to our own times, or to be struck by the splendid words that follow: "Liberty . . . is the greatest good fortune, the only glory of the social order; history is embellished by the virtues of free peoples alone; the only names resounding across the centuries for all generous souls are the names of those who have loved liberty."[1]

Scholars have yet to explore fully Mme de Staël's thinking on the subject, a singularly important task given the quality of her thought.

Translated by Avriel Goldberger.

They must examine the abundant material to be found in her oeuvre, which juxtaposes moral questions, philosophy, religious thought, literary criticism, and fiction.

Through her father, Jacques Necker, Mme de Staël discovered at an early age the importance of liberty in the public sphere. Since Necker came from the Republic of Geneva and had a marked preference for English ideas, he was well prepared to understand parliamentary regimes and to wish for their establishment. To a still feudal Europe, it was England that offered the model. Further, it must not be forgotten that although France was the advance post of the Enlightenment, her people were less educated than the Germans and her aristocracy was less cultivated and less suited to playing a role in important matters of state. Thus, as Mme de Staël remarks, it was in France that revolution was to break out all the more violently for the greater degree of misery suffered by her people.

Mme de Staël's acts in the name of liberty were confirmed and sustained by her quest for personal liberty. There is no doubt that it is a delicate matter to assess the degree to which the young girl was hampered by the demands of a mother gifted in making her daughter feel guilty, to know precisely how hard it was for the girl to assert herself in the face of her prestigious parents. We can sense it in her letters, and we can glimpse it at the root of her two great novels, *Delphine* and *Corinne.*

By chance as an adolescent, and by choice later, she lived in the milieu that was to be the point of origin for the spread of political activity throughout the nation. Early on she met the advocates of the new ideas, people who had fought in the American Revolution, the progressive segment of the nobility, the aristocracy of talent, those who would turn over the first pages of the French Revolution. Twenty-three years old in 1789, she shared in the general enthusiasm, and later wrote some remarkable pages on the events she had witnessed. She watched her father's efforts to establish liberty and justice and tried to contribute on her own through her eloquence and in her salon—the original instruments of her power before her genius as a writer gave her a still more effective voice.

To achieve her goals, she was very quickly obliged to face a major difficulty: that of being a woman. Men too, of course, faced dreadful attacks in spite of their dominant position. But the violence directed at women was of a distinctly sexist nature and all the more hurtful in that women were more vulnerable, and Mme de Staël returns to the subject frequently.

In the nineteenth century, women were locked inside the phantasms of the dominant male society. The discourses of religion, morality, jurisprudence, medicine, and fiction of the time had a common goal: it was inadmissible for a woman to meddle in politics, literary criticism, or philosophy, inadmissible for her to dare emerge from the assigned sphere to which she was confined by her lack of education and rationality.[2] The servitude under which Mme de Staël's female contemporaries lived, even at her own level of society, was painful to her. She describes their weakness and their need to lean on the alleged strength of men, strength they rely on and ultimately find disappointing. This is a statement of fact and not acceptance of that fact. We watch Mme de Staël herself struggling courageously to reach the point where she can live her own liberty. In every one of her books, she calls for women's right to education and self-determination, at a time when society sought to confine them to the role, respectable in itself, of wife and mother.

Already evident under the Old Regime, the situation grows worse under the Revolution and the Empire. Even in her highly privileged position, Mme de Staël, aware of the restriction, seeks to contravene it by writing, and so brings down on her head the anathema of society and of governments. Thus we see how part of her counter-legend was shaped. Like many men, she was attacked for the positions she took in religion and politics: the conservative hostility to Romanticism as breeding disorder, the revanchist mentality following the Franco-Prussian war—it is all there. And to that must be added a violent and undeniable antifeminism which even today is receding at an unspeakably slow pace.

Every biography of Mme de Staël tries to show her political activity on behalf of liberty and in support of her father, the members of the constitutional party, later on the republicans, and then the opponents of the Napoleonic dictatorship. She herself maintains an astonishing discretion in her books with respect to the role she played. She prefers to adopt the role of the informed witness, to picture herself as a victimized woman—an image more suited to the ideal of the time.

Primarily, she assumes the role of the commentator who draws a philosophy from events. It must be emphasized that even in so doing, she goes well beyond the place assigned to women.

There is no time here to explore a book with the scope of the *Considerations on the French Revolution*.[3] However, we shall take from it the example of the Constituent Assembly because, imperfect though it was, its roots were in the party supported by Mme de Staël. Her full approval is evident when she describes the work accomplished to restore equality in taxation and in the military through the abolition of privilege. She was pleased with guarantees of civil rights, the elimination of *lettres de cachet,* and the abolition of torture, and indeed she protested capital punishment for political activity; she was pleased that judicial procedure was made known to the public and that the jury system was instituted. She was also pleased with the Assembly's work in the religious domain: the confiscation of church property, freedom of worship. Thus, she writes, the country has been freed from "the triple chains of an intolerant church, a feudal nobility, and unlimited royal authority" (*Considerations,* 2:IV).

Despite the problems encountered by her father during those first revolutionary days, and despite his progressive disappearance from public life, her memories of the first stages of the Revolution are full of joy: "We breathed more freely, there was more air in our chests; and the undefined hope of a boundless happiness had powerfully seized the nation just as it seizes young men with illusions and without foresight" (*Considerations,* 2:XVI). However, the violent turn taken by the Revolution struck a serious blow against liberty. Mme de Staël was opposed to the terrorist mentality, but also to extravagant royalism, political and religious fanaticism, violence, and dictatorship. The book she wrote in 1798 but did not publish—*On Current Circumstances which Can End the Revolution*—clearly shows that she was anxious for France to emerge from the state of revolution, of anarchy, and to found the Republic on the positive acquisitions of the first Revolution, taking into account the lessons learned.

As the philosophical theory underlying the revolution in France is in itself not open to question, the only remedy for the abuse of that theory is to shed torrents of light on its principles and on their explanation. . . . The philosophers are the ones who made the Revolution; it is they who will bring it to an end.[4]

STAËL AND LIBERTY: AN OVERVIEW

This can only happen with the restoration of free speech. Mme de Staël opened herself to criticism, however, by adopting a contradictory position: liberty for books but censorship of a press made more dangerous by the rapidity of circulation. It must not be forgotten that in her time there was no recourse to the courts, since slander and libel were not yet considered crimes. Further, the press had no code of ethics then as it does in modern democracies.

Another key idea increasingly asserted in Mme de Staël's work is not only freedom of religion, but also the spread of Protestantism. In her view, the latter is the only religion that can guarantee enlightenment and public spirit, thanks to its principle of free enquiry and the absence of the coercive hierarchal priesthood.

To speak of liberty of thought is to speak of the writer in terms of her relationship with power; it is to speak of the importance of literary talent for the future of republican ideas. As she says in her treatise, *On Literature:* "Only in free states may genius for action and genius for thought be combined."[5] Elsewhere I have treated at length the vast subject of the writer's relationship with power. Mme de Staël has explained that genius cannot tolerate political interference which restricts its inspiration and full realization. "Provided that it respects religion and morality, [genius] must go as far as it wishes: it extends the empire of thought." These words figure in *On Germany*, thus demonstrating the undeniable political content of the work.[6] I have shown that the same is true for *Delphine* and *Corinne*.

Mme de Staël also attaches great importance to certain specifically literary genres like the theater, particularly tragedy, which she judges useful for educating the people and depicting great ideas forcefully. Oratory becomes the means of persuasion par excellence in democratic regimes, and Mme de Staël sees it as the literary genre of the future.

The rules governing writers since the seventeenth century are yet another servitude in her eyes: "Good taste in literature is like order under despotism in some respects; it is important to consider carefully the price for their purchase" (*On Germany*, II, 220). Thoughts of that nature could hardly suit the Emperor, who was specifically in favor of returning to the age of Louis XIV as well as to Catholicism and other restrictive institutions of the Old Regime.

Liberty also means the search for new ideas beyond the borders of France. Thus Mme de Staël would be led to explore the Germanic

realm, which seemed curiously richer than French philosophy and literature of the time. To make progress, she said, each country needs the
knowledge all others have acquired. Napoleonic power could not be
pleased with that set of ideas.

Yet where liberty is concerned, there is a marked difference between
philosophy and the "positive sciences," according to Staël. In her view
scientists are not interested in the "events of life," and they "disregard
the moral order" (*On Literature*, 1:33); the arts also betray by giving
shape to subjects which "by the very pleasure they afford," are what
tyrants wish them to be (*On Literature*, 1:35). Staël wrote remarkable
pages in this vein, opening up domains considered far more important
today than was the case in her time. To a much greater degree, we now
see researchers who reflect on the enormous moral consequences of
their discoveries and artists who are conscious of the messages they
can impart to everyone. *On Literature* is a great book precisely because it demonstrates this awareness so strongly. In 1800, Mme de
Staël wrote: "The spoken word would also be an act if it fully conveyed the soul's energy, if feelings were lifted to the lofty height of
ideas, and if tyranny saw itself under attack by everything that denounces it, generous indignation and inflexible reason" (*On Literature*, 1:36).

Bonaparte saw to it that *On Literature* and then *Delphine* were
violently criticized in the press for their literary, political, and social
ideas. Worse still, in 1810 he had *On Germany* ground to pulp. We
have here the clash of two mind-sets, two systems. For Napoleon, the
writer has no role in politics other than as propagandist for the regime
in power. Literature thus loses its social and political function. Considered useless, the writer will come to know the suffering of scorned
and unrecognized genius.

This is precisely Mme de Staël's situation. She is a victim of the
despotic regime under which she lives and of which she disapproves.
She speaks with great moderation in her books, but that is still not
enough to protect her from the imperial thunderbolts. A political reading of her nonpolitical works is very instructive on the positions she
took; even where she thinks she is being careful, she is still not careful
enough. *On Literature* shows her as an advocate of Republican ideas.
In *Delphine*, she attacks society (divorce), the Catholic religion (super-
stition, religious vows), and politics (the *émigrés*, the reaction). Her
admiration for England is implicit in this novel; in *Corinne*, however,

the nation is richly celebrated. In *On Germany* a second conquered and despised country is held up as a model. Thus Mme de Staël did much more than the other writers of her day. We discern only caution when we look at them, and we discover that it was a woman who set the example, an example they were very careful not to follow. The consequences she suffered show that their fears were justified indeed.

Napoleon's attitude toward Mme de Staël grew out of his scorn of women, his abomination of all opposition—warranted, it must be admitted, by the difficulties of his position. It is conceivable that after 1802, the date of Baron de Staël's death, his natural harshness was no longer moderated by the diplomatic status of the now widowed ambassador's wife. He could easily have considered her to be French; but if his annexation of Geneva appeared to confer citizenship on Mme de Staël, her marriage to a Swede also permitted its denial. Thus the way was open to the servitude of exile with Paris declared off limits by a simple edict of the police.

Mme de Staël took advantage of her new "liberty" to become better acquainted with other countries—Germany, Italy—and to write books about them. The results were *Corinne* and *On Germany*. In the Emperor's view, these works, as well, expressed too many displeasing ideas, and he closed France to Mme de Staël, permitting residence in Geneva alone, while dangling still more serious threats over her head. She was truly afraid of prison. Thus she chose escape so that she might recover her liberty to publish and to act. Crossing Europe once more in 1812, she added the Russian Empire, Sweden, and then England to the countries she knew, all her travels extending her thought to new areas for reflection. Finally, in 1814, the Emperor's defeats reopened her pathway to liberty.

Mme de Staël was in the right places at the right times and waged her personal battle within the general war—a battle for liberty *against* Napoleon and *for* France, even if for the moment the fate of the nation and the fate of the ruler were linked. Her role as propagandist for liberal ideas must not be underestimated. In her books, in her letters to the people in seats of power—sovereigns, ministers, and politicians— she says and repeats that the war against Napoleon is religious and moral, the fight against the spirit of evil, the scourge of the world, the man who wanted war so that he might conquer peoples and impose peace in order to destroy them. Her struggle was indeed liberty's fight against tyranny; it was fought in the name of progress, it was not waged to bring back, along with the Bourbons, an old order which she condemned. It was her wish that Bernadotte govern France, Bernadotte the crown prince of Sweden, Protestant but born a Catholic. To her dismay he backed off, and she would judge this a personal failure and one of her major disappointments.

Returning to Paris in 1814, heartbroken by the Allied presence there, she exerted all her influence to lighten the burden of the occupier's hatred weighing on France, just as she would do in 1815–1816. She witnessed the promulgation of the Charter which, she said, "includes almost all the articles guaranteeing liberty that Monsieur Necker had proposed to Louis XVI in 1789" (*Considerations* V, VII); she pointed out its inferiority to the English constitution, and took note of the mistakes of the first Restoration government, which came as no surprise to her. Although she lived through only the beginning of the second Restoration, she saw enough to take sides against the Ultras.

Chance willed that the last pages ever written by Staël, pages which she carefully revised for her final book, *Considerations on the French Revolution*, are a hymn to liberty. They end with these words:

It is a remarkable thing that among all men, given a certain depth of thought, liberty has not a single enemy. These opinions are so manifestly true that people who have accepted them will be forever unable to give them up, and from one end of the earth to the other, the friends of liberty communicate through knowledge as do religious men through feeling; or rather knowledge and feeling join together in the love of liberty as in the love of the Supreme Being. Whether it is a question of abolishing the slave trade, of freedom of the press, or religious toleration, Jefferson thinks like La Fayette, La Fayette thinks like Wilberforce; and those who are no longer with us are also numbered in the holy band. Doubtless we need knowledge to rise above prejudice; but the principles of liberty are grounded in the soul as well: they make the heart beat, they give life to love and to friendship; they come from nature, they give character its nobility. A whole order of virtues as well as of ideas seems to form the golden chain, described by Homer, which binds man to heaven and so frees him of all the iron shackles of tyranny. (VI, XI)

The need for liberty was infinite, and one woman stood up for it, and courageously spread it abroad for the sake of humanity in the tyrant's grip.

At first Mme de Staël observed her milieu, experiencing a degree of surprise. But she refused to be hampered by prejudice. She chose to rethink everything and she joined in the battle men waged for the liberty that must become the goal of humanity's struggle today, the duty it must assume. There lies the greatness of Mme de Staël.

GERMAINE DE STAËL AND OTHER POSSIBLE SCENARIOS OF THE REVOLUTION

Michel Delon

Joseph de Maistre's *Considerations Regarding France,* and twenty years later, Germaine de Staël's *Considerations on the French Revolution* agree on at least one point: the Revolution was no accident. "The first condition for a revolution decreed from on high is that everything that might have prevented it simply does not exist, and that no success could have crowned the efforts of those seeking to keep it from occurring," affirms Maistre, for whom all things are decreed by God.[1] A glance at the principal crises in history is enough, Staël tells us in her turn, "to convince us that they were inevitable, that in some fashion they were tied in with the ongoing development of ideas."[2] Necessity borrows the scientific language of the day, the language of Newtonian physics: the very same formulae are used by Necker's daughter to trace 1789 back to the vices of the aristocracy, and by the nobleman from Savoie to proclaim the inevitability of the counter-Revolution. The former argues this way: "Civil disorders have not been analyzed thoroughly enough if one fails to observe that reaction exactly mirrors action. The furies unleashed by revolt parallel the vices of institutions" (3:16:304). The latter prophesies: "Since reaction tends to equal action, don't be in such a hurry, oh impatient mankind. Consider that

Translated by Madelyn Gutwirth and Marcel Gutwirth.

the very extent of the evil presages a *counter-revolution* the like of which you have no conception" (40).

The justification of the Revolution by the one on grounds of the excesses of feudalism or of absolutism, or, by the other, of the counter-Revolution on grounds of the excesses of the Terror, ought not mislead us, however. Progress, for the friends of liberty, is not simply a mirror-image of Providence. The Enlightenment is not a substitute for traditional religious dogma. Staël sees the Revolution as a phenomenon both necessary and contradictory: necessary inasmuch as it opens up the possibility of a liberal regime in France, contradictory in that its violence postpones the dawn of a lasting and stable freedom. While nothing could have stopped the Revolution from coming to pass, its criminal trespasses could have been avoided. A reflection on the Revolution as possibility thus allows Staël to explain the past while preparing the future.

From "Sidération" to "Considération"

We quote once more from Maistre's *Considerations Regarding France:* "'I just can't understand'—these are the words on everyone's lips" (32). The first impressions of the Revolution's contemporaries, of those immersed in its events, is a loss of all bearings, a dissolving of all their certainties. There are many who assert the impossibility of making any global historical sense of what is taking place. Strong in her religious, philosophical, and political convictions, Staël means to move beyond this stage of fascination, whether of admiration or of revulsion, the stage of *sidération,** to reach a broad vision of these events. The title she adopts for her book on the Revolution reflects such an intellectual effort in its will to formulate this kind of global view of history.

It is in evoking the darkest moments of the Revolution that she gives point to the term *considération:* "It must be feared that such a story cannot be entered into without our imaginations being spattered ineradicably with stains of blood. We are forced therefore to reflect

*Sidération: Deviating slightly from its original meaning denoting the effects of malign influences of astral bodies, the author uses this term to mean the state of being stupefied by events [Eds.].

philosophically about events that might drain all indignation from eloquence, without ever giving an adequate sense of the inner feelings they arouse" (3:16:303). As she goes on to explain it, "the searing indignation of contemporaries must be supplemented by an enlightened scrutiny capable of offering guidance to the future"; we must "observe as thinkers" (3:16:304). To consider, therefore, is to adopt the point of view of the future, of the general march of history, without letting oneself be fixated on the personal and the particular: it is to understand what at first blush might appear as aberrant and peculiar.

This intellectual stance is notable in a text that is at once personal testimony, historical narrative, and philosophical treatise. The account of the Estates General and the portrayal of Robespierre owe their power to the autobiographical dimension of the work. On May 5, 1789, Staël is seated next to Mme de Montmorin; that lady had spoken one day at her father's house with a little lawyer from Arras named Robespierre.[3] Memory brings the scenes to life. The two chapters entitled *Particular Anecdotes* (part 3, chapters 10 and 25) situate the narrator in the midst of events, no longer as a witness but as an actor in spite of herself: "The details of these horrible massacres repel the imagination and offer no food for thought. Consequently, I shall limit myself to retelling what I myself saw at the time. That may well be the best way of giving some idea of it" (3:10:280). What she has seen and what she has personally undergone—the book extracts its own rhythms from this to-and-fro between the general and the particular, between memories that do not quite delineate a historical narrative, and reflections and considerations that reach beyond it.[4]

Recognizable stylistic and intellectual features characterize this endeavor of understanding. The first of these is a reliance on historical analogy that seeks not so much to reduce differences as to situate epochs in relation to a general and theoretical evolution of humanity. The eighteenth century had witnessed the growth of a historical genre, that of the history of the revolutions of certain foreign lands. Thus pluralized, revolution was to designate all the political variations that had affected that land, referring readers back to the old cyclical principle of the rise and the ineluctable fall of empires.[5] Political regimes were subject to the corruptions of all earthly things subject to nature, and therefore doomed to revolutions. The events after 1789 impose the notion of a peculiar nature of the Revolution in France which will turn into the French Revolution. Louis-Sébastien Mercier insists upon this difference between the revolutions which until then had been but "a change of vices and abuses," "a mere permutation of tyrants," and the Revolution which had been made "for the people, that is to say for the universality of the French citizenry" and which presents a "unique model of philanthropy, of perseverance, and of courage."[6]

Such a claim of singularity as this did not deflect the enterprise of reflection from its path of comparison and analogy. In an attempt to defend the uprising of the French people, Volney writes *Ruins, on a Meditation on the Revolutions of Empires* (1791), Frédéric Ancillon his *Tableau of the Revolutions of the Political Systems since the End of the XVth Century* (1803–1805), and Count Ferrand *A Theory of Revolutions in Connection with the Principal Events that were their Origin, their Unfolding or their Sequel* . . . (1817).

Staël rejects comparisons with Greece and Rome, that is, with civilizations founded on slavery. She shrugs off in like manner any primitivist nostalgia, any backward turn, any basic questioning of economic progress.[7] A reference to England is preferred over an analogy with antiquity: "A like impulse produced the English Revolution and that of 1789 in France. Both belong to the third epoch of the forward march of the social order, that of the establishment of representative government, toward which the human spirit has everywhere begun its voyage" (1:1:69). Her book opens with "Considerations Concerning the History of France," and one of its last chapters is entitled "A Glance at the History of England." The comparison, explicit at times, at times implicit, but ever present, operates to discriminate between the positive elements of the French Revolution and its criminal transgressions. Analogies between the violence of the past and that of the present, the St. Bartholomew's massacre and those of September, seek to explain what would seem *a priori* to be inexplicable: these upsurges of irrational savagery remain susceptible to rational analysis.[8]

A second feature is the distinction drawn between principle and circumstances, the general and the particular. The book starts out with an enunciation of the law of the three epochs: feudalism, despotism, and representative government. The Revolution appears as the crisis that may allow access to the third of these epochs. The principle to which all the analyses of the *Considerations* refer is liberty, in its political, religious, moral, and economic forms. It is liberty that gives the Revolution meaning and that constitutes it as a stage in the progress of history. The Enlightenment had made the distinction between the history of the human spirit, that harmonious ascent of an ideal humanity, such as it was celebrated by Condorcet, and the history of actual human beings with their relative progress and their backslidings, in all of their dispersions and contradictions.[9]

Sénac de Meilhan gives as an epigraph to his *Principles and Causes of the Revolution in France* a celebrated sentence of Montesquieu's on the subservience of the particular to the general cause.[10] Staël herself wrote *On Current Circumstances Which Can End the Revolution and of the Principles by Which to Found the Republic* (1798; 1906), thus distinguishing among the circumstantial, the causal, and the structural, that which pertains to principles and to foundations. Three chapters of the *Considerations* also bear the title *Of the Circumstances that . . .* (1:9; 5:3; and 5:5). They signal an attempt to fit a global historical explanatory grid over concrete realities, to hold together a philosophy of history and the management of the everyday, to bring the human spirit into accord with mankind as it is. Some somewhat vague postulations characterize this truce proposed between purity of principle and the perplexities of lived experience: the course of things (272), the nature of things (538, 576). The slow evolution of nations, with their delays and turnings-back, will end up resembling progress and eventuating in freedom. Such is the ideal Staël never tires of verbalizing afresh.

A third feature completes the analogies among eras and the distinctions made between principles and circumstances. It consists in rewriting history in light of the unreality of the past, in perceiving what might have been. Faith in an ineluctable progress cannot be assimilated to any sort of fatalism as long as each period presents itself as one in a series of possible states among which human freedom has to choose. According to the legacy of the Enlightenment, militant action is fully justified by such a gap between progress proposed and the vicissitudes of chance. For Pascal, Cleopatra's nose was emblematic of the world's vanities and the absurdity of all of political history: "Had it been shorter, the entire face of the world would have been changed" (*Pensées*, #162, Brunschvicg). The hypothesis here opens up no signifying variable to men; on the contrary, it encloses them within the narrow circle of their condition. Enlightenment thought, and in its wake Staël, breaks with such fatalism: it gives back to the possible its powers of explanation over the past and its hopes for the future. The *Considerations* thus characterize 1789 as a time of near-universal enthusiasm and 1793–1794 as a tragic bloody parenthesis: in this way, it points to those missed opportunities that replaced liberal evolution with the violent upheavals of terrorism.

The Failed Encounters

Necker's daughter's struggle is a dual one: against those who were nostalgic for the old regime, who would deny all necessity for Revolution and would look for the men and events that would have favored its avoidance; and against a fatalism which, either in invoking Providence or justifying the Terror, denies all possibility of an effect by men upon their history. Another king, another minister would not have sufficed to alter the course of events: "If Louis XVI had been a man of genius, some say, he would have put himself at the head of the revolution; he might have prevented it, say others. Can such suppositions matter?" (1:3:83). One man, even were he king, could not alter what was a function of public opinion, of the whole of the nation. A later chapter, on Charles I and Louis XVI, underscores how differences of conduct between these two sovereigns nonetheless led to an identical catastrophe: "Such is the invincible force of revolutions whose cause is the public opinion of the majority" (3:13:292). The same species of argument is useful to Staël in defending her father against the accusations of those who held that "a man like the Cardinal de Richelieu would have known how to prevent the revolution" (294). The Count of Strafford, Charles I's favorite minister, was no more able than was Necker to impede revolution's march forward.

Yet, even if the French Revolution was necessary, it was still not fated to be violent. To those unrealities of the past which bespeak the illusions of some is opposed an unreality of the past by which Staël paradoxically expresses her faith in the future. Although she exclaims, "What is the use of such suppositions?" they still sometimes do seem germane to her. If only they had listened to her father, "if they had adopted his administrative projects, it is possible that this same crisis might have produced only a just, gradual, salutary reform" (1:5:94). "The dissension that we saw break out between the privileged classes of the nation might never have occurred if, long before, the three orders had come together and discussed the affairs of a province in common" (1:6:96). *Il se peut que, n'aurait peut-être pas* (*It is possible that,*

might perhaps not): rhetorical prudence does not prevent us from en-
visaging another possible story in which the Revolution would have
been only a radical Reform.[11] Staël thus responds to nostalgia for the
survival of an old regime that powerful men would have known how
to defend with a countering utopia of Enlightenment, that is, the
spread of progress under the aegis of an enlightened government.

Until August 10, such a Revolution, which would have perpetuated
the euphoria of 1789 and allowed a new regime acceptable to all to be
formed, remained possible. An equilibrium between king and nation,
tradition and *Le Peuple,* would have established the foundation for a
constitutional monarchy on the English model. "We cannot help but
feel profound grief as we rehearse the phases of the revolution in which
a free constitution might have been established in France, for we see
not only that this hope was dashed, but how the most sinister events
came about instead of the most wholesome of institutions" (3:3:263).
Staël enumerates these unexploited possibilities, these missed engage-
ments, these spoiled chances: if the Girondists had allied themselves
with Lafayette (3:6:274), if the nobles had not emigrated and had
instead become reconciled with the friends of liberty, "one might still
have saved France and the throne" (3:9:278). But on the 10th of August
the bell tolls the end of such hopes. The assault on the Tuileries had to
eventuate in the despotism either of the king or of the assembly. In
either case, "the creation of an infernal necessity" put an end to possibility (279).

After the failure of constitutional monarchy, the second great missed
rendezvous is the one during the Directorate, with a liberal republic.
There the elements that failed to appear were:

—understanding on the part of foreign nations: "We cannot help
regretting that at that date the powers still at war with France,
that is, Austria and England, did not consent to make peace"
(3:21:323).

—a better constitution: "If only the government had had the right
to dissolve the 500, the mere threat of using such a prerogative
would have sufficed to contain them. Finally, if the executive
power had been able to oppose a veto, even a suspensive one,
against the decrees of the councils, it would have been satisfied
with the means the laws had provided to protect and maintain
itself" (3:24:330).

—maturity in public opinion: "If the French nation, instead of choosing that fatal foreigner who exploited it so grievously and in his own interest, if the French nation, I say, still so imposing at that time in spite of all its flaws, had constituted itself according to the lessons that ten years' experience had just given to it, it would be still the light of the world" (4:2:360–361).

We hear in the repetition of a formula such as "We cannot prevent ourselves" (263, 323) the regret of the woman who cannot act directly and of the liberal who takes stock of the Revolution's disorderliness and of France's historical laggardliness. A militant will prevents her from ever accepting the fait accompli. The historian in her must record the facts; but the inheritress of Enlightenment substitutes for them a possibility which might yet enact an always present ideal.

The discourse she engages in about the Empire is not always devoid of ambivalence from this standpoint. While she denounces the illusions of those who believed in a republican or democratic Bonaparte, sometimes she cannot keep herself from dreaming up a good Napoleon:

—"I don't share the view of some persons who claim that if the English ministry had then accepted the proposals of France, Bonaparte might immediately have adopted a peaceful policy. Nothing was more contrary to his nature and to his interests" (4:5:370).

—"People have often repeated that if he'd been moderate, he might have stayed in power. But what do they mean by moderate?" (4:11:395).

—"Many people are pleased to claim that if Bonaparte had attempted neither the Spanish nor the Russian campaigns, he would be emperor still. . . . I've already said . . . that Bonaparte needed war to establish and to hold on to absolute power" (4:19:435).

It was necessary to discern beneath the mask of the revolutionary general the "profiteer-knight" (366), that is, the man devoid of principle, the oriental tyrant.[12] Without letting herself be taken in by this mirage that had gulled too many of her friends and that tempted even her, Staël at least dreams of what the effect of a victorious general at the head of a truly revolutionized France might have meant: "An able chieftain, at the beginning of this century, would easily have been able to render France happy and free, had he possessed merely a few virtues. . . . Had he felt himself hemmed in, in his huge appetite for action, even in the fairest of all monarchies, if this was deemed too wretched a fate for one who had been a Corsican sub-lieutenant in 1790 to be the emperor merely of France, even so, in provoking all of Europe, he might at least have done so in the name of some benefit to it"(4:12:401).

All of these nonrealities of the past make sense only insofar as they prop up hypotheticals about the present. Experience of the past authorizes these prospects and grounds political choices. The France of the Restoration, during which the *Considerations* were written, must become a truly liberal nation. And if internal politics keep Staël from describing her ideas in detail, she still manages to express the hopes she places in a sovereign resembling Czar Alexander. Here are prudent hopes, a wager on the future: "If he accomplishes his plan, posterity will accord him the honors due to genius: but if the circumstances in which he finds himself, if the difficulty of finding the proper instruments to sustain him fail to allow him to effect what he wishes, those who have known him will at least be conscious that he had conceived great ideas" (5:4:452). Here circumstances rise up to limit the freedom of the individual as well as the power of principle.

History of Peoples; History of Individuals

Even if the grammatical forms of the conditional furnish the *Considerations* with one of the elements of its rhetoric, the category of the possible does not seem to have been theorized about as such by Staël. The distinction between power and acts, so useful to Aristotle for giving an account of motion, still seems operative when it becomes imperative to formulate a concept of history that would be neither the result of pure chance nor a simple operation of Providence—of progress or any other transcendent plan. The play between the uniqueness of the real and the multiplicity of the possible opens a space for militant action, for a work of signification that escapes both the absurd and all established dogmas of meaning. Staël's reflections and those of her liberal friends seek to protect against the double dangers of an immobilism which would freeze mankind and block its perfectibility (nothing is possible) but also the terrorist vertigo according to which man is transformable at will, infinitely malleable by government decree (all is possible).[13]

The theoretical will to define history beginning from its unrealized possibilities in the past and its still open possibilities in the future is contemporaneous with autobiographical reveries that explore the detours and meanders of a life, express wonder at its course, and raise questions about individual identity arising from existential choices. Staël's eloquence is her heritage from Rousseau, who found that the pathetic offered new legitimacy and effectiveness to philosophical and political speech. At this same time, reflection about the self begins to pursue parallel paths.

Rousseau had dreamed of what he might have been so as to better understand what he was. To the wanderings that followed his departure from Geneva, he contrasted the alternative hypothesis of a tranquil life devoid of writing or of adventure: "Before abandoning myself to the fatefulness of my destiny, allow me to cast my eyes back to what would have awaited me quite naturally had I fallen into the hands of a better master. Nothing was more congenial to my character or more likely to make me happy than the quiet and obscure station of the good artisan. . . . I would have been a good Christian, a good citizen, a good father of a family, a good friend, a good worker, a good man in every way. I would have loved my state."[14] The *Essay on the Origins of Language* summons up a divine finger that tips the earth's axis and thus transforms random existence into a story rendered rhythmic by the seasons, devoted, for better or worse, to an irreversible becoming. This finger that pushed humankind off into the dangerous and desirable road of progress similarly tossed the young Jean-Jacques out upon a road to Europe and to literature.

As we advance toward the end of the eighteenth century this meditation on irreversibility becomes inseparable from the questions that the Revolution evokes. Far from France, full of sound and fury, Casanova writes his *Story of My Life* so as to resuscitate a lost aristocratic innocence, a royal libertine freedom in pleasure, a lack of consequences or an unconsciousness that might keep the possible open in perpetuity.

The Revolution represented the termination of the possible to the Venetian adventurer; it coincided with his aging and imprisonment in the library of the chateau of Dux. All that remains to him is a dream of what his existence might have been if he had settled in Rome or Constantinople, if he had married or retired to a convent with a fine library. Restif de la Bretonne, too, once *Monsieur Nicolas or the Human Heart Unveiled (1794–1797)* was completed, undertook to pen his re-lives, those lives he'd had neither the time, nor the occasion, nor the nerve to live. The idea of a *re-life* helps to multiply his existence, but this infinity of lives goes hand in glove with death and that schism that is the Revolution. Two of the pseudonyms that Restif adopts in recounting his fantastic re-lives—or challenges flung against human limits—are the names of contemporaries who died on the Revolution's scaffold: Linguet and Cazotte.[15]

Finally, Chateaubriand identifies that species of alternative destiny evoked by both the *Confessions* and the Revolution. He imagines an English gentleman, quite indifferent to the Revolution that strikes down the neighboring country or, on the contrary, a French gentleman cut down by the violence of the populace in 1789. He wonders at each crossroad of his existence about the life that might have been his: "In marrying Charlotte Ives, my role on earth might have changed: buried in a county in Great Britain, I would have become a hunting *gentleman;* not a single line would have come from my pen; I might even have forgotten my own language."[16] The writer seems to take pleasure in evoking such silence, his exclusion from the French language, his death to letters so as better to bring out the miracle of his prose. The *Memoirs from Beyond the Grave* accept to record the real only on condition that the entire spectrum of the possible be set out; a lived life becomes a score orchestrated by all the possible variants of this biography. Chateaubriand's eloquence draws its effects from a skillfully controlled hesitation between old and new worlds, tradition and Revolution, the possible and the real.

One can only wonder what the echoes of these practices might have produced in the autobiography Staël never wrote. In any case, the mastering of an individual or collective event will henceforth pass through an exploration of the possibilities that give the real its depth, its resonance, its sense. If Aristotle turns to the possible to understand movement, the women and men of the nineteenth century raise questions about this category as they reflect upon individual or collective history, having unmoored themselves from ancestral certainties only to float away to some unknown Progress of the Species, toward some unknown relative Eternity of literature. The Revolution and writing made them, made us, enter irreversibly into modernity as the place of construction of a meaning forever provisional.

GENERATIVE FACTORS IN
CONSIDERATIONS ON THE
FRENCH REVOLUTION

Charlotte Hogsett

The literary career of Germaine de Staël amply demonstrates that she did not let her gender interfere with the range of genres in which she worked. A close reading of her writing suggests, however, that it was not entirely without misgiving and malaise that she ventured beyond the kinds of writing traditionally associated with women.[1] Her final work, *Considerations on the French Revolution,* is a brilliant inter-weaving of a variety of genres. Yet a close reading of the text suggests that this virtuoso performance was not easily accomplished. Inter-nalized interdictions against writing women bid fair to weigh down the soaring of her considerable talent. The strategies by which the *Considerations* present and resolve the resulting conflict are the sub-ject of this inquiry.

In the United States, one speaks of George Washington, Thomas Jefferson, and others as the "fathers of their country." When Ger-maine de Staël looked at the attempts of the Constituent Assembly of 1789 to make a new government, she saw men engaged not in an act of paternity, but in an act of authorship.[2] In Staël's view, as the mem-bers of the assembly set out to write the new France into existence, there stood before them one clear model, the English constitution. They had only to follow it, and their dilemma, "to reconcile republi-can institutions with the existing monarchy," as Staël stated it, was resolved (115). Unfortunately, they suffered from what Staël called "an almost literary obsession with vanity" or, to borrow Harold Bloom's phrase, an "anxiety of influence."[3] This obsession or anxiety "inspired the French with a need to innovate in this matter. They feared borrowing, as would an author, characters or plots from already existing works" (115). This fear is well-founded, Staël tells us further, in the case of a fictional work, but in the matter of real institutions, experience is the best guide. Thus, despite all of their quite positive contributions, the members of the Constituent Assembly did not discharge their task as well as they might have.[4] She likens their failure to that of an author unable to work creatively within an already established tradition.

The metaphor of authorship is somewhat perplexing. The "already existing work" to which Staël refers—the English constitution—is not properly speaking a "work" at all.[5] To be sure, it relies partly on a collection of written documents and statutes; however, these do not form a single document. Moreover, the constitution is partly unwritten, dependent on orally transmitted custom and tradition. To what "already existing work," then, was Staël, knowledgeable as she was about British government, referring? Was she thinking of the "constitution" in the more general sense of the way in which an entity is constituted or made up? Or was she calling for the French to write that which in England was only partly written? The latter possibility implies that Staël is valorizing written language over spoken language. Her position on this matter is a complex one; in *Considerations* she addresses it most interestingly.

To some degree Staël's valorization of the spoken word is quite clear, for she proposes that the French emulate not only the constitution of England but another British practice as well. She states that in England it is forbidden to *read* a public discourse; the speaker must improvise. In the French assembly, however, orators could read what they had previously prepared or what had been prepared for them. The English procedure ensures that only the most talented persons will be able to lead the assembly because only they will possess the art of improvisation. Under the French system, a larger number of men will be able to make themselves heard. Staël concludes that leadership, when dispersed among men who are not necessarily very gifted, is weakened (115). It seems that whereas earlier Frenchmen were criticized for a failure to write, here they are denigrated for an inability to speak extemporaneously. Speaking is presented as a skill superior to that of writing.

During the early years of the Revolution, Staël tells us, French society was uniquely brilliant, owing in large measure to the genius of French women for the art of conversation.[6] In the "salons," women in France, more outspoken than their quiet English sisters and more adept than their French brothers, directed conversation. "Their minds were trained early in the facility demanded by this talent. Discussions over public affairs were softened by them in this way and often intermingled with agreeable and saucy pleasantries" (140). This softening effect even enabled Staël herself to invite to her home persons representing quite different political opinions. The possibilities of understanding and compromise inherent in such encounters were never to be actualized, of course, because of the Terror which was approaching all too rapidly. Nevertheless, it was Staël's belief that the supple and flexible medium of conversation might have been able to move France in a less troubled and more fruitful direction.

Once the Terror had taken hold in France, again it was this flexibility which made it possible for women to play, at least on an individual level, conciliatory and even life-saving roles unavailable to the men who were more publicly associated with specific parties. Staël recounts several occasions on which she was able to appeal to men in power on behalf of friends and friends of friends. Her own political positions allied her in many cases neither with the representative of the government to whom she spoke nor to the individual for whom she pled. Nonetheless by finding the language that might move the listener, this woman—skilled as few have been in the art of speaking—succeeded in apparently impossible situations. The spoken word gave to women, then, a power and sphere of activity that the written word denied them. However, Staël viewed their undertakings as secondary to or as following after those of the men, and thus relatively ineffective. In this scheme, the deeds brought about by written words must occur first; only then can those which the spoken word can cause to happen come into play. The masculine sphere of influence takes temporal and spatial priority. Woman can act, but only once male action has created a propitious setting for her.

It seems, then, that though Staël does in some ways valorize spoken over written language, in the final analysis the former is found to be inadequate. As woman depends on man in the social system Staël experienced, so also must effective speaking have its foundation in writing. Therefore the "already existing work" to which Staël referred seems indeed to be a written piece. But one will try in vain to reconstitute what that work was, I will argue, unless one takes into account that as she was elaborating her interpretation of the Assembly's work, she came to see it in terms of the writing she was engaged in herself as the author of the *Considerations*. That is, the difficulties involved in authoring a country became conflated with those she encountered as she wrote her book.

In her foreword, Staël tells the reader that the original idea for her book has undergone a number of transformations. At first she intended only to examine the political acts and writings of her father. We may imagine that she would have entitled such a work "The Public Life of M. Necker"; certainly we find lengthy sections of that projected book in the book as it stands now. But that initial subject led her, she says, to treat two related matters: the principal events of the French Revolution (hence the eventual title of the work) and "the portrayal of England, as justification of M. Necker's opinions" (55). Her subject matter changed, then, from a specific one (the public life of Necker) to more general topics (the Revolution, English political institutions).

The book itself contains elements both more specific and more general than what the foreword promises. Staël does not speak only of the principal events of the Revolution; such a book would have been a historical narrative only. Staël also analyzes the advantages and disadvantages of different forms of government. Further, she demonstrates her knowledge of both French and English political theorists and contributes her own ideas on political theory. Finally, she frames her work with an introduction and conclusion that express her theory of history. The book is indeed about a number of abstract or general matters.

On the other hand, it also contains more passages that may be categorized as personal memoirs than any other work of hers, with the possible exception of the much shorter *Ten Years of Exile*.[7] Here she writes concretely, although one tends to associate Staël with the abstract, in that her most well-known works (*On Literature, On Germany,* and *Corinne, or Italy*) are characterized by striking syntheses and generalizations. Nonetheless in the *Considerations* she shows prodigious talent in the art of recounting personal stories, so exciting that the reader does not want to put the book down and so specific that one can visualize the scenes clearly. Staël's contemporaries never tired of saying—and her critics have never ceased to repeat—that Staël was a superb conversationalist. In these passages of the *Considerations,* the twentieth-century reader catches at least a glimpse of what it must have been like to hear her talk.[8]

In the spectrum of Staël's writing, ranging from the most abstract to the most concrete, two genres most particularly echo the writing/ speaking dichotomy toward which Staël showed such mixed emotions. The written word is represented in her book by her father, its original subject and the seed from which all of its eventual manifestations grew. Staël not only tells about his public life, but she includes in her book long quotations from Necker's works and, in a few cases, judgments of Necker by others. In doing this, it may be said that she behaves as she says the Assembly should have behaved. She regrets that they did not simply put the British constitution into a written form appropriate for the French. When there is a perfect model to follow, why not follow it? In like manner, when Jacques Necker has already stated certain positions or opinions as well as they can be stated, why not, she seems to imply, quote them?

To some extent, then, Staël allows Necker's writing to stand for itself in her book. She has made way for it, showing off her father's brilliance by sacrificing her own writing space for his as a dutiful daughter should. She gives him the priority which she associated with male/written language. Her point of departure for discussions of events and ideas is frequently a word or deed of Necker's. She seems to exist as a conduit for his life and thought. Even when she tells of her own experiences, they are often, at the outset always, generated by his adventures. He had temporal priority and in her book a great deal of the space is his.

That a woman writer might find herself intimidated by an impressive and forbidding male presence is not surprising. We owe the work of Germaine de Staël to her refusal to accept the silent and private world of the English woman (which she characterizes briefly in this book and a great deal more acerbicly in *Corinne*) or to remain in the secondary and dependent position of the French woman.[9]

That she viewed herself as taking the linguistic initiative away from the father who might seem to have staked prior claims is suggested in the passage in which she criticizes the Assembly for failing to adopt the

English constitution as its own. She attributes to them the motivation that must have been her own as she proceeded with the writing of the *Considerations:* the desire not to copy, not simply to transcribe into her work that of another, albeit her own father, but to do an original piece of writing. Like them, she wanted nothing—not her father's superiority in political experience, not his temporal priority, and not even the considerable veneration she had for him—to interfere with her own creativity. His work seems to have stood firm in her mind, but she had to find ways of moving it aside in order to make way for her own writing. In the *Considerations* she seizes the written and spoken word and wields them both on her own behalf. But the encounter between her own intense desire to establish herself and her misgivings about that enterprise can be glimpsed as one watches her using covert ways of writing her own work where her father is the explicit topic of her discourse.

While quoting Necker, Staël both does and does not let him speak for himself. Obviously the reader can see Necker's own words. But at the same time, Staël brings to those words her own interpretations, which become the light in which the reader will view them. The second chapter of the third part of the book is an excellent example of the interweaving of paternal and filial thought into one new thought, that of the daughter (154–157). After a lengthy quotation in which Necker calls for "the effective intervention of the monarch," Staël rephrases his thought to make the claim that he was speaking of a House of Peers. The change does not precisely distort the thought of Necker, but it does extend and interpret it. Later she characterizes a passage which seems dominated by Necker's apparently considerable ego as one in which he demonstrates a remarkable love of France. By completing his thoughts, by making exaggerated claims, by covering over his egotism, Staël creates her own image of her father, not allowing his words alone to create it. The Necker we see here is a Necker of Staël's imagination. It may well be that he appears in a better light for having passed through the prism of his daughter's imagination, but that she has, like the Assembly, invented rather than copied is clear.

There is something other than excessive praise here. The verbs that Staël uses to speak of Necker's deeds and words are predominantly in the past conditional. We learn what would have happened if the English constitution, which Necker favored, had been adopted, what would have happened if his advice had been followed, and especially how the dark side of the Revolution could have been avoided if he had continued to be minister. The second predominant tense is an implied future. Necker is said to have predicted laws and events. What is lacking here is clearly a strong simple past, the recounting of effective deeds actually carried out.[10]

With respect to this relative void of actual accomplishment when compared with past or future eventualities, Staël seems to move into still another conditional tense—what would have happened if she had had the opportunities afforded her father. Although Staël's respect for her father was considerable, the reader of the *Considerations* has reason to suspect that the daughter would have liked to have taken over her father's responsibilities, and perhaps believed she would have discharged them better. She addresses the words of Ben Jonson to her father: "I pray God that he may grant you strength in adversity, for as to grandeur, you could never be lacking in it" (155). Above all, in submitting his resignation to the king in 1781, Necker did not demonstrate strength, but rather yielded to his own excessive sensitivity to criticism ("susceptibilité"). Strength in this event would have involved resisting the "traps set for his character," but Necker, whose self-concept was rooted in the abiding and yet easily shaken idea of his own grandeur, could not endure disapproval and did not manage to resist. Another salient characteristic in Staël's description of her father is resignation to his fate, a trait which she distinctly associates also with women, as in this commentary concerning the king's sister: "Her courage became manifest in her religious resignation; and this virtue, not always an adequate one for men, is a kind of heroism in women" (133). The claim here is not that such characteristics are negative nor that Staël necessarily viewed them as faults, but rather that they caused her father to act in ways that undercut the influence which she believes, rightly or wrongly, he might have had at this crucial moment in French history.

Neither Staël nor anyone else can redo history, to be sure, but one can rewrite it. Unwilling simply to transcribe, Staël gave literary existence to a new and original story. In so doing, she demonstrated once again and finally the impressive range of her linguistic and literary talent. The *Considerations on the French Revolution* provide one last opportunity for the reader to observe strategies for paying homage to admired models even as the author undermines them in order to build a work of her own. Here she displays her talent for this delicate but necessary maneuvering while expressing her disappointment with a France unable to follow creatively the example of England in its early efforts to constitute a new nation. In her creative imagination the building of the work and the building of the nation become mutually illuminating metaphors.

DELPHINE AND THE PRINCIPLES OF 1789: "FREEDOM, BELOVED FREEDOM"

Eve Sourian

In her preface to *Delphine*, Staël states that she deliberately omitted from her novel everything that might relate to the events of the Revolution, not in an effort to hide her political opinions (of which she was very proud), but rather to center attention on the characters of her novel. This concept of the novel reflected the ideas she expressed on this subject in *Essay on Fiction*, written in 1795, where she rejects the idea of a purely realistic historical novel. Does this mean that the novelist takes no note of history? Certainly not. "I would be guilty of absurdity," she wrote, "if one could say that I fail to take account of history, preferring invention, as though such inventions were not rooted in experience, as though the delicate nuances that novels can bring out were not, all of them, derived from the philosophical results, the parent ideas inherent in the broad picture of public events."[1] Furthermore, for Staël "the morality of novels relates more to the development of the rhythms internal to the soul than to incidents recounted" (69). It was for both these reasons that Staël refused to write "the great novel of the Revolution."[2]

And yet, as a work of fiction, *Delphine is* the novel of the Revolution, even though Staël's contemporaries did not understand it to be so:[3] for de Villers there was simply no reason for the novel to have been set during the Revolution at all, and Benjamin Constant was unenthusiastic about its historical framework. Sismondi was the only one to perceive its importance; he saw that the clash of prejudices against liberal ideas was one of the principal springs of the novel, and that it took place at that moment when the tensions between these two forces were strained to the limit and clashed with the most intensity. The Revolution is not only the historical framework of the novel: it is its subject.

Delphine is the novel of the Revolution, first, because it is a novel, the democratic genre par excellence in which the English, a free people, excelled, whereas in the France of the *ancien régime* the novel was not yet a consecrated form. For the illustrious disciple of Montesquieu, the novel blossoms especially under a free government where thought may be translated into action and where literature is more moral than philosophical. "A novel such as we might imagine, of which we have several models, is one of the most beautiful products of the human spirit, one of the most influential on the morals of individuals, which must thereby establish the public morality" (68). Staël made a conscious choice when she decided to write *Delphine* as a novel unfolding under the Revolution. As Henri Coulet so aptly remarked, the difference between *Delphine* and the novels of the *ancien régime* "lies in two interrelated facts: public events play a role they never played before; the characters do not belong only to social class or society but to a nation."[4]

The presence of Mme Necker is felt from the beginning to the end of *Delphine*. Indeed the novel begins with the epigraph: "A man must know how to stand up to opinion, a woman to submit to it."[5] This quotation comes from the unfinished "Commencement d'un éloge de Mme de Sévigné." Mme Necker firmly believed that no one could outdo Mme de Sévigné's epistolary style, not even the English authors whom her daughter admired so much. In her choice of the epistolary novel, Staël perhaps wanted to prove to her mother that she could succeed where Richardson had failed. Furthermore, in choosing the democratic genre of the novel, Staël might very well have sought to challenge Mme Necker's antirevolutionary ideas.

Delphine is dedicated to freedom, to freedom in all its forms. "If I were a man," Delphine exclaims, "it would be as impossible for me not to love freedom, not to serve it, as it would be to close my heart to generosity, to friendship, to all the truest and purest of feelings" (1:470). According to the first article of the Declaration of the Rights of Man and of the Citizen: "All men are born and are entitled to remain free and equal." This is the catechism of the new order to which the young wife of the Swedish ambassador would enthusiastically adhere, in contrast to her mother, Mme Necker, who wrote:

> In creating man, God left him freedom because he could not have virtue without it; but there were so many conditions, insuring that he would not abuse this blessing! Reason, conscience, limited forces, feelings which propel us toward others, the balance of physical and moral powers, the fear of resistance or retaliation; yet despite so many counterbalances, man still abuses this freedom. This observation should have predicted the consequences for a government where freedom was regarded as the primary goal and took the place of the happiness of all, which is in fact the only term which men wish to attain. (*Mélanges* 3:40–41)

Seen in this perspective, *Delphine* is a response to Mme Necker's skepticism concerning freedom.

The novel takes place between April 12, 1790, and the beginning of October, 1792.[6] The narrative unfolds during the National Assembly and the Constituent Assembly, ending with the deposition of the King and the demise of the Legislative Assembly. The September massacres, the victory of Valmy, the secularization of the civil state, the institutionalization of divorce, the September 22nd proclamation of the first year of the Republic serve as the settings for the tragic outcome of the novel. It is interesting to note that Staël set *Delphine* in a period when she was herself not only at the center of events but attempting to promote revolutionary ideas.

Staël advocated the abolition of the feudal system. Like her constitutional friends, she sought to replace the society of orders and privileges of the ancien régime with a constitutional system. This was an "impossible compromise," doomed to fail;[7] for the monarchy, there was but one class that counted. *Delphine* is the novel of this failure. The heroine, Delphine d'Albémar, a partisan of the Revolution, and the hero, Léonce de Mondoville, a representative of that aristocracy frozen in the past, suffer and fight so as to be able to love each other and remain together, but their union is impossible; death alone can unite them because for Léonce, there can be no compromise. The novel describes the conflict between two moral codes: Delphine's democratic morality based on honesty and integrity; and Léonce's aristocratic concept of honor born of feudal society. Delphine's moral standards have been instilled in and bequeathed to her by her tutor and husband, the late M. d'Albémar, a veteran of the American War for Independence. Her preeminently Kantian morality is that "Truth must win the suffrage of others or teach us to do without it" (1:320).

Spanish on his mother's side, French on his father's, Léonce de Mondoville reminds us of Corneille's *Le Cid*, torn between love and duty, a duty that his honor imposes on him. As he writes to his democratic American tutor, Mr. Barton: "Thanks to you, I've had an enlightened education. And yet, the strongest motivations for all the actions of my life are grounded in a kind of military instinct, prejudiced if you will, yet congruent with the prejudices of my ancestors and perfectly expressive of the pride and impetuosity of my own spirit" (1:89). Politically, it is obvious that this call to duty would thrust Léonce into the camp of the defenders of the *ancien régime*. In his letter of April 20, 1791, he explains: "My mind understands very well the motives that inspire the defenders of the Revolution. . . . I myself would not have made it a point of honor to maintain the privileges of the nobility, but since so many old gentlemen have decided it must be so, that is quite enough to make it unbearable for me to pass for a democrat" (1:486). Alexis de Tocqueville observes that men use two separate and distinct means for passing judgment on the actions of their fellow man: "Sometimes they judge according to the simple notions of right and wrong, which are widespread throughout the world; at times they value them using quite specific notions which are proper to one country or to one era. It often happens that these two rules differ; sometimes they are at odds; but they never completely coalesce or cancel each other out."[8]

Léonce, lucid about the existence of the two codes, admits to his preceptor that if ever his sentiments regarding honor were to oppose "true morality" (1:90), morality would triumph, thanks to the lessons of his master. As Léonce has understood it and as Tocqueville later wrote: "Honor is simply that specific rule based on a specific state by which a people or a class apportions blame or praise" (Tocqueville 2:317).

As for Delphine, hers is the true morality, that which comes down to the principle of not doing harm to others. As she writes to Léonce: "Your morality is based only on honor; you would have been happier if you had adopted the simple, true principles which, in subjecting our actions to our conscience, emancipate us from any other yoke"

(1:416). Her values are democratic, because universal, and do not call for a complete and detailed code that preordains.

Throughout *Delphine*, democratic virtue and aristocratic honor are in direct opposition. The conflict increases in concert with the progression of the Revolution until the final catastrophe, which marks the deposition of the king and the disappearance of the nobility as an aristocratic caste. Honor then no longer has a raison d'être and Léonce's death becomes inescapable: this is so through his own will, for like the king he had refused to compromise. As each conflict between love and honor arises, he wants to die, and each time it is Delphine who gives way to love and generosity, supporting and reviving him until the final tragedy, where, at least in the novel's original ending, she gives him hope and faith in another world as he succumbs, a victim to that sense of honor which prevents him both from lying or from telling the truth. In the second ending, after a terrible internal struggle, he decides unenthusiastically to marry Delphine, but his honor is saved by her death; he then joins the army of Vendée composed of aristocrats and peasants devoted to King and Church. There he meets his own death.

In the original ending, Léonce is condemned to death by a revolutionary tribunal and shot by republican soldiers. We should keep in mind, however, that he had not joined the army of the émigrés; therefore he demonstrates an awareness that they were identifying themselves with their peers and not with the nation. As Tocqueville remarks, feudal honor "never passed a strict law that one must remain loyal to one's country" (2:321). In the *Considerations on the French Revolution*, Staël herself states: "The French nobles unfortunately considered themselves more as compatriots of the nobles of all countries than as fellow citizens of the French."[9] Furthermore Staël, who admired the patriotism of the French Republican Army (*Considerations* 180–181), depicts the French soldiers as generous and capable of pity.

In the second ending, Léonce will die fighting for the Royalists in the Vendée. This ending also conforms to Staël's opinions. "Nothing," she wrote, "brought more honor to the Royalist Party than the Civil War they attempted then. . . . They (the Vendéens) did not compromise the independence of their country. The leaders of Vendée were so regarded even by the opposing party" (*Considerations* 181). For Staël, "there are inflexible political duties as well as moral ones, and the most important of these is never to deliver your country to foreigners" (152).

The concept of patriotism is not the only issue raised in *Delphine:* since democracy destroys or changes the various inequalities in society, what will its effect on the inequality of men and women be? All the women in *Delphine* are unhappy, whatever their position in society. As Mme de Vernon aptly expresses it: "I firmly believed in the idea conceived from my childhood, that I was, by my sex and by the small fortune I possessed, an unhappy slave, prey to all the trickery of her tyrant. I did not reflect on morality, I didn't think it could be of any concern to the oppressed" (1:331). From a social standpoint, there is little difference between a woman and a pauper. Delphine represents an exception because she is without a family, therefore independent, and rich besides. She also represents the enlightened woman, thanks to the education she has received, an education which in the mind of her tutor, M. d'Albémar, was supposed to help her deal with the problem of the inequality of the sexes. Her tutor had prepared her for the problems independence might create for women in this particular society. He believed that "women more than men were in danger of being misjudged and therefore they had to fortify their souls in advance against misfortune" (1:94).

In a society where women are under the yoke of men, a woman's freedom is fostered by divorce. The plea of M. de Lebensei for divorce is a refutation point by point of Mme Necker's treatise against divorce, a treatise she had written just before dying and which provoked heated discussions between mother and daughter, since Staël was contemplating divorce. Mme Necker had little love for the Revolution, whereas M. de Lebensei, speaking for Staël, remarks: "It is true that divorce seems to some people the result of a revolution which they detest, and they resent it more for this than for any other reason" (2:79–80). Mme Necker thought that the legalization of divorce would not contribute at all to the happiness of marriage, that it burdened the couple with the threat of separation and infidelity. She believed divorce to be disastrous for children and cited as an example Medea, who stabbed her children under the eyes of Jason, who was about to abandon her for Creusa. To this Suzanne Necker's daughter replied that children suffer as much as their parents "when they are locked with them in the unending circle of pain caused by a mismatched and indissoluble union" (2:78–79), and that these same children would one day be adults, relieved to have benefited from the laws on divorce.

Mme Necker was in fact against freedom in all its forms: "Freedom," she wrote, "a dangerous word for all ages, for all states, for all sexes, but especially for ours, whose virtues are dependence, feelings, the relinquishment of the will."[10] This need for freedom is particularly harmful to women, according to Mme Necker, for it drives them to become virile, revolutionary:

> Then women coming down from their pedestals and mingling with the crowd want to play a role in the world. Soon they are imitating men in their rage, soon they become intoxicated with passions that they should have calmed; they soon end up neglecting the graces of their sex and like the bacchantes, they break Orpheus's lyre to let in the cymbals and the bugles; they parade themselves before the grandstands, armed with lances and bloody thyrses. (*Reflections* 58–59)

Woman's destiny, all her aspirations, should be to become the complement of the destiny of others. Mme Necker thinks there are true victims of husbandly tyranny, but laws are not made for the exceptions; we cannot fail to see a warning to her daughter in these words:

> The confederacy of women seeking the divorce law today numbers quite a few; they follow the devouring restlessness of their nature, in believing they can escape from mismatched unions; they claim that by this change they can avoid the unhappiness they carry within themselves, but it still awaits them in their new commitment, for a common wrong never makes a new bond, while virtues and sacrifices bring the most distant and the most opposite natures closer together. (*Reflections* 64)

As for Staël, though an advocate of divorce, she remained faithful to her own moral code. Thus, Delphine will not accept the idea of Léonce divorcing Matilde, as M. de Lebensei advises her to. Mme de Lebensei's divorce, on the other hand, is presented as perfectly acceptable. Married to an evil man who had become rich in the slave trade and who didn't love her, it was natural that she should benefit from the divorce laws of Holland so as to be free to marry M. de Lebensei.

A plea for divorce—and what is more, divorce for the freedom of men and women in marriage—the novel is Staël's side of a dialogue with the deceased mother who had refused to see her daughter before she died and never mentioned her in her will. The novel certainly develops the epigraph borrowed from Mme Necker, but in a particular, complex sense, as Claudine Herrmann notes: "Not accepting the prejudices of a society is to judge it. That is how Delphine does not submit, and why she continues to atone, as the epigraph of the novel anticipates."[11]

The democratic morality of Delphine goes hand in hand with a democratic religion opposed to Catholicism. Staël favors Protestantism as a state religion, for it is not based on a suffering calculated better to imprison the spirit. "In the Protestant countries, in England, Holland, Switzerland and America, morals are more pure, crimes less heinous, laws more humane" (2:74). She thereby rejects atheism: it flourishes in Catholic countries, especially among the aristocrats of the *ancien régime* for whom, as for Léonce, "religious ideas are nothing . . . ; that must be so, since honor in the world is everything" (1:92).

But what *is* Delphine's religion? Baptized a Catholic, she does not practice that religion, nor is she Protestant. In the original ending to the novel, Delphine does not mention either the Old Testament or the New, so dear to the Protestants. When she chooses readings to fortify Mme de Vernon as she faces the terrors of death, she turns to the ancient and modern religious and philosophical moralists. Moreover, she tries to lead Léonce to a "natural religion" (1:419). It is only in the second ending that Delphine dies as a Christian, having the Psalms and passages from the Gospels read to her.

In accordance with the terminology of the era, Delphine calls upon the Supreme Being. The novel reflects the fact that under the Revolution, dechristianization was about to increase: on February 13, 1790, there was the Constitutional decree forbidding perpetual monastic vows; then on November 27, 1790, came the civil constitution of the clergy; and on September 20, 1792, the secularization of the civil state and the institution of divorce were promulgated.

Delphine affirms a universal faith, a faith in which dogma plays no role, a positive faith based on a God of goodness whom we assume wishes the happiness of mankind. The religious revolution could occur only by eliminating theology in the same way that the *ancien régime* had been overturned. Thus, in France in 1793, Christianity had given way to the cult of the goddess Reason. Inaugurated on the 20th Brumaire in the second year of the French Republic in Paris, this cult reached its peak in France among Protestants and Jews as well as among former Catholics. Its goddess was portrayed as lively and animated, and her representative was chosen from among the most beautiful and notable citizens. This republican religion gave the country some of the unity needed to resist the counter-Revolution. Thus a religion was created whose only dogma was equality. Although these cults were developed in 1793 and 1794, subsequent to the novel's time frame, they do make us think of *Delphine*. Perhaps Staël was inspired by them, for her heroine resembles a priestess of the principles of 1789.

True to her name, Delphine is also the sibyl of Delphi who collects the words of Apollo, god of all science and the highest religious and moral authority, a mediator between men and other gods. Throughout the novel, Staël prepares us for the original ending, where Delphine succeeds in converting Léonce to her own conception of God. She becomes the intermediary between God and men. Staël elaborates at some length on her "inspired character" (2:411), on her perfect goodness, the true sign of her "divine nature" (1:377). Thus, Sophie de Vernon, during her agony, refuses the dismal apparatus of the Catholic religion and declares, pointing to Delphine: "This angel will intercede for me with the Supreme Being" (1:354).

Apollo was god of light and truth; he was also a purifying deity who prescribed measures for ending national disasters by eliminating the defects that caused them. Thus it was appropriate that Delphine should accompany the chariot of Léonce to his death and act as his priestess. Her own death and Léonce's, in the midst of a bloody Revolution which was to weaken virtue, freedom, and nation for a long time to come, reflect on one hand the failure of constitutional monarchy; on the other hand these deaths also represent an apotheosis that could not be realized on earth. Delphine plays the role of priestess of Apollo, the god who delights in the foundation of city-states and the establishment of civil constitutions, the purifying god who cleanses the national stains and allows the triumph of freedom. M. de Lebensei writes: "That Revolution, which has unfortunately been soiled by many crimes, will be judged by posterity for the freedom it will assure France. . . . All that is noble in the human race—happiness, glory, virtue—is so ultimately linked to freedom that the centuries have always pardoned those events which furthered it" (2:338).

The novel with its original, non-Christian ending, forms an entity that Simone Balayé has justifiably restored to the critical edition that she and Lucia Omacini have prepared. Devoted to freedom and to the Revolution, *Delphine* thus ends on a line first quoted by Mme Necker herself in her *Mélanges*:[12] "No one answers me, but perhaps someone hears me." Here the irrepressible creative spirit of Staël speaks, appealing to those who, as exemplified by her own departed mother, would distrust freedom in all its forms.

ARTICULATIONS
OF INWARDNESS

COMMUNICATION AND POWER IN GERMAINE DE STAËL: TRANSPARENCY AND OBSTACLE

One of the results of absolute power which most contributed to Napoleon's downfall was that, bit by bit, no one dared any longer tell him the truth about anything. He ended up unaware that winter arrived in Moscow in November because none of his courtiers was Roman enough to tell him something even that simple.[1]

Because of this remark, and many others like it, I shall try to present here an overall view of a major problem in Staël's writing, which she never analyzes in a systematic way, but where her thought is very rich: how communication is impeded or interrupted by silence, lying, hypocrisy, the debasement of language.[2] We tend, incorrectly, to associate the problematics of language and communication solely with the crisis of modernity; they were also of great concern for the Groupe de Coppet. The problem is linguistic, but also moral and political, and Staël discusses it in all her various sorts of writing. My goal is in part to demonstrate the homogeneity of her thought as novelist, critic, philosopher, and political theoretician. For lack of space, I shall have to be schematic; the subject merits a book.

Adelaide and Theodore, an early work, (1786), prefigures in many ways the obstacles to communication typical of Staël's later writings. Adelaide is secretly married to Theodore. His mother's opposition makes declaring that marriage impossible. Because a friend of hers is in love with Count d'Elmont, Adelaide often entertains d'Elmont; Theodore is understandably jealous, but she cannot betray her friend's secret. She becomes pregnant, but does not dare tell Theodore, whence the crisis scene:

> Adelaide, who was on the point of telling him about the new tie between them, was deeply wounded by his coldness, and so kept silent. They moved toward each other, their secrets were about to be revealed, but some strange eagerness for unhappiness imposed silence, and Theodore rushed off with the painful cry, "Adelaide, adieu."[3]

She runs after him, shouting, but "her voice could not be heard." He falls fatally ill with pulmonary trouble (other heroes get wounded in the chest, all interfering with speech). She goes to see him, but in hiding, does not even dare ask where he is. When they do get together, his mother arrives, and she can say nothing. Theodore dies, and Adelaide stays alive long enough to bear their child and then commits suicide. She does leave her son an autobiographical text which tells all, but when communication is finally established, the protagonists are all dead. Otherwise, communication fails throughout the text, and each failure produces a new disaster.

The plot is quite similar to that of *Delphine* but, as Simone Balayé has shown, *Delphine* is also a political novel in which communication is impeded not only because of the amorous plot but also because of political and social factors and because of woman's status.[4] Staël was the first woman to obtain fame in France not only as a novelist but as an essayist, in philosophy, esthetics, history, and politics. In all these areas she is concerned with the problem of communication.

Despotism as an Obstacle to Communication

The clearest case is that represented by my opening quotation about Napoleon and the Moscow winters. Political theoreticians, from Machiavelli to Max Weber and Erving Goffmann, have lengthily analyzed how the possession of power prevents effective communication. It is one of Staël's major criticisms of Napoleon: "The fear he created was such that no one dared tell him the truth about anything."[5] She also

faults the ancien régime for the same reason, as she does the first Restoration; even a simple Swiss peasant knew that Napoleon was apt to
return, but court etiquette and ministerial pretensions were such that
no one could state the obvious.[6] There are historical exceptions: Louis
XII, Henri IV with his attacks on flattery, the English—who are "as
truthful about their failures as about their successes,"[7] but generally
despotism produces flattery, and he who is flattered cannot know the
truth.[8] The Duke of Mendoce in *Delphine* is a nice satirical portrait of
such a flatterer, and the play *Jane Grey* offers several others, but one
could say that in *Delphine* salon life is similarly vitiated by the despotism of opinion. Staël's thinking here is hardly original, except in two
respects. One is her thesis that the obstacles despotism poses to communication can be remedied by the use of allegory or the fantastic,
stating the truth in a veiled manner.[9] The other is that, despite flattery,
the truth will out, history will destroy the lie, it will snow in Moscow
in November.[10] I leave aside the related but well-known matter of her
opposition to censorship to discuss how political abuse of language
can create obstacles to communication.

The Debasement of Language

Staël is primarily concerned here with two phenomena: the abuse of
revolutionary language during the Terror and the problem of calumny—of which women, including Marie Antoinette and Staël herself, are particularly victims. But she reflects the same concern with the
debasement of language in her discussion of what we have referred to
since Heidegger as "inauthentic discourse," in salon life as well as
elsewhere. Here she is a precursor of Flaubert: the abuse of language
deprives words of their proper meaning and results in a reversal of
moral values, where virtue becomes associated with the weak and
duped, vice with the strong.[11] Calumny and revolutionary eloquence
"deprive words of their natural power and reason, exhausted by error
and sophistry, can no longer perceive the truth" (*On Literature* 405).
On Literature contains a long and violent attack against revolutionary
eloquence, which abuses the names of all the virtues to justify every
crime (407–409). In a close analysis of a sentence by Couthon, she
shows how it is well organized and logically constructed, but only to
the end that reason can become the arm of crime. And here, in contrast

to what happens with flattery, history tends to espouse and realize the abuse of language. These false ideas, dressed up in exaggerated images, lead to the most sanguinary furies; all proper judgment is destroyed.[12] Words that are so abused become arid and powerless to move, and the language of liberty particularly loses that power.[13] A special study should be made of Staël's proposals for controlling calumny, where she and Constant had some trouble reconciling their hatred of libel with their love of the freedom of the press. But the main problem for her was that words and eloquence, which should be instruments of freedom, had become the instruments of terror and oppression. As an example of her deep concern, I cite one of the few really cruel passages she ever wrote, about Robespierre's death. "His jaw was smashed by a pistol shot; he could not even talk to defend himself, he who had talked so much in order to destroy others! One might say that divine justice does not refuse, when it wishes, to strike the imagination by powerfully moving circumstances" (*Considerations* 315).

Under Napoleon, matters became worse in the sense that he not only censored the press and speech but also created a controlled press that spewed forth lies and falsehoods, creating "a despotism which took its delights in language" (*Circumstances* 294). Napoleon manipulated language, indulged in the "active lie."[14] He practiced political dissimulation not by silence but by floods of words; it is easier to mislead by speaking, by lying actively, than by silence.[15] To the tyranny of gossip he added the gossip of tyranny.[16] And this abuse of language, created by the Revolution and intensified by Napoleonic despotism, she felt, was now invading all forms of discourse; one can only learn what it is safe to say, and not what is.[17]

The Treatise On Good Eloquence

A contemporary reader is astonished by the importance Staël attributes to eloquence in *On Literature*, but for her, eloquence is a necessary and indispensable political instrument badly in need of rehabilitation. And Staël, a firm believer in perfectibility, does not despair; indeed, with progress in literacy and democracy good eloquence will become more and more necessary, for "reason and eloquence are the natural links of any republican association."[18] Her recipe for rehabilitating the eloquence that the Revolution and Napoleon had perverted is a simple one; one must have recourse to reason, imagination, and sentiment, and the three must be harmoniously combined.[19] The spread of printing, as opposed to oral communication, has made right reason even more essential: geometric precision and logical ordering are required when the text can be read closely and reexamined.[20] But truth and the ornaments of truth must be effectively combined, expression and sentiment derived from the same source.[21] Also, one must be brave and dare to speak the truth. Notably, truth is for Staël necessary not only in political discourse but also in the novel, a theory she has already developed in *Essay on Fiction;* fiction must also harmoniously combine reason, sentiment, and imagination.[22]

But the task is not a simple one, and we must make a detour here to discuss another problem.

The Powers and Dangers of the Ironic Wit of the Enlightenment

Eighteenth-century authors, particularly Voltaire, says Staël, employed "an allegorical manner of expressing the truth effectively in an age when error reigned."[23] *On Literature* offers an interesting historical explanation for this phenomenon in France. The power of the French monarchy was limitless in fact but uncertain and limited in principle (*droit*). Power could be arbitrary, but at the same time liberty of thought and expression was both possible and necessary when it took the form of wit and even ridicule, and could contribute to the progressive struggle against error and oppression. This wit is peculiarly French: in Russia, the nobility is too uneducated, the government too despotic; in Italy, again for political reasons, wit can only deal with matters of love, esthetics, and so forth; in Germany, people are too concerned with the truth to practice wit; in England, there are no intermediate conversational bodies between the family and Parliament where wit could find political play.[24]

Elsewhere, however, Staël can be quite negative about this ironic wit, which is too often used to attack behavior that does not conform to social norms. The "noble simplicity" that should characterize speech in a republic has been replaced by this clattering of syllables, the product of despotism. It is a discourse of vanity and not of energy.

In the novels it is often the weapon of slander.[25] More interestingly, she associates language of this sort with that "metaphysic which links all our ideas to our sensations." Staël is convinced to the contrary, that the superficial comes from outside impressions, serious discourse reflects the depths of the soul.[26] Her rejection of eighteenth-century wit is connected with her option for transcendental rather than sensualist or ideological philosophy. But that choice raises another question.

Is a Purely Transparent Language Possible?

Staël associated Transcendentalism first and foremost with Kant, including the categorical imperative and the Kantian injunction to refuse lying in all its forms. Kant, as she notes, respected truth to the point where one should not even lie when a scoundrel asks you if your friend whom he is pursuing is hidden in your house.[27] Staël concluded, in the context of the Terror suggested by the above example, that there are occasions when one must lie in order to protect others, whence her preference for Jacobi over Kant, for a somewhat flexible ethics inspired by religious sentiment over logical rigorism.[28] Delphine echoes this debate in her preference for religion as opposed to honor as the ethical principle. In ethics, Staël, a novelist, thinks about concrete, not abstract situations, as she does in politics, and concludes that good must often compromise with evil.[29] It is noteworthy in this respect that, in her essay on Rousseau, she does not praise his claim of absolute sincerity in his *Confessions*. Her minor literary texts are full of "white lies"; indeed Jane Grey's excellence stems from her lying about her political attitudes, from the lie she tells in order to save her husband's life, and *M. de Kernadec* is all about the invention of a rather preposterous white lie so that crossed lovers can be married. Elsewhere, she is more ambiguous. Her comments on Rousseau's *Nouvelle Héloïse* on the one hand admire Julie's refusal to tell all to M. de Wolmar, but then she adds, "How I should appreciate a movement which would lead her to reveal everything."[30] Her *Story of Pauline* offers an exemplary illustration of this ambiguity. Mme de Verneuil, who is good, encourages Pauline to lie in order to get out of the clutches of her seducer and start a new life, then to lie about her past in order to marry her true love, Edouard; but when Edouard does discover the past, the result is a duel where he is fatally wounded. The text concludes that what most caused his despair was Pauline's silence about her past failings.[31] In the same way, in *Delphine* the "white lie" is usually the lie of silence—Léonce about his would-be assassins, Delphine about her political opinions, about the love of Thérèse d'Ervins for M. de Serbellane, about her gifts to Matilde, and her refusal, at Barton's suggestion, to tell Léonce what she has discovered about Mme de Vernon. But many of these lies of silence, while morally justified, eventually produce disaster; Delphine's silence about Thérèse, for instance, leads Léonce to marry Matilde. The absolute refusal to lie demanded by Kant is then not only impossible, but can even be immoral. When one must lie, it is best to lie by silence, and even then the "virtuous" lie exacts a price of suffering. Nor was Staël unaware that almost everyone thinks that his or her lie is virtuous; Mme de Vernon gives a rather good speech to that effect on her deathbed.

English Eloquence and Lucile's Silence

The Anglophilia which dominates much of Staël's thought is less strong when it comes to the problem of communication. On the one hand she admires the seriousness of English political discourse, the fairness of legal eloquence, the absence of a declamatory style and of sophistry.[32] On the other, she not only criticizes, as noted above, the absence of political discussions outside Parliament, but above all she deplores the silence that women in England are reduced to. They do not participate in discussions, creating a lack of general conversation, of familiarity.[33] *Corinne* offers an ample case study of this English failing, not only with Lady Edgermond but with Edgermond himself and above all with Lucile. Lucile's refusal to tell Oswald about the dangers of crossing the Alps is all too reminiscent of the courtiers' refusal to tell Napoleon about the November weather in Moscow. Staël interestingly (if incorrectly) complains that in England there are no memoirs, confessions, autobiographical literature; a too severe refusal to talk about the self vitiates English literature.[34] According to Staël, silence, particularly the silence imposed on women in England, is not golden.

The Forms of Impeded Communication

I should now like to propose a categorization of the forms of impeded communication in Staël's texts, though I must admit that my categories are heteroclite and not watertight. The "degré zéro" would of course be what I have already discussed, Silence. In addition to the white lie of silence, it should be noted that in many cases silence is either anodine or clearly virtuous—Oswald's silencing of praises about his heroic conduct at the fire of Ancona, for example. It should also be noted, however, that silence is often imposed by an excess of emotion, or more importantly by someone who is more powerful (Mme de Vernon on Delphine, Lady Edgermond on Corinne, or the way in which Corinne cannot improvise in front of Edgermond, the incarnation of English power).

Nonverbal Communication

In many cases, communication is effected by nonverbal means, particularly when an excess of emotion imposes silence. Staël was familiar with de Gérando's theory that language was not the only or even the most important system of communication—one recalls the rather comic Kalmouk prince of *Ten Years of Exile* who, unable to converse with the ladies who delight him, gives them diamonds instead—but the innumerable instances where gesture or glance replace language in Staël's novels should be studied, particularly because they are associated with

Communication by Displaced Discourse

Direct discourse is often replaced by singing a song, often accompanied on a harp (usually in order to declare one's passion), or by citing a poem, or by evoking a work of literature, or, most importantly and frequently, by discussing a painting or a sculpture. Delphine is as much a master of this art as Corinne. Sophie and Pauline also use displaced discourse, and in her esthetic writings Staël discusses at length the communicability of music. But all these are instances where straightforward verbal communication breaks down, usually because of varying degrees of emotional intensity or incompatibility.

To Speak or to Write?

The same problematics of communication appear in the numerous discussions in Staël's writing about the written versus the spoken word. Here again, her thought is complex. Serious subjects should be treated in writing, she feels, not in conversation.[35] Yet, the spoken word is often more sincere than the written word, and she admires the English obligation to improvise rather than read a speech. (She does not seem to have known the considerable discussions of contemporary theoreticians of eloquence about the relative merits of improvising, learning by heart, reading, or speaking from a detailed outline.) Both Léonce and Geneviève de Brabant insist on speaking rather than writing because it is more sincere, but Corinne, Mme de Lebensei, and Mlle d'Albémar know moments when they must substitute writing for speaking, out of timidity, *pudeur*, or intense emotion. Mme de Vernon prefers writing to speaking because it is easier to manipulate and control what one writes. And, of course, there is the problem of the extent to which the form of the epistolary novel requires that one substitute writing for speaking.

Opinion as an Obstacle to Transparent Communication

In the salon, opinion reigns, and, even if the salon exists for conversation, opinion imposes silence and lying. *Delphine*'s epigram is a quotation from Mme Necker, "A man should know how to defy opinion, a woman how to submit to it," a theory repeated in the novel not by Delphine but by Matilde.[36] In politics, it is necessary but also difficult to go counter to opinion; one must know how to flatter, how to please.[37] But generally Staël attacks the way opinion imposes dishonesty and lying, to the extent that this reader at least likes the jesuitical proposal of Mme d'Artenas that Delphine should become publicly reconciled with Mme de Vernon and at the same time be as nasty as possible about her behind her back. To do so would be to enter into the world of submission to opinion, of hypocrisy and lying. The Staël heroine refuses even if Staël's mother recommended it.

Inauthentic Discourse

Staël refuses this, much as she does ironic wit. She considers it "bavardage qui use l'esprit," chit chat which destroys the mind, gossiping sprinkled with name-dropping, a waste of time where the soul is sacrificed to the taste of the day.[38] The exigencies of inauthentic conversation destroy sincerity of character and treat thought as a sickness that requires a strict diet of pap.[39] In *On Germany* she gives some nice examples, including the man who begins by fulsomely praising an actress he has just seen; the sardonic smiles of his audience make him temper his praise bit by bit until he ends up saying, "The poor devil did what she could" (1:103); inauthenticity leads to lies. The problem is fully represented in the novels, epitomized in *Corinne* by M. d'Erfeuil who, though *sympathique,* claims that proper form can justify any kind of content. It is more nefarious, more widespread and vitiating in *Delphine*, where it is associated with slander and suffering. But my favorite example is in the play *The Mannequin*. Sophie practices a white lie in order to avoid marriage with the egotistical and loquacious Count Erville (Erfeuil, Ervins—*air vain?*). Erville, who chatters and never listens, is put before a mannequin who pleases him endlessly; she is beautiful, never interrupts him, and admires everything he says. He asks her hand, freeing Sophie. Inauthentic discourse is here not the chirping of birds, but a means of reducing the other to a mute object.

Impeded Communication as a Principle of Plot Structure

Often in Staël's novels, it is lies, silence, and hypocrisy which create misunderstandings but also determine the action and create suspense for the reader—all the more so because of dramatic irony: the reader knows what the characters cannot say or be told. Almost all of *Delphine* is constructed on this principle: the heroine's unspoken love for Léonce, the unsaid reasons why she receives M. de Serbellane, the occultation of Mme de Vernon's perfidy, the silence toward Matilde demanded by Mme de Vernon on her deathbed. It is noteworthy that it is a child, Thérèse's daughter, hence an innocent outside the social system, who reveals the truth. The purest case is probably the play *Sappho;* but there, as in *Delphine* and elsewhere, the anagnorisis, far from solving matters, produces tragedy. When the obstacle disappears and communication becomes transparent, tragedy and death result.

Impeded Communication and the Crisis Scene

Significantly, the crisis scenes in Staël's writings occur when communication is impossible: Corinne, hidden spectator of Lucile and Oswald's marriage, where at the most she can communicate by sending a ring; Delphine, at Léonce's marriage to Matilde (with its tense build-up), hidden behind a pillar, veiled. One could add many others—the scene in the garden at night, the scene at the theater when *Tancrède* is being played, and so on. As Simone Balayé notes, a symbolic system of hidden gestures, veils, masks, and separating screens, governs the whole novel, showing that Delphine and Léonce can never get together.[40] It is this symbolic system which comes into play in the crisis scenes that articulate the plot.

The Mother as Impeder of Communication

The classic case is surely Lady Edgermond. Silence reigns in her house, and what conversation there is is completely inauthentic and concerns the weather. Corinne cannot talk to her; moreover, here again, Staël weaves a symbolic system to underline Lady Edgermond's role—her silencing the Italian musicians, the fact that she becomes mute a month before her death. Mme de Vernon is a more complex case. She will not let Delphine reveal her love to Léonce, or to Mme de Vernon herself, and she manipulates what can and especially what cannot be said, practicing both hypocrisy and censorship. "I'll hear," she says, "Delphine's confession of her love when I want to, but I don't intend to for a while, so I have freedom of action."[41] She has an intense dislike for moments when one says what one thinks or tells all.[42] She does tell all on her deathbed, but only in order to impose a new kind of silence on Delphine and Léonce. One could do a similar analysis of the mother in *Sophie* or *Sappho* or elsewhere. It is often, of course, the mother not of the heroine but of the heroine's enemy. This is a comforting kind of transference, but still the epigram of *Delphine* about how women must bend to opinion is from Mme Necker. Grist for the mill of psychoanalytical critics . . .

Hypocrisy Done and Undone: From Obstacle to Tragic Transparence

Mme de Vernon could take as her motto Talleyrand's supposed quip, "language was given to man to hide his thoughts"; indeed, she has often been read as a caricature of the famed diplomat. Among the vices, hypocrisy in particular provokes Staël's wrath. In a noted attack in *On Literature* hypocrites are described as charlatans of vice, mockers of the sensitive soul, of all moral principles, who should themselves be ridiculed, handed over to the mockery of children.[43] Elsewhere she emphasizes how hypocrisy perverts its practitioners.[44] The exemplary hypocrite in her political writings is less Talleyrand than Napoleon, particularly in his dealings with the Poles and Czar Alexander. Once more, however, I underline that when Mme de Vernon does at her deathbed drop her mask of hypocrisy, she does so only to ask Léonce and Delphine to practice hypocrisy, thus heightening the tragedy. The same thing happens elsewhere, notably in *Jane Grey*, where Surrey and Northumberland are both consummate hypocrites; the latter, like Mme de Vernon, unveils all the horrors of his crime but in so doing only precipitates the tragedy. If hypocrisy is the worst of vices, is it perhaps also a necessary vice?

That Love Which Cannot Be Expressed

Love should create total transparency between two beings, but more than any other relationship in Staël's writings, it is vitiated by the obstacles to communication. Oswald does not dare declare his love for Corinne to Edgermond, to Erfueil, or to Corinne, creating endless misunderstandings; she cannot declare her love, nor the details of her past, not even her name, to him; Lucile finds herself in a similar impossibility. From her first meeting with Léonce, Delphine cannot talk with him, and if Léonce can declare his love for her to Barton, he cannot to Delphine. The preface evokes "those sentiments of affection which cannot be stated" and the plot is created by the obstacles to the communication of love. The play *Sophie* probably offers the quintessential treatment of the theme. The Count cannot declare his love for Sophie, or Sophie hers for the Count, and the Countess refuses to state anything concerning these loves. When the love is revealed, it is without saying for whom, or the revelation is created by breaking taboos.

The obviously incestuous overtones of the play may explain why love cannot be declared here in so intense a fashion, but as Sophie herself observes, "When passions achieve a certain degree of violence, they are almost always veiled in silence."[45] The main obstacles to communication are located on the *Carte du Tendre*.

Conclusion

I have probably exhausted my reader's patience, but I have not exhausted the subject. One could analyze those occasions where people refuse to speak because to do so would be to wound, to create suffering; the cases of blackmail, where saying does destroy; the refusal to state what the hero must discover on his own (see *La Sunamite*); the way in which transparent communication can deteriorate into the trite and the inauthentic, and then into silence. I have not discussed Staël's correspondence here, which would offer rich material for the subject. The problem in Staël should be compared to incommunicability in Constant (well studied) and in Mme de Charrière. Much of what I have been describing is a commonplace of political discourse and indeed of the tradition of the novel and the theater, but I do think that Staël's texts reveal an exceptionally high incidence of preoccupation with the failures of communication. For her, the problem is a central one. "Nature created me for conversation," she says in her proposed panegyric.[46] She loved to converse and to communicate, and her fear of exile and hatred of despotism were deeply motivated by the fact that both provided obstacles to communication. She lived in an age that was very aware of the problematics of language and of communication, of the uses and abuses of eloquence. In many texts, she suggests an almost frenetic confidence in the potential and power of language. Language offers an inexhaustible resource and no sincere word is every wholly lost.[47] In her political writings, however, as in her fiction and plays, she shows an intense and acute awareness that there are obstacles to communication and also that transparency can be dangerous. My title is derived from Starobinski's remarkable study of Rousseau, but the world of Staël's fiction is not the utopia of the *Nouvelle Héloïse*, and she never chose to strive for transparency the way Rousseau did in his *Confessions*. Between the two occurred the Terror (where many, like Corinne, did not dare give their names) and

Napoleonic despotism, under which *On Germany* was given more drastic treatment than that given the *Encyclopédie* under the ancien régime. Rousseau was a man, Staël a woman, and, as Marie-Claire Vallois says, her novels exemplify "the aphasic character of feminine discourse."[48] She is reported to have said of her second husband, John Rocca, that "words were not his language"; perhaps Rocca is to be envied. But in *Corinne,* as Madelyn Gutwirth notes, and often elsewhere, silence conquers language.[49] The result, if inevitable, is nonetheless tragic.

SUICIDE AS
SELF-CONSTRUCTION

Margaret R. Higonnet

"Whatever does not annihilate itself, is not free and worth nothing."—*Friedrich Schlegel*

"Modernity must be under the sign of suicide, an act which seals
a heroic will. . . . It is *the* achievement of modernity in the realm
of passions."—*Walter Benjamin*

Suicide, in cutting short the natural span of a life, turns existence
into a metaphoric ruin, a fragment. Paradoxically, however, a person
may stop linear time in an attempt to give her life definitive shape as a
whole. As Walter Benjamin put it, "a man's knowledge or wisdom,
but above all his real life . . . first assumes transmissible form at the
moment of his death."[1] Suicide, then, can be understood as a form of
self-construction.

The way I understand this paradox differs sharply from that offered
in a previous analysis of Staël, the brilliant essay by Jean Starobinski.[2]
The main lines of my own inquiry lie buried in his analysis, but in
order to bring them to light, I want to break open some of his evalua-
tive assumptions.

Starobinski traces a systolic-diastolic rhythm, both in Staël's life and
in her works.[3] At the outset, he finds in the portraits of her heroines an
overflowing abundance of faculties and "a radical lack"; as a result of

this fundamental, contradictory character, her heroines couple an exuberant devotion to the other with the avid need for possession of the other. "At the limit of the expansive impetus, devotion and the bounteous gift of the self become the inseparable twins of a capture" (JS 244). In this master plot of the lives of Staël's heroines, devotion tends toward the asymptote not so much of self-sacrificial death as of manipulation. Staël wishes by a perpetually renewed rhetoric without substance—mere threats or attempts—to "aggravate" the wrongs of the beloved (JS 246). Or when the suicidal act is indeed accomplished, its narcissistic aim is to inscribe oneself on the other. Staël's emotional ideal, he suggests, "can only arouse endless suspicion and terror—a Terror whose formula would be not *la liberté ou la mort,* but *attachment or death"* (JS 245). In the theme of suicide, he finds "the ultimate arm of possessive desire, entrapping greed. Staël and her heroines contrive to turn the void that they confront into the currency that permits them to keep all of the loved being" (JS 246). Suicide, in short, is blackmail.

As systematic and psychologically plausible as Starobinski's analysis may be, it also poses a few problems. First: the "lack" Starobinski attributes to Staël is not merely a perversely innate craving for power over another that happens to occur among women. If Staël writes of faculties that devour us as the vulture gnaws on Prometheus, because they have no outlet outside the self, she most often has in mind not some universal, sexless, frustrated genius, but the woman artist, who is denied an appropriate "point of action."[4] Staël consistently theorizes and analyzes the social reaction to women's other (unmentionable) "lack": namely, women's disbarment from speech and other forms of public action. The point is critical. For under the circumstances Staël describes, suicide may ultimately become for a woman the only available means of speaking or acting.

Second, Starobinski seems to assume that the only characters in Staël's novels who deploy what he calls the "perpetual allusion to suicide" are female. Yet many men in her novels not only mull over ways of finding death for themselves, but also accuse their mistresses of effective murder and threaten them with double suicide: Vallorbe and Léonce, Erfeuil and Oswald all manipulate what Staël calls this "sublime resource."

Third, it seems to me that in his discussion of her erotic desires and representations of suicide, Starobinski lets Staël have it both coming and going. To commit suicide is to turn oneself into an Erinnye. But not to commit suicide is equally a fault; she "hesitates," he says reprovingly, at the threshold of absolute annihilation, for she clings to a desire for immortality. Incapable of true resignation or "moral suicide," she retains a faintly ridiculous love of life—and takes new lovers.[5] "She takes on the burden of her own survival, she will survive herself in her own devastated life" (JS 249).

Taking charge: survival amid the ruins. These are the ideas enfolded in Starobinski's intrinsically hostile essay that I would like to turn around and apply positively to some texts by Staël. In broad outline, we can say that the prospect of autonomy ("l'empire de soi-même") that the Staëlian protagonist hopes to attain through suicide takes three forms. The first is retrospective: by becoming one's own Atropos and cutting the thread of life, the suicide redefines the past as a whole. The second, more positive, orientation is prospective. Only by shattering the old order can a new order emerge. Here suicide is often a metaphoric transition between two lives, or an actual displacement, in which the dying heroine yields to her double. The third form is the most desperate and politically explicit: what we might call linguistic or poetic suicide. Here the character has recourse to the most absolute of human gestures, in lieu of speech. In this third moment, the problematic relationship between control and authenticity comes to the fore.[6]

Eighteenth-century writers often quoted a passage from Pliny, in which he remarked that the possibility of suicide gives us a freedom beyond that even of God. For those who accepted the idea of a natural instinct of self-preservation, to commit this act was also to step outside natural law. In a rather simplistic move, one could say that Staël throughout her work pursues the liberating possibilities of suicide. *On the Influence of the Passions* (1796), for example, written out of the shards of her relationship with Narbonne, broods insistently over the theme of suicide.[7] She exhorts us to admire "the man larger than nature, when he rejects what it has given him, when he uses life to destroy life, when he can master by his spiritual power the strongest human impulse: the instinct of self preservation" (*Passions* 187). Suicide, then, is a form of mastery.

One direction this assertion of control over life may take is to define the past by cutting short the otherwise inexorable processes of corruption, decay, and disillusionment marked out for the future. It is this type of suicide to which Starobinski's analysis best applies, although he sees in it only the desire for mastery of another, not that for mastery of oneself and one's environment. The woman whom Staël imagines condemned to the guillotine next to her lover suicidally "cherishes death" as a form of permanent union that will eliminate the possibility of future loss.[8] It is a theme Staël used in an early verse epistle about lovers thwarted by their parents and the accidents of the Revolution. At its close, as she sees her lover at the tribunal, Sophie throws herself into the arms of soldiers, with a cry of counterrevolutionary sympathies in order to join Edouard: "This bloody chain links me to my husband."[9]

Likewise, the heroine of *Jane Grey* (1790) greets death, for as she reminds her husband in the fifth act, their ardor might have cooled. By choosing to die rather than escape, "We die still entire; our last sigh can yet be heaved by a heart that burns with love" (act 5, sc. 4).[10] The wholeness of the marriage is underwritten by a willing surrender of both to death.

Zulma (1794) sums up the notion that death can cut short the slip of perfect love into imperfection. The Indian heroine, Zulma, has been shaped by her love and by her lover's instruction into his mirror, his second self. Naturally, she is ready to sacrifice her life to save his, whether from intra-tribal conflict or from a mortal poison. When she discovers his infidelity, she murders him.[11] As she explains, by killing him, she preserves the past: "I have saved my lover, he remains immortal."[12] At the same time, because to kill him is to kill herself (to become "my own enemy"), at the moment of her public testimony, she is already among the living-dead: "Since this time I have lost my identity, the very recollection of my existence" (*Zulma* 344). This loss of life makes it possible for her to confront her accusers with calm dignity, indeed it enables her narrative. Her final act, then, culminates her turn inward upon and against the self, as she draws one of her own arrows to inflict a mortal wound in her side. In this ultimate gesture of autonomy, she closes the circle of her life.

The idea that suicide—or a double suicide—will offer a substitute for marriage and can foreclose further suffering recurs in the two great novels, *Delphine* (1802) and *Corinne* (1807). The pathetically divided Monsieur de Valorbe proposes a double suicide to Delphine, laying out pistols on the table of the room in which he has locked himself with her.[13] Such a suicide/murder scene clearly exposes the motives that Freud diagnosed:

For analysis has explained the enigma of suicide the following way: probably no one finds the mental energy required to kill himself, unless in the first place, he is in doing this at the same time killing an object with whom he has identified himself, and, in the second place, is turning against himself a death-wish which had been directed against someone else. . . . The unconscious of all human beings is full enough of such death wishes, even against those we love.[14]

Though a similar twin impulse, both homicidal and suicidal, may be detected in a figure like Zulma, it seems most clearly imaged in scenes where a double suicide is threatened.

But Staël also represents the longing for perfected love through the motif of double suicide, twice proposed by Léonce. Leaning over the Seine after Delphine has been insulted, he asks her, "Would you like to flee with me from these cruel people, into the bosom of death? One word, and we will leap together into these waves. . . . Is it not certain that nothing remains for us but pain?" (*Delphine* 2: 124). And later, "Unfortunate woman! Do you wish to die with me, do you? To leave life together seems something like happiness; I will give you the dagger you must plunge into my heart; you will feel this heart, in its terrible palpitations; I will guide the blade and your hand. Soon afterwards you will follow me" (2: 332–333). The imagined palpitations leave little doubt about the sexual import of double suicide. *Liebestod* lures the protagonists of *Corinne* as well. During her nearly fatal illness, when Oswald nurses her in Rome, Corinne imagines that they will be able to preserve their love in death; shortly afterwards, Oswald invites his beloved to "leap into another life" in order to join him (with his father!) in heaven.[15]

This first mode of suicide is dominated by the desire for self-defini-tion and for continuity with all one has adhered to in the past; it is allied to political suicide or the suicide of principle, such as that of Cato. Matilde, the cousin of Delphine, suffers from a rigorous cult of religious purity and social correctness that we might diagnose as *ano-rexia religiosa*. Ultimately, she responds defiantly to the threat of her husband's infidelity by a secret but rigorous fast, at the risk of her health and the life of her infant. Her mother-in-law pessimistically predicts: "If she persists in nursing her child, she certainly will not be able to survive two months" (*Delphine* 2: 278). In addition, Staël weaves constant references to heroic suicide, such as that of a Curtius or Cato, into her texts.[16] By contrast to modern actions dominated by personal "interest," Corinne dreams, for example, of heroic self-sacrifice and faithful wives like Portia, whose ancient "traces" remain among the ruins of Italy (*Corinne* 244). Characteristically, Staël juxtaposes a political and a feminist theme.

The second broad orientation of suicide in Staël is prospective. Here the act—or the idea of suicide—serves as a condition for freedom. Thus M. de Serbellane explains why he has carried a ring with Italian poison in it—the ring he will give to Delphine: "I felt calmer and freer in thinking that if life became unbearable, I had with me that which could easily save me" (*Delphine* 2: 399). By reflecting on suicide, he can take control of life, in order to go on.

The attitude is one that Léonce shares. Indeed, Léonce says, death grounds all knowledge. "The presence of death has shed light for me on what is real in life" (*Delphine* 2: 402). He plunges into battle, because he knows that in combat, "chance belongs to me." Because he can direct the operations of chance in order to obtain an "easy death," he can support a few more days of life, consecrated to winning honor (2: 390). During Delphine's illness, he similarly retains self-control by thinking of this ultimate act of self-mastery. "Do you think that to stay calm, it suffices to resolve to commit suicide if she dies?" (2: 9). The very *thought* of suicide is enabling.

Staël sees the imagined possibility of suicide as an existential anchor. The insight has a philosophic dimension, as Staël herself ironically suggests in her introduction to *Delphine:* "Some nineteenth-century text says that the secret of the philosophic attitude is suicide."[17] For Staël this anchor above all permits emotional risk taking. "If one knew how to die, one could still take the risk of hoping for such a happy destiny. . . . Only men capable of resolving to kill themselves can, with some shadow of wisdom, attempt this highroad to happiness" (*Passions* 121). Once one has embraced the idea of death, life can be constructed into an artistic curve.[18]

To embrace the idea of suicide is in some fashion to fracture the past and to violate old laws, in order to give another self room to develop. For as Staël herself says in her analysis of suicide, the vast majority of us do not commit suicide, but pass on through these crises to a reflexive consciousness, "as if one were two" (*Passions* 230). That *dé-*

doublement, that alienation from both self and world, may in turn become an enabling, creative moment.

We see just such a pairing of two selves around a moment of symbolic voluntary death in *Corinne.* When the talented Miss Edgermond decides to pursue her career, she effectively "dies." Her stepmother has declared that she owes it to her family to change her name and pass for dead (*Corinne* 267).[19] Only by dying to her English family and breaking social rules can she become Corinne and find freedom as an artist. To kill her English self is to lift the lid of the sarcophagus, "to cast off my shrouds, and repossess nature, my imagination, and my genius!" (268). As Miss Edgermond becomes her own female double, Corinne, she renames and reconstitutes herself.

But in this allegory about the dead hand of history and the inexorable law of the Father, once is not enough. If, in the latter part of the novel, Oswald reunites with his father over the rejected body of Corinne and the frigid body of Lucile, at the very end, Corinne must break his patriarchal line of transmission by uniting with her sister and niece over her own dying body. After her second, self-willed, literal death (an echo of Clarissa's corrective remaking of her self), the only resurrection available to Corinne is through the little Juliette, Corinne's physical double or "miniature," to whom she transmits her talents and knowledge.

The third moment in Staël's analysis of suicide concerns speech. Where women's words and actions are persistently misread and repressed by men, suicide becomes the final authorizing signature that guarantees transmission of a message. Suicide, of course, is also itself a message, a figure of life traced through death. And if women speak through a rhetoric of the body, their means of communication are predetermined: this is a language which in "speaking" them, also silences them.[20]

As a convention of drama and sentimental romance, suicide is the exclamation point that reinforces the sincerity of one's emotions. The play *Geneviève de Brabant* (1807), written the same year that *Corinne* was published, reinforces this theme by its medieval frame. Geneviève de Brabant, a figure who fascinated Proust as well as Staël, has survived in solitary exile with her child, after a false accusation by the villain Golo, who had tried to seduce her and been rejected. In a dream attempt to appease her husband Sigefroi, who still believes her to have been unfaithful, the angel of death appears to her and says, "Unfortunate woman, do you wish to die? At that price, your husband will believe you" (act 3, sc. 1).[21] The angel, it turns out, is right. Sigefroi will not believe Geneviève's assertion of fidelity, and she tries to stab herself. (Luckily her son has the sense to send for a doctor.) Woman's truth can only be read and grasped in her death.[22]

Misreading by Sigefroi in effect generates Geneviève's attempted suicide, and one could say that Delphine's progressive exile from the world and from life is caused by Léonce's attempts to imprison her within a falsifying grid of interpretation. Perpetually distanced from her lover by a libelous public opinion, she is driven to take conventual vows, which her friend Henri de Lebensei describes as a form of "suicide." The ceremony in which she takes the veil calls for death to this world. Self-sacrifice can be a means to withdraw from the laws of the social world. But to submit to another, even more repressive set of laws is not a solution Staël can endorse. Significantly, she permits her heroine to revoke her vows.

More generally, the woman artist's desire to exercise her talents conflicts with the social order, a lesson Corinne learns twice over. Entrapped in a provincial English town, she resists the internalization of rules that would mean little other than self-silencing and therefore suicide: "'What else is happiness but the development of our abilities,' I thought to myself. 'Is not killing yourself morally the same as killing yourself physically? And if mind and soul must be smothered, what is the point of going on with a wretched life that stirs me up to no purpose?'" (Corinne 254). Not to speak is to die, which is what happens on the second round, when the withdrawal of Oswald's affections silences Corinne's love and forces her second exile from England, from song, and from life.

Is it fundamentally suicidal for a woman to possess genius?[23] According to Virginia Woolf, any woman born with a great gift would have become crazed or shot herself.[24] Staël's Sapho laments on a similar note, "What a fatal present is this genius, which seems like Prometheus's vulture to gnaw insatiably on my heart!" Genius arises from "this spirit that devours me, from love, from grief" (act 2, sc. 7).[25] Having sung the sweet lessons of ethics and philosophy, Sapho, we are reminded elsewhere, leapt from the rocky heights of Leucade (Passions 103).

Language begins with suicide,[26] but not for the reasons given by

Starobinski, who regrets Staël's failure to carry through with a literary suicide, the suppression of the author on the model of Flaubert or Mallarmé (JS 251). The "strange analogy" he notes between her definition of suicide from despair as "le deuil sanglant du bonheur personnel" and her definition of literary glory as "le deuil éclatant du bonheur" tells us more than he was ready to admit.

As Starobinski rightly points out, the loss of "gloire," or, for a woman, the ruin of love, causes a kind of living death. We might say that a heroine like Sapho experiences a first, emotional death for which the second death, or suicide, is simply the inevitable consequence. "All your being has passed from life to death. What resource remains in the world against such pain? The courage to kill oneself" (*Passions* 127). In both instances, the heroine translates herself, as if she were physically becoming a figure of speech. Sapho explains her plight, her reasons for hesitating to attend Apollo's festival. "Would you like me to be there like a funerary monument, which retraces death amid all the delights of life?" (*Sappho*, act 1, sc. 3). In living her loss, she has become a sign of death, an allegory of absence made presence, like Baudelaire's Andromaque, "bent in ecstasy beside an empty tomb."[27] She doubles death, represents it, tracing it visually in her visible sorrow, and as she moves toward death she becomes its synecdoche.

Thus in the play *Sappho*, suicide appears to be the only act that will permit the heroine to possess herself. Love has turned her into the possession of another, dependent on the kindness of one who does not in fact reciprocate her love. The social definition of women's role in love reduces her as well to passivity, for women's love is supposed to be receptive rather than threateningly active. Sapho therefore laments, "I would like to possess myself; but the gods have made me the toy of love" (act 4, sc. 2). Victim of Venus, just as Phaedra was (and Staël admired Racine's play), Sapho can achieve freedom only by her own self-annihilation. But this classic motif acquires a secondary elaboration in the works of Staël, a self-consciously reflexive, textual dimension.

Sapho retakes possession of herself through self-inscription. *On the Influence of the Passions* explains that to love means to become the site of inscription for the Other, whose responsiveness in turn preserves one's status as subject; hence to be abandoned means to become an alienated sign, object of the Other. In this state of abandonment, as

one revisits sites where love had been shared, one discovers its mutilated traces within oneself: "The marks of sympathy remain in you
alone, their point of reference has been erased" (126). In order to
escape from this dilemma of reduction to a signifier cut off both from
its signified and from its privileged audience, the woman must become
a speaking memory. She must re-textualize herself, inscribing herself
spectacularly and publicly on the landscape, in order to retrieve the
possibility of signifying action. "Oh thou whom I have loved so much!
Can you see this bank again, without the memory of Sapho stirring
your heart!" (*Sappho* act 5, sc. 6). Ironically, the removal of the lover
through death or infidelity creates a secondary domain of communication through absence and erasure. In this negative realm, by unmaking
herself, she also remakes herself.

"In narrative," as Peter Brooks puts it, "death provides the very
'authority' of the tale, since as readers we seek in narrative fictions the
knowledge of death which in our own lives is denied to us." Or, citing
Benjamin, "death is the sanction of everything that the storyteller can
tell."[28] "Sanction," of course, has a double meaning: it is both the
penalty, the inevitable cost of rupture that every narrative must pay in
order to achieve its form, and it is the ultimate guarantee of authenticity. Suicide is a quintessential "simulacrum" of natural death, and
as such, suicide is a gesture that gives a point simultaneously to a life
and to a narrative, summing up and transmitting it as message.

In lieu of a conclusion, I would like to raise the problem of the
rhetoric of suicide. Staël herself was vividly aware of the possibility of
our dramatizing ourselves through our sentiments. She suspected bad
faith in the double suicide of Heinrich von Kleist and Henriette Vogel:
"Man has so much difficulty imagining the end of his existence, that
he associates even the tomb with the most wretched interests of this
world. In effect, we cannot help seeing sentimental affectation, on the
one hand, and philosophic vanity on the other, in the way the double
suicide of Berlin was orchestrated" (*Reflections* 352). Similarly, *On
Germany* held that one cannot write of feelings with perfect truth,
since all self-representations obscure as they construct the self. "The
human heart is still far from being penetrated in its most intimate
relations. Perhaps some day someone will tell sincerely all that he has
felt, and we will be astonished to discover that most maxims and observations are in error, and that there is an unknown soul in the depths
of the one we have been talking about."[29]

In *Delphine,* the figure of Valorbe embodies not only Staël's distrust of suicidal rhetoric, but her awareness that melodramatic uses of suicide taint its authenticity, so that one may not know what one truly intends. After stabbing himself, Valorbe vacillates: he tears open his wounds, then calls for a doctor, too late.

The staging of suicide, indeed, becomes a leitmotif in *Corinne*: the protagonists witness both a melodrama whose villain shoots himself in a parody of real remorse and a tragedy acted by Mrs. Siddons, who stabs herself in a mad frenzy. Corinne's orchestration of her own death, like Delphine's insistence on dying before Léonce, may well remind us of what Staël observed: "Women try to arrange themselves like a novel, men like a history" (*On Germany* 3:18, 215). Far from a mere betrayal of Staël's tendency to narcissistic manipulation, as Starobinski would have it, this mise-en-scène of suicide explicitly exemplifies for her the unreliability of speech and the indeterminacy of sentiment.

How is Staël to escape from the dilemma of inauthenticity that returns even in the most absolute effort at truth-speaking, inscribed on one's body and grounded in one's death? Benjamin again provides a link and explanation in his discussion of ruins in *Origins of the German Trauerspiel*. The baroque leitmotif of the ruin was, of course, a *memento mori* reminding us of the mutability of this world. At the same time, Benjamin argues, ruins figure the allegorizing procedures of the *Trauerspiel* itself. Baroque dramas not only take advantage of ruins for the stage setting, as in *La vida es sueño,* a favorite among the romantics; they also "ruin" or rupture their own narrative line. They fragment the apparent "organic" order, in order to let an alternate insight shine through. By breaking an order that is illusory, fragmentation forces us to look elsewhere and permits creative reinterpretation.[30] Although Benjamin never discusses Staël's novel in his work on the romantics or on ruins, we can see that she too links her pervasive images of ruins to the problems of authenticity in language and in life, problems at the core of the theme of suicide.

Ruins have a peculiarly important significance in *Corinne,* where tourism punctuates, or even fractures, the narrative rhythm. As in the baroque drama, each fragmentary monument the protagonists visit, indeed Rome itself, is a memento mori: "All that—it is death!" Numerous commentators have observed that the visits by Corinne and Oswald to both natural ruins like Vesuvius and archeological ruins

like the Colosseum prefigure the inevitable ruination of the love relationship between Corinne and Oswald.[31] The mutually destructive relationship between public life and private love finds its expression in
sublimely scarred stones that not only bear the traces of time but also
mix public and private functions in their composite reformations. On
both counts—her pursuit of an artistic career and her pursuit of
love—Corinne was doomed from the outset. The layers of tombs they
encounter bespeak the multiple realms of death through which Corinne
will pass.

More interestingly, Corinne haunts ruins because they can serve as a
catalyst and model for interpretation of the other—of the past, of
one's love, or of oneself. The very fragmentariness of ruins triggers our
recreative activity, our effort to seize the character of a nation by a
fact, or a fact through a word (*Corinne* 205).[32] Ruins provide material
for physical and imaginative bricolage: "A portico standing beside a
humble roof, small church windows cut out between columns, a tomb
sheltering a whole rustic family, evoke an inexplicable mixture of
great and simple ideas" (*Corinne* 64–65). Just as the Romans build
their churches and huts among the columns of the past, Corinne and
Oswald build their mutual understanding through encounters with
these crumbling landmarks—an instance of what Frank Bowman has
called displaced discourse.[33] The gaps between their two responses to
the ruins dramatize the hermeneutic struggle to wrest significance
from difference, and wholeness from incompleteness. Significantly,
however, when Corinne tries to shake the monument Oswald has built
in his mind to his father, she fails; she cannot turn the memories of the
past into material for building a new world. Like the stones, she is
mutilated by history.[34] Unable to rework the past, she turns to a symbolic dismemberment of her own gifts, which she disperses between
Lucile and Juliet.

This allegorical, suicidal conclusion confirms Marie-Claire Vallois's
reading of *Corinne* as a drama of displacement and substitution that
deconstructs language itself as privileged cultural edifice.[35] At the
metanarrative level, a further set of ruptures reappears in the obsessive
change of locus and in the novel's generic instability, as it hovers between poetry and prose, romance and travelogue, toponymy and anatomy.[36] In place of language, gestures of fragmentation, grounded in
the ultimate ruin of the self that is suicide, convey the struggle for
authentic communication.[37]

I would like to make a fragmentary gesture myself here, toward Corinne's own art, which through its breaks and turns seems to me to embody another version of this instability. Her improvised bricolage in response to her audience brings us back to the problem of staging one's own cessation, for Corinne uses poetic breaks to provide points of entry for her listeners.[38] She stops, for example, to observe Oswald, then turns her spontaneous effusion in a direction that will be responsive to his melancholic state. By linking the genius of her heroines to the public performance of inspired dialogue and fragments, Staël underscores the dynamic role of reception that is central to her social theory of art. The fragmentariness of women's art finds its figure, too, in the allegory of suicide.

OLD IDOLS, NEW SUBJECT: GERMAINE DE STAËL AND ROMANTICISM

Marie-Claire Vallois

When we consider the texts of Germaine de Staël in the context of romantic writings we are running the obvious risk of judging her work less for its originality than for its ability to fit within a literary canon from which it has been, in some sense, excluded. Staëlian criticism and feminist studies of the last twenty years, however, have provided another context in which to read her, a context that has allowed us to determine in what ways the Staëlian text has brought the entire institution of literature into question.[1] Starting from this double context, I will analyze the inaugural moment of Staël's peculiar exclusion which, as we modern readers might expect, appears problematic. To study the canonization of literary figures—a canonization which becomes for the romantics a monumentalization—discloses in effect what is at stake in the ritual of literary consecration. The literary deification of male writers such as Chateaubriand and Byron is very specifically determined ideologically. To question the sexual politics that preside over the erection of the romantic Olympus in the nineteenth century and its consolidation in the twentieth inevitably leads us to an undermining of its gods.

Translated by John Galvin.

Writing *On Literature*: A Mythological Battle

If we are overly fond of citing Guibert's first literary portrait of Staël as author-to-be, it is because while prefiguring her scandalous secret, it fixes through a mythological image what will become the charm, or rather the spell, of Staëlian writing, her prophetic voice:

> Zulmé is but twenty, and she is the most celebrated of the priestesses of Apollo; it is she who is the favorite of the god; it is she whose hymns are always the most pleasing to him. . . . During my youth I have seen the Delphic Pythia; I have seen the Cumean Sibyl. . . . This young priestess was inspired without alteration . . . her words and her music were not prepared beforehand. . . . What nuances in the tone of her voice! What perfect accord between thought and expression! She speaks, and if her words do not reach me her inflections, her gestures, her eyes tell me enough for me to understand her.[2]

Presented as the idol of that Parisian salon, of that small society which had the brief good fortune to gather peacefully into its circle, on the eve of revolutionary turmoil, nobleman and bourgeois, philosopher and politician, men of finance and men of letters, man and woman—the young Germaine recalls the ancient Pythia at Delphi and the Cumean Sibyl, not only for the language of her hymns, dear to the gods, but for that other language, transmitted by gesture, expression, and tone of voice.[3] One can hardly be surprised, then, that Staël places the heroines of both her novels—Delphine, whose name evokes etymologically the Delphic oracle, and Corinne, who is often represented as a sibyl—in the tradition of this feminine genealogy of inspired priestesses. One can wonder, of course, whether Staël underestimates or fully evaluates the danger of this mythological ancestry to which she herself is attracted.

Against the neoclassical backdrop of the Consulate and the Empire, the choice of the sibyl/pythia as a literary model is an act of provocation. The celebration, even in the mode of fiction, of these inspired women and of these female figures as objects of public worship in pre-Hellenic times ill-accorded with the new worship of those ancient Roman gods of the hearth, the Penates, recently reinstituted by the Napoleonic Code.[4] Is Staël preparing to restage, on her own behalf, the ancient mythological battle which, with the dawning of ancient Greece, pitted new gods against old goddesses? As we know, the Pythia of the *Eumenides* became the priestess to Apollo only after Apollo killed the serpent Python, born of Gaïa, the Earth. Moreover, in the more primitive legends that Bachofen analyzes in *Du règne de la mère au patriarcat*, the name of the dragon Python was "Delphyné": she was half serpent and half woman.[5] The chronological order of the feminine genealogy evoked in the Staëlian novels seems to retrace an older mythological order. If the female dragon Delphyné antedates the Python, the sibyls antedate Pythia. The sibyls were the first in the genealogy of priestesses, depositories of primitive revelations of the Delphic oracle which was originally the shared possession of Gaïa and Poseidon. So, in raising from the ashes the specter of the sibyls, did Staël not take up once more the clash of the Titans, a clash dating from that mythological era when the heavens were apportioned to god and goddess alike?

Chateaubriand was among the first to grasp, from its very beginnings, the theological stakes in the Staëlian endeavor. Writing to his friend, de Fontanes, about the second edition of *On Literature,* the work with which Staël accomplished, so to speak, her rite of passage into the republic of letters, Chateaubriand wittily allegorizes the battle that pits them against each other: "You know of course that my particular lunacy is to see Jesus Christ everywhere, whereas Mme de Staël's is to see perfectibility."[6] Theirs is a metaphysical battle whose personal origin Chateaubriand soon discovers:

Alas, it would be nice to believe that mankind gets better from age to age, and that the son is always better than the father. If something could prove this excellent quality of the human heart, it would be by seeing that Mme de Staël had found the principle of this illusion in her own heart. Nevertheless, I am afraid that this lady, who so often complains about men, while celebrating their perfectibility, is like these priests who do not believe in the idols at whose altars they worship.[7]

This witty remark serves, curiously, to underline the sacrilegious side of the Staëlian enterprise. For Chateaubriand, Staël's work appears to be iconoclastic, a destroyer of paternal images.

It is against the background of this, as it were, mythological battle, and with this landscape of broken idols as a setting, that we might read anew *Corinne, or Italy,* but now with a view to a Staëlian poetics of ruins, no longer in terms of the traditional canon of the romantic ruin. After paying homage to the one woman to write or deal with ruins, Roland Mortier, in an implicit comparison of Staël's feeling for ruins with Chateaubriand's, concludes: "Romantic, she certainly is in her conception of femininity and love, in her sense of enthusiasm, and in her conception of religion and poetry, identified with the attraction of the infinite, but on the other hand, she is not romantic on the subject of ruins."[8] He considers a witticism of her daughter, then aged seven-and-a-half, which Staël herself delights in reporting to her friend, Monti, as the best example of her initial reaction at the outset of her trip to Italy: "Mother only liked two things in Italy, the sea and Monti."[9] Mortier does acknowledge that those two marvels, a few days later, became four, when she added to them Saint-Peter's and Mt. Vesuvius (letter to Monti, February 23, 1805). But he immediately identifies, in this same letter, that paradoxical moment when the quality of the feeling of melancholy is, as it were, perverted in the Staëlian text: "Things that are dead forever are finally not very important for her and it is the reason why she likes to gaze upon ruins in the moonlight."[10] He finally concludes, using Staël's own words: "In Rome, I especially like the moon at night. All that separates you from the ancient world is put to sleep and the ruins awake."[11] It is, then, at that very moment when the ruins, in their nighttime setting, cease to be ruins only, at that moment when the ruins seem to pass, as it were, from death to life, that the feeling of melancholy finds itself imperiled.

The moonlit walk occurs in the novel *Corinne, or Italy* at the moment when Corinne finally comes to say farewell to Rome. The feeling of melancholy is curiously mixed with enthusiasm:

The ideal language of music harmonized nobly with ideal expression of the monument. Enthusiasm reigned in the city while all commonplace interests slept. . . . As she drew near [Saint Peter's] her first thought was to picture the building as it would be when its turn came to fall into ruins, an object of admiration of the centuries to come. She imagined the columns now standing, half lying on the ground, the portico shattered, the vault open to the sky. . . . Dawn came at last, and from the top of Saint Peter's, Corinne gazed at Rome flung in the barren countryside like an oasis in the Lybian desert. . . . This city has an individual charm, as it were. One loves her like a living being; her buildings, her ruins are friends to whom one bids farewell.[12]

It is in this same passage, however, and just at that moment—when modern buildings, in an apocalyptic vision, become, in their turn, ruins—that Mortier recognizes that "visionary imagination" with which Germaine de Staël prevails, for once, over her rival, the Viscount.[13] Put back into its context, the passage takes on another meaning; it seems, rather, to replace that apocalyptic and thus, theological, vision of history, with the more archaic and more enthusiastic vision of an eternal destruction followed by an eternal return. In writing her novel, Staël seems to pursue the literary battle that pitted her, five years earlier, against Chateaubriand: a battle of giants that will take place, henceforth, literally against a backdrop of ruins, and with the death of civilizations as its horizon. Far from excluding the reality of the ruins, Staël, like Chateaubriand, makes of them an object of choice, since they become the subject of the novel. The presence of the ruins, however, seems to evoke for her the advent of another theogony, the celebration of new gods and of new men, and it is, perhaps, this difference that romantic critics have continually overlooked.

A Woman in the Ruins or a Story of the Uncanny

In a letter to Suard, Staël presents her second novel, *Corinne, or Italy,* as an echo of *La lettre de Chateaubriand sur la campagne romaine.* But she quickly underlines the curious reversal which, for her, makes the ruin a privileged object: "I shall write a sort of novel that will serve as a frame for a trip to Italy and I think that many thoughts and many feelings will find their place there."[14] A meditation on ruins cannot, for Staël, be effected without a novelesque staging. The description of the ruins, funerary remains, calls for the anthropomorphization of fiction—an anthropomorphic process that transforms the dead into the living, the inanimate into the animate. We find in this same letter an enigmatic sentence, which, while referring to Chateaubriand's letter, illustrates where she and Chateaubriand part company. "To visit Rome, as Chateaubriand puts it, appeases the soul; the dead inhabit it and each step here is as eloquent as Bossuet on the vanities of life."[15] It is precisely at this moment that, according to Mortier, Staël perverts romantic aesthetics. Although often occulted in romantic literature, this passage from death to life is present in the topos of "the voice of/in the ruins." Far from resembling Chateaubriand's glorification of ruins—the site where the subject celebrated, at the expense of its own death, a death of the self that serves to glorify the "work" as monument—Staël's fictitious ruins become the place of a renascence, of a rebirth of the self to the self, through the mediation of the voice. The journey to the country of ruins, far from ending in a melancholy meditation upon the dead, stages the enthusiastic creation of an origin: that of the voice of writing.

The Staëlian project does not seem to privilege fiction over the travelogue. On the contrary, Staël's presentation of her novelistic writing operates a curious reversal of the classical hierarchy: the trip to Italy is presented as the privileged subject of fictional writing—the personal fiction serving only as a frame. In fact, as Simone Balayé reminds us, until the end of the nineteenth century *Corinne, or Italy* was classified at the Bibliothèque Nationale in Paris under the rubric "travel guide."[16] This displacement of the fictional subject is disturbing because it questions the traditional anthropomorphic hierarchy in western (fictional) writing, where a thing, an inanimate object, cannot take the place of a person (except in the fantastic genre, where the passage from one realm to another—inanimate to animate—is the rule of the game).[17] Does that mean that Staël's novel should be read as an example of the (romantic) fantastic? Or rather, since the novel seems to invite us on an excursion into some ancient land, should we read it according to a mythological mode that does not distinguish between natural and supernatural? At first glance, nothing would seem to authorize us to do so, unless, perhaps, it is the figure of the double—person or country—so oddly emblematized in the novel's title: *Corinne, or Italy.*[18]

In the plethora of literary excursions so common to these eighteenth-century heirs to Fénélon's *Télémaque*, Staël's travelogue figures as one of the most successful. This success may be due as much to its connection to the genre as to its eccentricities. Not only does the goal of the voyage turn out to be a feminine figure, but in a curious twist of representation, the description of the country metamorphoses into the description of the woman. In a troubling transmutation, toponymy becomes anatomy. The romantic voyage of the exiled hero to the privileged country of ruins becomes, as if by magic, an idyll in the haunt-ingly familiar landscape of love.

The novel traps us in a dialectical movement from the strange to the "familiar," which Freud identified, in his study *The Uncanny*, as char-acteristic of the peculiar aesthetic feeling (a feeling which is neither melancholy nor enthusiasm but which entertains a curious relation-ship with both) that seizes those travellers who return to their "ancient homeland": "An uncanny effect is often and easily produced by effac-ing the distinction between *imagination* and *reality*, such as when something that we have hitherto regarded as imaginary appears before us in reality, or when a symbol takes over the full functions and signifi-cance of the thing it symbolizes, and so on."[19] The strangest charac-teristic of the novel *Corinne, or Italy* is the very particular way in which the transition from the inanimate to the animate produces an effect of the fantastic by oscillating between the two extremes, Co-rinne and Italy. This oscillation produces the indeterminate image of the "double."[20]

The very title of the novel *Corinne, or Italy* offers itself as a riddle to be solved by the reader. Read as a sibylline utterance, this title inaugu-rates a travel narrative that is partly the description of a land, partly the description of a woman. In the context of mythological references, it cannot but evoke that other figure of mythology who speaks enig-matically, the Sphinx at the gates of Thebes. The mysterious lineage between the Delphic Sibyl, the Italian Cumean Sibyl, and the Sphinx is betrayed by what they have in common: the association with a dragon who is half serpent, half woman, with the troubling gift of an enig-matic voice. The allusive presence of these two kinds of enigmatic languages in the novel, the Sibyl's and the Sphinx's, points to the ne-cessity of another logic of reading. One has to read the novel not only for the teleological unfolding of the storyline, but one also has to deci-pher the enigmatic language of this sphinx-like landscape in ruins.

The title of her first novel, *Delphine*, is a woman's first name with-out a patronym; in her second novel Staël compensates for the erasure of the father's name by indicating a place-name: *Corinne, or Italy*. This substitution of toponym for patronym cannot help but be prob-lematic for the reader. Is the loss of the paternal reference redeemed by the place-name "Italy?" Bound to the first name by the copula "or," is it, in fact, inscribed as another enigma? Do we have here the copula "or" in the sense of coordination "and" (Corinne and Italy), which would imply a metonymical relation—the proximity of the container "Italy" with the contained "Corinne"? Or rather, do we have a copula in the sense of the alternative "either/or," Corinne or/either Italy, a copula which would then suggest the metaphorical interchangeability of the person's name with the country's name? Is Staël giving us a travelogue to read, a book whose primary function is to be used as a complement to the real landscape, in a relation of proximity to the "referent"? Or are we to read it as a fiction defined as a pure imaginary "supplement" to the real?[21] This is a monumental question because it stages *Corinne*. Nevertheless the answer to this inaugural query can be found nowhere in the novel. The novel's title presents us, instead, with an "uncanny" linguistic game which has far-reaching and dangerous consequences for the literary Pantheon. For it puts into question, or rather reduces to ruins, the whole imaginary structure of language as a fetish object, in order to give birth, in its place, to a literary voice speaking the feminine.

A literary sphinx, does this fictional entitling not speak to the reader in words of stone, amid a landscape of ruins, to evoke all the better a woman's secret? From the beginning this riddle seems open to a double solution: on the one hand a metonymic performance—Corinne in Italy; on the other a metaphoric description—either Corinne or else Italy.[22]

The Enigma of the Double:
The Awakening of a Goddess

In fact, Oswald, Lord Nelvil, an English hero, is cast in the opening of the novel as the central character of the story, which at first appears as a typical romantic journey. Narratively speaking, the male protagonist, a traveler in Italy, is also the reader of the heroine's story.[23] In Italy Oswald discovers a mysterious woman; while she reveals Italy to him, he sets out upon the quest of loving and knowing her. Italy is the metaphorical double of the heroine. The key that would unravel her mystery is, moreover, suggested to him by Corinne's attendant and confidant, the Prince de Castel-Forte: "Gaze on her, for *she is the image of our beautiful Italy;* . . . an admirable product of our climate and our arts, an offspring of the past, prophet of the future" (2:2). It is not, however, given to everyone to understand this mysterious key.

The feminine mystery is revealed only to that specific spectator who can also hear. As the Prince de Castel-Forte reminds the public, Corinne is "someone you can have no real idea of until you have *heard* her" (2:20).

The word *heard* (*entendu*) must be taken here in its double sense: in the sense of hearing, but also of interpretation and deciphering.[24] Corinne, descendant of the Sibyl, speaks an enigmatic language which calls for an interpreter, in the same way that it was necessary to have a key in order to interpret the books of the ancient Sibyl. Thus it becomes necessary to read Corinne's story in the story of the ruins of Italy that the heroine narrates to the hero. There has been a substitution of stories through a delegation of discourse: instead of Corinne's personal (autobiographical) discourse we have the discourse of tourism. In the Italian descriptions, often it is no longer the heroine but the "stones" that "speak": "Perhaps I am mistaken, my Lord, but I think people become dearer to each other when they share admiration for monuments whose true greatness speaks to the soul! The buildings of Rome are neither cold nor mute, genius created them, remarkable events consecrate them (4:3)."

The heroine's lost Voice is inscribed in her stone double: a fossil Voice ready to live. The Corinne-monument substitution is poetically implicit from the moment of Corinne's first appearance at the Capitol. Does the narrative describe a sculpted Sibyl carved in an ancient "*bas relief*" or a being of flesh and blood? "Corinne sat on the chariot built in the ancient style and white-clad girls walked alongside. . . . She was dressed like Domenichino's Sibyl. . . . Her arms were ravishingly beautiful; her tall figure, reminiscent of Greek statuary, conveyed youth and happiness. In her expression there was something inspired" (2:1). Half-goddess, half-woman, the Sibyl-statue nevertheless comes to life under Lord Nelvil's and the crowd's admiring, loving gaze.

The tourist trip is thus transformed into a curious idyll between a human and a godlike woman: the romantic tale of a British Lord and a Delphic Sibyl. The statue becomes a woman, a commonplace of that period's fictional literature, some of whose veils Freud lifted in his reading of Jensen's *Gradiva*.[25] *Gradiva* is another magical fiction. In Jensen's story a woman of stone comes to life before the eyes of the hero and enables him to recover his health through the familiar sound of her voice speaking enigmatic sentences. There is an obvious archeological parallelism between *Corinne, or Italy* and *Gradiva*.

Likewise in Staël's novel, each monument, each statue, becomes the double of Corinne, a double made of stone but able to speak in her name when the human heroine loses her gift of language. A striking illustration of the delegation of speech that results from this doubling is given when Corinne, reduced to silence in Florence, lets Michelangelo's statue of Night speak for her in Italian: "I find it sweet to sleep, and sweeter still to be of marble made. As long as injustice and shame shall last, it is great happiness not to see and not to hear: so do not awaken me and, for pity's sake, speak softly" (18:3; in Italian in the text). Blessed with the capacity of "speech," the Italian stones also give the impression of a diffuse physical presence (5:2); the curves and the contours of the Italian landscape "caress" and comfort like a woman's embrace (2:3). Italy, "dethroned" and "mutilated by History" (4:3), still asserts its ancient grandeur, appearing once again as the double of the heroine: "For a long time Rome has been asylum to the exiles of the world: but is not Rome herself dethroned? The sight of her consoles kings who, like her, have been despoiled" (4:3).[26]

The metaphorization of the whole Italian landscape into a sleeping beauty of stone is not without risk. By assigning to the decor of ruins the task of refracting her image and presence, as if speaking in her name, the heroine risks not only effacing herself as the subject of discourse, but also positioning herself as object of the masculine gaze. By this feminine strategy, woman would only be able to inscribe herself as an object in ruins, a mutilated object. In this perspective the pleasure in ruins would depend more on the androcentric strategy of the melancholic observer and would disclose its fetishizing tendency. According to Freudian logic, the melancholic fetishist would maintain the fascination for the mutilated feminine love object using a double strategy: by denying its mutilation and by displacing its adoration onto fetishistic objects which function as "memorial substitutes": monuments, frescoes, statues.[27] But this transmutation of woman into stone, of life into death, as we have already seen, is never arrested or definitely fixed in a monumentalizing effect. It is always susceptible to its own reversal. In the Staëlian ruins the statues can always awaken. In the passage just mentioned, Michelangelo's "Night" is next to the statue of "Dawn," and, as the text reminds us: "A poet wrote verses on the statue of Night, concluding with the words: although she sleeps, she is alive; if you do not believe it, wake her, she will speak to you" (18:3).

The archeological quest of the hero for the feminine Other reveals itself finally to be tragic because he can look at Corinne's story only from the point of view of Death, the death of his own father. He can only read the story of the woman as a double of his own, the story of the transgression of the dead father's law, an androcentric reading which can result only in mourning and melancholia. But *Corinne, or Italy* is not only a story about death and mourning; it is also a story of love and coming to life, a story about transmission and generation, a story of "enthusiasm."

The travel to the country of ruins can be read according to two different modes, the mode of melancholia, but also as Staël suggested in her travel journal and in *On Germany*, the mode of enthusiasm.[28] We are beginning to recognize here the fundamental opposition melancholy/enthusiasm that Mortier identified with Chateaubriand and Staël, but this time as it is translated in fiction in terms of an opposition between masculine and feminine characters. Oswald, temporarily forgetting his melancholy, seems at first able to read the novel according to the other mode and to be receptive to the "feeling of enthusiasm" that Corinne brings to life among the ruins:

> "It is from here that Saint Peter's should be seen," Corinne went on, "and the columns standing in front were supposed to extend this far. That was Michelangelo's magnificent plan; he hoped it would be completed after his death at least; but these days, men no longer think about posterity. Once enthusiasm is made to look foolish, everything but money and power is undone." "You are the one who will bring that feeling back to life!" exclaimed Nelvil. (4:3)

It is only temporarily, however, that Oswald contemplates forgetting his sorrow and empathy for the dead father and accepts the possibility of a passage from death to life. The very fact of his reading in Corinne's autobiographical letter her voluntary transgression against the father's law reiterates his solidarity with the father and results in his return in England. In the end Corinne's story is not reducible to that of Oswald. The quest abandoned by the masculine hero at the end of the novel will be taken up by his wife, Lucile, another English double for Corinne as well as her sister. And finally Corinne herself chooses to transmit all the secrets of her art to a girl child who speaks Italian just like her—Juliette, Oswald and Lucile's daughter. The novel's riddle does indeed reside, as this proliferation of doubles attests, in the problem of identity, the actual lost object whose quest is tied to the name of the Father. But is this the real object of the fictional inquiry? If something is lost, the figure of feminine genealogy seems to imply that something is also found.

From the Monument-Fetish to the Voice of Literature

The novel *Corinne, or Italy* is, in fact, the story of a double voyage. The voyage of the hero's exile overshadows (in the first part of the novel) the heroine's return to her mother's homeland. If it is the father's voice and letters that Oswald seems to designate as the cause of his Italian trip, for Corinne it is the mother's voice. For the heroine Italy is the maternal land, or rather the maternal home. The reading process that is set up by the very enigmatic quality of Staëlian writing reminds us of the archeological deciphering that consists in uncovering the different layers of History. Under the story of Oswald's quest for the father's voice (which will reiterate the Father's law), we find the story of Corinne's quest for what had been lost earlier, the mother's voice.[29] Under the Oedipal scenario we find the pre-Oedipal one, with its blurring of the distinction self/other. Corinne both is and is not Italy, which is also her mother. We are in the presence of a new definition of a polymorphic identity or a strategy for escaping the romantic (male) schema. Departing from England for Italy, Corinne chooses to abandon the "cold letters" of her father's name. In its stead she takes the patronym-less name of a woman poet. In other words, the Staëlian fiction figures the locus of a loss, the loss of the connection of identity that is bound to the name of the father.

The failure of the romantic quest inscribed in the mode of melancholy thus shows itself to be only the first step in a return to the sources of a past buried even further down in the memories of civilizations, as in those of the individual psyche. Translated in psychic time, this mythic past would correspond, as we have seen, to what in psychoanalysis is indistinctly referred to as the stage of the "pre-Oedipal"; or to what we will identify as a certain kind of "primary narcissism." In this stage, according to Kaja Silverman's understanding of the "negative Oedipus complex," as expressed in her book *The Acoustic Mirror*, the girl child's entry into language is a moment where she is at the same time herself and her mother.[30] This archaic past, on the level of history (in Mycenian civilization), is that of the religion which preceded the cult of the Pythia: the religion of Gaïa, the mother goddess. We find this evoked in the novelistic theater of archaic loves, of infant loves, the religion of the first gods and of this first goddess, Cybele, which was reintroduced at Rome at the command of the Delphic oracle. In this religion the sacred seems to reside not so much in the erecting of idols, as in the transmission of the melody of the voice, which, from Cybele to Sibyl, and through the intermediary of the "oracles," never ceases to summon other echoes.

The linking of the oracles in the transmission of the voice is crucial in our reading of Staël's use of the Sibyl myth. It points to the necessary mediation of a certain kind of writing or rather of a certain kind of reading of what has been heard. We go back here to the advice of the Prince de Castel-Forte, who indicated to Oswald that Corinne needed to be "heard"—both in the literal and in the figural sense. The evocation and re-inscription of the myth of a "Sibylline voice" by Staël appears, in the romantic context, as essential to an understanding of the originality as well as the audacity of her writings. More importantly for a discussion of "feminine writing," it allows for a reevaluation—in a curious aftereffect of literary criticism—of the current discussions on the feminine voice in literature.

The return to the origins and the taste for the archaic that we have previously identified as characteristic of Staël's fictional writing dominates in the curious topos of the place-name—the mother as place-name.[31] Kristeva has shown all the power of evocation of the "mother as place-name" with the understanding that the mother is grasped then, not as an Other, but as an acoustic mirror (a resonant envelope), the house of voice. But in Kristeva's reading this stage of naming belongs to the pre-linguistic (or pre-symbolic), what she refers to as the "semiotic chora," using Platonic categories. The Sibyl's oracles, by contrast, not only bring the relation to the mother within the realm of language, but within the order of written language which is, nevertheless, still anchored in the voice. The Roman legend of the Sibylline Books illustrates this peculiar quality of the written oracles: the books must be interpreted because they are the transcription of a previous voice (the voice of the Hellespontic Sibyl and the Magna Mater) which in order to be understood calls for the interpretive reading/writing of other historical voices (the voice of the Cumean Sibyl, and after her of specially appointed priests).

The genius of Staëlian writing is to thematize, within the novel itself, a theory of language that would do away with, or put into ruins, the opposition written/oral in the same way that it does away with the opposition life and death, human and nonhuman, and ultimately God the author/father and man the reader—or God the creator and man the creature. But in order to do so Staël had to imagine a voyage away from the house of the "English" Father, which becomes an uncanny return to the home of the "Italian" Mother, a return which brings more enthusiasm than melancholy.

If the return to the strangely familiar (*un-heimleich*) ancient homeland produces less fright than euphoria, it may be that the house to which the subject returns is no longer the closed home of the Roman Gods, the Penates, but the palatial ruins of a previous "habitat," an open house of childhood memories which speaks (and asks to be heard) less about the dead than about the living. It is perhaps only in this childlike—some would say poetic—perspective that we might better understand the turn, in fiction, to the technical and rhetorical procedures of that writing which, for want of a better name, we call touristic. The travelogue descriptions become the spectacular, ostentatious, monumental presentation of the death and rebirth of the voice as writing/reading. Such would be the sought-for effect or rather aftereffect of the "deictic" dimension of the touristic writing which functions curiously as prosopopeia. The descriptive passages allow us to see (through the reiteration of the demonstratives) that which, by definition, is not in the text but which the text never ceases to interpellate as present (through the detour of reading the guidebook) in a relation of contiguity: the maternal landscape. This evocation of the dead Italian mother ends, however, in an unsettling evocation of the one who is forever absent from the text, but who is alive in a special connection of contiguity to the guidebook, in the trip to Italy: the author.

The last double, the double of the author (as the first voice of writing and of reading), reconciles all the doubles of writing. In other words, the touristic descriptions—in a way parallel to the riddle of the descriptive title—are valuable only in their demonstrative, deictic dimensions. They point to that dystopic and euphoric space wherein the girl child, placed in front of Oedipus's Sphinx, perceives herself simultaneously as self and other, in the acoustic mirror of this enigmatic place-name described in the novel. Receiving the first impression of her self as individual subject she, at the same time, identifies with the Mother and can therefore become, as if in a self-generating process, her own mother. The novelistic travelogue, which functions as a riddle, thus stands as the locus of the mother understood as the place of the engendering voice.

To bring about one's own birth against the backdrop of ruins, means, finally, to have found the capacity to be at once creature and creator—a new conception of literary creation—and means, moreover, to rediscover the Greek definition of enthusiasm, of that "god within us" to which *On Germany* makes reference; but this definition, in fiction, becomes highly unorthodox, since the god of enthusiastic writing shows itself to be a woman.[32] In the context of a rehabilitation of the Christian god like that found in Chateaubriand's *Le Génie du christianisme*, the spontaneous generation of the voice or the myth of self-generation in writing can only appear sacrilegious. Staël's writings would only serve to evoke, paradoxically, the birth of their author in voice. Chateaubriand's would extol them only as monuments erected on behalf of the death of the author. If, in Chateaubriand, writing becomes monumental, in Staël, writing presents itself according to the model of the ruin, of those monuments in ruins which, as we have seen, appeal to the voice.

In the end, we can only understand what separates the two writers at root by recalling their initial dispute about the function of literature. An instrument of Christian apologetics for Chateaubriand, it is, by contrast, an instrument of perfectibility for Staël. And though both conceive the legacy of literature as monument, and only as monument, both extol a very different notion of what this monument may be. Perhaps this is because they are finally, and fundamentally, so different in their respective conceptions of the relation of literature to language. Paying tribute, as early as 1800, to Degérando's *Des signes et de l'art de penser, considérés dans leurs rapports mutuels*, Staël praises the author's originality in having grasped that if "the history of language" is, as it were, "a succession of monuments," it is destined, then, to be constantly modified and put to ruin: "But if language modifies the qualities of the mind, it must be in its turn modified by them. In the phenomenon of understanding (*"entendement"*) as in the physical world, reaction is always inseparable from action."[33] The history of language can only be viewed, then, as a succession of monuments put to ruin, only to be raised again on those privileged occasions when the author finds his or her voice, or society, its own. This is an earlier version of the thesis that will be found in *On Literature Considered in Its Relationship to Social Institutions,* but this essay, in which Staël pays particular attention to the relations between signs and thought, helps us better apprehend the symbolic thematics of ruins found in the second novel. To return to the living source of literary activity is to find again, in the cemetery of literary monuments, the site of that euphoric moment when, believing we hear a voice, we find our own echo. In reviving, against the backdrop of ruins, the mythological figure of the sibyl, the novel *Corinne, or Italy* prophesies, it would seem, the end of the reign of the idols. The celebration of the character of the sibyl amounts, through the detour of fiction, to heralding the dawn of that new moment when each individual can be visited within by the genius of enthusiasm. The sibyl's message is that to speak the language of the god within us is to be both the receptacle and the transmitter of one's own interior daimon, a new genius enigmatically celebrating the birth of a new writing subject.

TRANSGRESSING
GENDER AND GENRE

CORINNE'S SHIFT TO PATRIARCHAL MEDIATION: REBIRTH OR REGRESSION?

Ellen Peel

Near the end of Staël's *Corinne, or Italy* the dying heroine makes a puzzling statement. It is easy enough to understand that Corinne is saying she wants her influence to survive her, but it is difficult to *evaluate* what she says. The statement is addressed to Lucile, who has won Corinne's lover, Oswald, away from her: " 'My only personal desire is that Oswald find some traces of my influence in you and your daughter, and that at least he can never enjoy feeling without remembering Corinne.' "[1] We can read this as a simple, benevolent wish for the well-being of others, but we can also read it as a jealous, malevolent wish to haunt them from beyond the grave.

Corinne's statement is typical of what she says and does near the end of the novel. As Vivian Folkenflik notes in an introduction to excerpts from Staël's writings, "At the end of *Corinne,* the artist heroine teaches a little girl to carry on for her after her death, and it sometimes seems as if every woman who read the book must have felt inspired to do the same. *Corinne*'s popularity was immediate and astounding."[2] Readers who have sympathized with her throughout will rejoice that something of the heroine will live on after she dies. Folkenflik is entirely justified in calling attention to the book's tremendous influence and to the importance of the ending. But the ending has not yet received the careful analysis it requires. A close reading reveals a sinister side to the *means* by which Corinne ensures her metaphorical rebirth.

I plan, in exploring this problem, to show that the heroine's final efforts to live beyond death consist largely of what I call *ventriloquism* and *indirect revenge*. As I shall explain, both are forms of *mediation*, which the rest of this particular novel associates with patriarchy (defined here basically as the system of male domination). Because Corinne has been striving against patriarchy throughout the novel, her ultimate adoption of its methods raises the tantalizing but unanswerable question of whether her rebirth is actually a regression.

Before turning to the unsettling ending, we must examine the patterns of patriarchy and feminism established earlier in the text. As has been pointed out by critics such as Madelyn Gutwirth, Corinne's struggle against patriarchal values is central to the novel.[3] A strong, talented artist, she initially thrives in sunny Italy, the land where she was born to an Italian mother and an English father (Lord Edgermond). In contrast, Oswald (Lord Nelvil) comes from melancholy, silent England. He is an extremely admirable character who loves Corinne deeply, but, when she refuses to confine herself to domesticity, he marries her English half-sister, Lucile Edgermond. Corinne loses much of her artistic ability and dies a broken woman.

The heroine's loss of both her lover and her artistic vocation, while rooted in individual circumstances, metaphorically represents the power of patriarchy over women's independence. In a sense young Lord Nelvil—who was himself oppressed by patriarchal values—was originally attracted to her because she offered hope of an alternative to those values. Yet, as Simone Balayé says in her introduction to the novel, "Oswald drew her into the prison that, thanks to her, he had thought he was escaping."[4] Despite his good intentions, he acts as an instrument of patriarchy. Staël sets up one correspondence between the heroine, women in general, Italy, and feminism, and sets up another between Oswald, men in general, England, and patriarchy.[5] The novel evokes sadness, and sometimes outrage, at the domination of the former by the latter.

The text links feminist values to immediacy and links patriarchal values to mediation. Like the novel's other major metaphors, these connections have no special validity outside the text; in reality feminism, for example, does not necessarily bear any relation to immediacy (or to Italy).[6] But Staël builds a metaphorical system that functions powerfully in this particular novel. In referring to immediacy as feminist and to mediation as patriarchal, then, I am not asserting some universal connection but following the schema of *Corinne*. The text associates the spontaneous heroine, Italy, and women with presence and speech, in contrast to absence and writing.[7] Corinne's unmediated communication culminates in her performances as *improvisatrice*. Not only does she speak directly to her audience, but what she says is spontaneous, composed on the spot instead of read or remembered from some preexisting script.[8]

In contrast, since the written word is a silent form of communication, it fits into the cluster of traits that typify quiet, distant Oswald, and, according to this novel, England and men in general. The Englishman uses a "strong and concise language that seems to suggest far more feeling than it expresses" (16:4:316). Because he rarely declares his emotions explicitly, Corinne is left to deduce them (3:1:38; 8:4:151).

Oswald leads Corinne toward more mediated forms. For instance, when she tells him of her past, she switches from oral to written communication. Perhaps in a (futile) attempt to make her story more palatable to him, she retreats from her natural oral expression and recounts her history indirectly, in a letter delivered by someone else. She is not even present while her lover reads it. When Oswald later returns to England, leaving her in Italy, she is forced to write letters instead of speaking. She fears the change, for "her charm was the source of all her power, and what power could it exert in her absence?" (15:2:278). Next she retreats a step farther: she stops writing to him altogether. When Corinne then follows her lover to England, she either remains silent or communicates in an indirect way. Her major communication there, her release of Oswald from his vow, takes the extremely mediated form of a brief note conveyed by a blind stranger.

At the end of the book, Corinne's final silence—in death—might seem the ultimate defeat, for her and for the feminist values she represents. Yet, as Folkenflik says, death might signal a new beginning. Readers are encouraged to wonder whether the heroine lives on in other guises, because the entire book has suggested that the past is kept alive in a variety of ways—through history, memory, art, and ruins. In a sense the heroine herself has already been resurrected once, when a false tomb was dedicated to "Miss Edgermond" and the former bearer of that name rechristened herself "Corinne."

Although the heroine literally dies at the end of the novel, there are hints of hope for women as a group, because she lives on in female relatives: in Lucile, her half-sister, and in Juliette, the daughter of Lucile and Oswald. Even before the little girl proves to be a talented pupil under her aunt's teaching, Corinne leaves her mark, for Juliette has looked like her from birth. The dying woman also teaches Lucile how to be more like her in order to please Oswald. Since neither woman alone completely pleases him, artistic Corinne uses malleable Lucile to create someone who combines both women in one. While giving pleasure to Oswald may not at first seem the most antipatriarchal motivation for Corinne's work of art, her effort has other, more feminist ramifications as well. It transforms English Lucile into a more "Italian"—and thus liberated—woman, and it is the fruit of a collaboration between women who literally rediscover their sisterhood.

Just before the heroine dies, she prepares another type of immortality for herself. Since returning from England to Italy, she has ceased to give oral improvisations. No longer capable of sustained expression, she has composed only fragments. Yet, when she is about to die, she rallies enough to compose a "last song." Too weak to improvise while performing, she must commit it to paper, and, too weak to perform at all, she entrusts her work to a young girl who will recite it in her place. The heroine's physical weakness matches her lack of control over other people and over her own life, but at least she finds a way to speak, if only through another. The youth of the girl, like that of Juliette, suggests some sort of rebirth.

Now, however, we must turn to the more disturbing undertones in the ending, those that suggest Corinne's final actions may not be wholly consistent with her previous antipatriarchal values. For example, like the treatment of Juliette, Corinne's treatment of the girl who reads for her is questionable. Why does the girl's individuality matter so little that we never learn her name? The idea of a continuing female heritage, especially one that can go beyond the limits of biological parenthood, may be attractive, but it is curious that the girls are almost clones of Corinne. Her very effort to duplicate herself in them defeats itself, because her domination deprives them of the independence that defines her.

More specifically, Corinne's treatment of Lucile, Juliette, and the anonymous girl is a type of *ventriloquism*, the first of the two mediated forms we shall be examining. In ventriloquism, one character speaks through another instead of speaking directly.[9] As we have seen, the heroine arranges to have her words read by the nameless girl, and, after Corinne dies, she speaks through Lucile and Juliette, whom she has profoundly influenced. The final sentences of the novel suggest she may have become a chastising voice in the mind of Oswald as well.

Corinne's practice of talking through others is strangely similar to the power exercised earlier by her father's second wife—an Englishwoman who conscientiously follows patriarchal rules. Every day at evening prayers, Lucile reads a prayer that her mother has composed:

Lady Edgermond had written it using a harshness of expression that contrasted with the timidly sweet sound of her daughter's voice as she read, but that very harshness heightened the effect of the last words that Lucile pronounced tremulously. . . . "Grant that [my] mother who must soon return to Thee obtain pardon for her own sins in the name of the virtues of her only child." (16:5:320)

The last phrase is conventional enough but also suggests Lady Edgermond is attempting to use Lucile as a vicarious source of virtue.

The passage bears a disquieting resemblance to the description of the girl in white who reads the last song of Corinne, a dark woman who sits in shadow, herself already a shade:

A young girl dressed in white and crowned with flowers came out. . . . It was she who was to sing Corinne's verse. There was a touching contrast between that soft peaceful face, that face still wholly unmarked by life's pain, and the words she was to speak. But this very contrast had pleased Corinne. It suffused the too-somber thoughts of her downcast soul with a kind of serenity. (20:5:415)

Both passages stress the poignant contrast between the woman who has written the words and the girl who speaks them. Corinne, who has acted in her youth as a mother to Lucile, comes to resemble Lucile's real mother here. Although the ideologies expressed in the two scenes differ greatly, both women are using the girls who speak for them.

Still more unsettling than Corinne's resemblance to a patriarchal woman is her resemblance to a patriarchal man. Her ventriloquism oddly recalls that of her nemesis, Oswald's father, and the dead weight of patriarchy he represents. The late Lord Nelvil is already dead when the book begins, but he symbolically speaks from beyond the grave in several ways, among them the recollections of most of the English characters.

In particular, Oswald has internalized the voice of his father, so that it has become the voice of his own conscience, a voice that speaks against Corinne.[10] The young man's conscience first condemns him because he feels the affair he had in France with Mme d'Arbigny was responsible for his father's death. Oswald's relationship with Corinne reminds him of his French affair and is therefore doomed by the voice of the dead father, which interrupts the son's hopeful thoughts of Corinne right after he meets her: "Putting his hand to his chest, he felt for the portrait of his father he always carried there. Taking it out, he gazed at it, and his momentary happiness along with the cause of that happiness reminded him only too clearly of the feeling that had once made him offend his father so badly" (2:4:33). Nor is the voice of the late Lord Nelvil confined to his son's mind. Later, at the moments when Oswald speaks out against Corinne, she is in effect hearing the dead man speaking aloud, for the son is expressing the father's attitudes.

The late Lord Nelvil also communicates in written form. Oswald, for example, always carries the manuscript of his father's reflections with him (12:2:229). The dead man speaks even through Corinne, for Oswald twice has her read aloud from the manuscript (8:1:136–138; 12:2:229–230).[11] The most important of the father's other writings is a letter that Oswald discovers late in the story, a letter his father wrote to Lord Edgermond, urging him to give Lucile rather than Corinne to Oswald in marriage (16:8:329–330). Exemplifying the late Lord Nelvil's narrative power, this letter outlines the entire course of the novel.

Although the original sender and receiver are both dead, the letter manages to reach Oswald by mediated means—through Mr. Dickson, a sort of double or zombie controlled by the young man's deceased father: "In no way was Mr. Dickson on a level with Oswald's father . . . , but he had been with him at the moment of his death, and since they had been born the same year, it would seem that he had stayed behind a little while to bring his friend news of this world" (16:8:328). Just as Lady Edgermond speaks through Lucile and Corinne speaks through the anonymous girl, so the late Lord Nelvil also speaks through a weaker version of himself.

Thus, by analyzing ventriloquism, a mediated technique epitomized in the practices of Lady Edgermond and Oswald's father, we have found its close ties to patriarchy, as constructed by this novel. These ties make it an especially suspect technique for Corinne to adopt.

The second sort of mediation is *indirect revenge:* one neither enacts vengeance openly nor truly renounces it. Corinne may seem to forgive Oswald for leaving her, but—as scholars have noted—she exhibits traces of anger and vengefulness.[12] She is taking indirect revenge, perhaps without realizing it.

We should look beyond her appearance of forgiveness, for female anger has been bubbling inside the novel without a way to reach the surface. The presence of anger has been hinted at earlier, in Corinne's description of Vesuvius, deep in Italy, the land of women (13:4:242). The volcano is described by the narrator as well (below I quote the passage). If one reads the following by interpreting "man" as "male human being" and by noting the traditional female imagery and the feminine grammatical gender of the major subjects—nature and lava—the passage becomes an image of female rage:

> On this site, nature is no longer in touch with man. He can no longer believe he is her master; she escapes her tyrant through death. . . . [T]he lava itself is dark, just as you would imagine a river in hell; it rolls on slowly. . . . As it approaches, you hear a small sound of sparks, all the more frightening for being slight, and for the feeling that guile is joined with strength. . . . The lava advances without haste, without losing a moment; if it meets a high wall or any sort of building in its path, it stops and piles up black, bituminous torrents in front of the obstacle to bury it at last under its burning waves. . . .
>
> We fear what goes on in the bowels [literally, "breast"] of the earth. . . . [The colors] torture one's sight, as hearing would be rent

by the shrill sounds of witches at night, calling upon the moon from earth. (13:1:232–233)

After the image of Vesuvius as a hostile breast comes a reference to shrill witches, whose presence makes sense only if they are considered figures of female rage. The grotesqueness of the last sentence clashes with most other metaphors in the novel, so that it represents the pain of the witches' struggle to help the terrifying female powers of the night, moon, and earth express themselves. Once deciphered, this allegory of volcanic female anger suggests that we would be wise to look for a vengeful face behind the heroine's forbearing mask.

Mediated revenge is normally indirect in one of two ways: it is *disguised* or it is *displaced*. A major example of the former is Corinne's ostensibly benign relation to Oswald's daughter and wife. Juliette's inborn physical resemblance to Corinne suggests Oswald's unfaithfulness—if only in emotion—to his wife.[13] It means that Corinne will always alienate Lucile from her husband and daughter, since all his affection for the child justifiably strikes Lucile as a form of affection for his lost lover (19:4:386).

Juliette's total resemblance to her mother's half-sister also means that she looks no more like her father than like her mother. Corinne has substituted herself for both parents, or she has thoroughly possessed them. Her possession of Oswald could be explained as a form of romantic love, but her possession of her rival Lucile seems more unsavory, especially in view of the younger woman's weakness and malleability. Thus a shadow falls over the dying Corinne's project of making her half-sister more like her.[14] In reply to the younger woman's thanks, Corinne makes the disconcerting comment (quoted at the beginning of this essay) that she wants Oswald to find her in his wife, his daughter, and all his enjoyment of feeling. As Gutwirth has said, Corinne "seizes and enchants all three Nelvils," who are "scarred by the hand of death that Corinne . . . puts upon them, saying like Dido, 'remember me.' "[15] Beneath a friendly surface, the heroine's possession of child and parents constitutes a particularly ironic, and therefore exquisite, form of ghostly revenge. She has inserted herself into each of their possible relationships with each other, so that whenever this family feels most nuclear, she will show herself to have been there all along.

Corinne gets revenge in another disguised way near the end of the book when Oswald, unhappy with his wife, begs in vain to see his former lover. Corinne's refusal to see him is not an act of direct revenge, because she is motivated by her recently increased piety, instead of (or at least in addition to) hostility. Without expressing anger openly, she nonetheless has the satisfaction of turning down his request.

The second kind of indirect revenge shows hostility more directly but displaces it from the original object onto a new one. A common type of displaced indirect revenge is self-destructiveness, in which characters turn their anger away from its initial target, back to themselves. To perform self-destructive acts is to exercise the "powers of the weak," powers that are negative.[16] They may be completely unintentional or unconscious and may include withdrawal, sulking, silence, and inaction.

Self-destructive practices have a certain appeal. They can be satisfying to people with little conventional power, such as the fading heroine: "Her enthusiasm was kindled in the midst of suffering by the very sacrifices she made to [Oswald]" (15:4:288). Because the weak cannot unleash the anger they feel against the strong, they must find someone weak on whom to vent it, and the weak self is a handy target. In addition, this form of revenge sometimes takes a still more indirect path, back to its original target—when the harm that the weak inflict on themselves manages to induce guilt in the strong.[17]

Oddly enough, self-destructiveness can attract the very person at whom the revenge was originally aimed. Because self-destructive acts weaken the person who performs them, the harm that Corinne does herself may represent an effort to charm Oswald, who likes weak women. He says of his former lover, Mme d'Arbigny: "'She was never more attractive than falling in a faint at my feet'" (12:2:222), and he is touched by Corinne's weakness when timidity prevents her from improvising (6:4:110). A woman who wants to attract Oswald does well to become weaker, though in the process she enters a traditional female double bind: "Oswald . . . had said that he could not resist a woman's suffering, but . . . that the sacrifices made for that suffering cooled his feeling" (16:3:312).

Corinne's death culminates her self-destructive efforts to please, and indirectly punish, her lover. The ultimate power of the weak, the ultimate self-destruction, is suicide, which runs through all Staël's work.[18] Corinne does not literally kill herself, but by the end of the book she does wish to die. Even if the heroine does not die so as to *cause* Oswald to feel guilty, her "willful self-destruction" certainly has that *effect*.[19] (The effect may not last long, though: the novel ends with questions about his remorse rather than with "he lived guiltily ever after.") Pierre Fauchery places the heroine's willed death within literary convention:

> Rather than contingent death, . . . a great heart will be haunted by the idea of a death that is necessary, unique, and as if under control. Doubtless one can "take one's own life," but . . . morality as well as aesthetic convention makes that way out even riskier for heroines than for heroes. . . . [The solution is] that kind of "technical" suicide, without violence and not forbidden, whose formula will be taught by Clarissa or Corinne to a number of plaintive souls of the nineteenth century.[20]

Ventriloquism is one major mediated technique that patriarchal characters share with Corinne; indirect revenge is the other. Once again, Corinne bears a curious resemblance to Oswald's father, the arch-patriarch. She cannot stop Oswald from marrying Lucile, nor could the late Lord Nelvil stop him from having an affair with Mme d'Arbigny, but the heroine and Oswald's father both haunt him, their revenge disguised as benevolence.

Indirect revenge typifies other patriarchal characters as well. For instance, Lady Edgermond does not refuse outright to bring up Corinne, the child of Lord Edgermond's first marriage, but her harsh treatment of the girl may be the stepmother's displaced way of punishing her husband for having been married before (especially to an Italian).

Instead of expressing anger directly, Lady Edgermond and Lucile frequently displace it onto the self, using self-denial as manipulative martyrdom. For example, silently resenting the attraction that Corinne holds for Oswald, Lucile takes on the role of martyr, particularly when she conceals from her husband her knowledge that the mountain pass they are to cross is dangerous (19:5). His anguished reaction to the incident, like the paralysis of their marriage in general, indicates that the advantages of martyrdom soon reach their limits. Like other powers of the weak, self-destructiveness helps one acquire half a loaf but prevents one from having more.

In such ways, patriarchal characters employ indirect revenge—either disguised or displaced. And, as we have unexpectedly found, so does Corinne.

Ventriloquism and indirect revenge are disturbing in the context of this particular novel because of a contradiction: the text links these actions with patriarchy and yet shows them in use by a heroine who has generally opposed everything patriarchal. Moreover, the two techniques have their own inherently disconcerting characteristics, regardless of this text's symbolic system. In addition to the contradiction just mentioned, Corinne's use of such innately troubling techniques conflicts with her role as admirable heroine.

In ventriloquism, one person uses another as an intermediary to address a third. We have seen that ventriloquism is troubling in several ways. To begin with, it can enable the originator of the message to interfere in matters that do not concern him or her, as when Oswald's father uses his son's voice to criticize Corinne. Furthermore, the originator of the message can overpower the intermediary, as when Mr. Dickson seems to live on only to carry messages to and from the late Lord Nelvil. Finally, ventriloquism can make the ultimate addressee—and even the intermediary—unaware of where the message actually originated. This problem arises, for example, when Corinne and even Oswald are unaware of the extent to which he is speaking for his father.

While the concept of ventriloquism is defined by its verbal form, the concept of indirect revenge is defined by its hostile substance.[21] The vengeance is indirect in one of two senses. It can be openly hostile but can be displaced onto a different target, as when Lady Edgermond feels bitterness against her husband and vents it on her stepdaughter and herself. Alternatively, indirect revenge can appear innocent but can be a masked form of hostility. As we have seen, indirect revenge can be disguised as a harmless act (as when Corinne trains Lucile and Juliette); it can be disguised as a harmful act with a laudable motivation (as when Corinne cites piety as the reason she refuses to see Oswald); or it can be disguised as a harmful act for which one seemingly is not responsible (as when Corinne punishes Oswald by willing her death). Thus indirect revenge is troubling either because it is displaced and harms the wrong person, or because it is disguised and is therefore difficult to combat.

We can now understand why evaluation of the ending of the novel is radically undecidable. The otherwise admirable heroine uses ventriloquism and indirect revenge, which have the disturbing traits just summarized. Since the novel has, moreover, linked mediation to patriarchy, Corinne is using mediated, patriarchal means to reach feminist ends.

When a patriarchal character uses a mediated technique, the narrator sometimes draws attention to the harm it causes (as when Oswald's father makes him suffer) or explains how the character's past history has led to this regrettable action (as when Lucile plays the martyr). In contrast, the narrator never identifies, much less evaluates, the disturbing means that the heroine employs to ensure the survival of her principles and, metaphorically, of herself. Readers are left on their own to evaluate Corinne's behavior: Could she have reached the same ends by means that the novel associated with feminism? Or was patriarchal power the only power remaining to her? If so, should she have eschewed patriarchal means and given up all chance of survival? Or was she right to use the only means of survival available to her? In other words, does the ending bring rebirth or regression?

Because the author lived in a male-dominated society, it may have been impossible for her to imagine an ending less shadowed by patriarchy. Even if she could have, it may have been implausible to include such an ending in *Corinne*, a relatively realistic novel placed in a contemporary setting dominated by men. In fact, nearly two centuries after the publication of *Corinne*, impassioned debate still surrounds the question of how to work toward feminist goals in a patriarchal society. In this novel, Staël does not solve the problem, but she poignantly brings it to life. And, in spite of the questions raised about how to work toward feminist goals, *Corinne* does not ultimately cast real doubt on whether one should work toward those goals. The book, including the ending, has had an inspirational impact on generations of readers.[22]

NARRATING THE FRENCH REVOLUTION: THE EXAMPLE OF *CORINNE*

Doris Y. Kadish

Critics have acknowledged, but not fully explored, the political elements in *Corinne,* which Simone Balayé characterizes as "quite clearly evoked in the novel."[1] Similarly, they have observed, but not sufficiently delved into, the focus in that novel on the facts and symbols of the French Revolution. Staël herself alerts us to that focus when she states, "Whenever our train of thoughts brings us to ponder human destiny, the Revolution inevitably comes to mind."[2] And Henri Coulet warns us not to forget, in reading Staël,

> to what extent revolutionary events were crucial to her thinking, with the hopes they aroused in her and the disappointment their outcome caused her, and how, without appearing in the forefront of her works of fiction, the Revolution inspired the creation of her characters, their relationships, and the structure of her plots.[3]

The focus on the politics of the French Revolution in *Corinne* is, however, only indirect, a fact that is consistent with the role of politics generally in the works and lives of women writers in the late eighteenth and nineteenth centuries. Staël's strong political views found other such indirect means of expression through the influence she exerted in her salon or on the careers of her husband and her lover Narbonne. As Carla Peterson remarks, "Exiled by Napoleon, relegated to the sidelines of history, condemned to watch helplessly as power-wielding men determined the direction of French history, Mme de Staël had only the recourse of writing her own female epic."[4] And Charlotte Hogsett notes, in a related vein, that whereas Staël's model Rousseau or her contemporaries Constant and Chateaubriand wrote both confessionally and politically, following the rhetorical rules of accepted literary genres, such writing was considered inappropriate for women. She concludes, "Perhaps one reason why the writing of many women has not been adequately appreciated, why not as many works by women find their way into those canonized as the great classics, is that in many cases women writers do not work according to that kind of rhetorical rule."[5] Efforts currently being made by feminist critics to restore women writers to their rightful place in the canon will perhaps be furthered by the recognition that their "female epics" and "rhetorical rule" were distinctly, albeit indirectly, political in nature.

The political focus of *Corinne* is developed largely through its treatment of the female protagonist as allegorical, a political strategy manifest generally in cultural productions of her era. It is important to remember the highly significant role of allegory in the revolutionary period, especially in the representation of women. As Mona Ozouf points out, "the lesson of the Revolution was conveyed by a swarm of allegorical figures. Many of these figures were female."[6] There is also textual justification for an allegorical interpretation in the fact that the novel presents Corinne less as a fully developed subject than as a kind of neoclassical object, as Madelyn Gutwirth has so thoroughly demonstrated.[7] In this paper, I attempt to build on Gutwirth's studies of allegory by introducing into the discussion of neoclassical, allegorical elements in *Corinne* a Marxist focus on issues of politics and social class. As I have already suggested and shall amplify subsequently, that focus has important ramifications for a feminist interpretation of the novel.

I would like to add that even the surface romantic interest of *Corinne* is not unrelated to the political thrust of the novel. As Nancy Armstrong shows in her important recent book *Desire and Domestic Fiction,* focusing on a woman, defining her, and describing her amorous conflicts served potent political ends in nineteenth-century novels by and about women: through such activities, writers "seized the authority to say what was female, and that they did in order to contest the reigning notion of kinship relations that attached most power and privilege to certain family lines. . . . the female was the figure, above all else, on whom depended the outcome of the struggle among competing ideologies."[8] Armstrong credits Foucault with enabling us to see "sexual relations as the site for changing power relations between classes and cultures as well as between genders and generations."[9] To unify the interests of non-aristocratic groups, to reject the aristocratic values of status and material versus moral worth, to assert the worth of a new economic model: these are some of the issues at stake, according to Armstrong, in the treatment of love, marriage, and gender in nineteenth-century novels. As Armstrong helps us to understand, instead of viewing the domestic issues treated in the surface plot of *Corinne* as outside of history, they too can be seen as determining history, as much as battles, treaties, legislative policies, and the like.

We can turn now to the first of three narrative strategies through which political issues are indirectly raised in *Corinne*, the treatment of Corinne as an allegory of the Republic. That a woman assumes such a role is not surprising, for, as Marina Warner points out, whereas men have been treated historically as specific individuals, women have tended to be treated as generalizations and abstractions, especially in France, where "from the *ancien régime* through a succession of Republics, kingdoms and empires, French governments have used the human form, and especially the female form, to decorate the seats of authority and prestige." She adds, " 'La France' traditionally personified royal France, while Marianne bodied forth La République, representative of liberty."[10] In a related vein, Lynn Hunt observes that during the revolutionary period, it was necessary to promulgate certain symbols, notably female symbols of the Republic, in order to provide a basis for the new class. The need arose because of the absence of any stable French constitution or tradition of common law that would anchor the nascent political forces.[11] What was at issue in female allegories during the revolutionary period was thus not only woman as liberty and the republic, but woman as representative of a new, non-royal, non-aristocratic class. In Staël's novel, Corinne embodies certain of the new values of that emerging class, in sharp opposition to the fixed, traditional values of her aristocratic lover Oswald, Lord Nelvil. In the nascent system of bourgeois values with which she can often be identified, superiority is based on talent and merit, not on genealogy and tradition, as in his older system of aristocratic values.

One key scene in *Corinne* presents a salient illustration of that character's allegorical presentation as a figure of the republic and the newer system of non-aristocratic values. In chapter 2 Corinne appears before the adoring eyes of Nelvil and the Italian people as what Madelyn Gutwirth has identified as Niké,[12] seated on a "chariot built in the ancient style,"[13] ascending the stairs of the Capitol, to the sound of music and canons. In addition to personifying talent and merit, she emerges in this scene as a figure of liberty and the Republic, not only by the repeated emphasis on the adulation of her by the people, with whom she shares the virtues of simplicity and spontaneity, but also by the tricolor setting in which she appears: white and blue in her clothing ("She wore a white tunic with a blue drapery fastened beneath her breast") and red in the background ("Everyone came forward to see her from their windows which were decorated with potted plants and scarlet hangings") (p. 21). Corinne's clothing in this scene recalls the "imagined simplicity of classical republican dress" designed by David, which Warner describes as follows: "The style was patriotically termed 'en gaule,' and was created by muslin-like shifts, usually white to connote purity" with a sash under the bust, to emphasize woman as nurturer.[14]

Corinne's appearance can also be linked to the use of living allegories during the revolutionary period, that is, the use of live female models as participants in revolutionary festivals. Through that use, the revolutionary governments attempted, with only partial success, to replace traditional religious symbolism. In this regard, one critic observes, speaking of the pietà structure of David's celebrated painting of Marat's death: "The gradual elision of the boundaries between sacred and profane is one of the most fascinating stylistic accomplishments of the Revolution."[15] Not surprisingly, then, one notes that, while appearing as an allegorical representation of freedom, Corinne also appears constantly in a religious, divine guise: "She is a goddess among the clouds" (21), "a priestess of Apollo" (21); "No longer a fearful woman, she was an inspired priestess" (32).

Whether as a divinity, Niké, a personification of liberty, or an object of adulation by the people, the triumphant Corinne at the beginning of the novel is clearly associated with the positive, moderate, non-Jacobin side of revolution and with the lofty goals and aspirations that Staël conceived after 1793 for a Republic controlled by the emerging middle class. Corinne's symbolism points to the first stage of the Revolution, before the Terror, when hopes for genuine and lasting freedom were possible and when an ideal synthesis of the best in aristocratic and bourgeois values seemed feasible. Madelyn Gutwirth sums up Corinne's revolutionary significance when she designates her as "a goddess of excess who, like the revolution, was guilty of having expected too much from mankind."[16]

The second narrative strategy to be considered here is closely associated with the first; it is the treatment of Corinne as an analogue of Italy. Like the Revolution in its positive phase, and like Corinne as a representative of non-aristocratic values, Italy represents freedom, liberation from oppressive traditions, enlightenment through artistic achievement, and classical simplicity and humility.[17] With respect specifically to tradition, Italy stands in sharp contrast with England, which is depicted in *Corinne* as embodying an aristocratic commitment to the past, family lines, and property. This is not the England of liberalism and constitutionalism that Staël strongly admired at other points in her writing career, but rather the England at war with France after 1793, harboring French émigrés and menacing France with the restoration of the *ancien régime* through force.

The symbolic value of Italy in contrast to aristocratic England is enhanced by the novel's further identification of Italy with the feminine, which has already been seen to have privileged links with the newer, non-aristocratic class. Not only is Italy tied to the maternal in the novel by virtue of Corinne's mother being Italian, but there are also repeated references to the feminine nature of Italy and Rome as a female ruler of the world ("Liberty made her queen"; "Queen, too, by her scepter of thought"; and so forth [27]) and to Italy as the country of artistic rather than military power. Marie-Claire Vallois notes in this regard the appropriateness of the full title *Corinne, or Italy* for a work in which Italy and woman are intimately related.[18] The non-aristocratic significance of Italy is also enhanced by the values and aspirations of its people. If the Italian people worship Corinne it is because, as the embodiment of the Republic, she is the ideal of a country whose people hark back to the Republic of ancient times. Common to Italy, the people, and Corinne as the feminine embodiment of the Republic are such qualities as simplicity, spontaneity, and imagination. Thus it is not surprising that the art of oral improvisation, "an essentially female art form,"[19] is identified as especially appropriate for the people: "It lends something poetic to the lowest orders of society" (44). Moreover, the people, Italy, women, and the Republic are presented in the novel as similarly lacking in power and autonomy, and accordingly as subject in like fashion to oppression. Italy in *Corinne* is a mere shadow of its former glory, and its interest in the arts reflects its political and military impotence. Thus it is unable to resist such nefarious forces of power as Napoleon, whose oppression of women like Staël and whose destruction of the Republic constitutes, as Vallois reminds us, the true "unsaid" of *Corinne*.[20]

Further evidence that Italy is far more than a geographical and cultural entity in *Corinne* can be seen in its declining narrative importance during the course of the novel. Italy shows its most resplendent, enlightening side at the beginning of the novel, as did the Revolution in its early phase. The novel then depicts the gradual period during which the wonders of Italy are exhausted by Corinne, a period analogous to the decline of the Revolution after 1791. That decline is expressed thematically through the consistent emphasis in the novel on the bad air in Italy. Revealingly, the pernicious effects of that bad air are most pronounced in Rome, the site of the ancient Republic, and are experienced in the form of contagious disease by Corinne, the embodiment of the Republic. Finally, the novel suggests the triumph of England over Italy, as toward the end Oswald assumes full control of the novel and asserts English male virility by assuming the role of war hero. At the close, Italy, like Corinne and the positive early side of the Revolution, have been totally eclipsed.

The third narrative strategy to be considered here is the treatment of Corinne as a substitute and alternative king and father. That the patriarchal roles of king and father have been inextricably linked throughout history is well known and is stressed within the pages of the novel itself, when, in an aristocratic spirit of allegiance to family and king, Oswald designates paternity as a "noble image of a supremely good master" (182). Although not referred to as such within the pages of the novel, the national loss of the king Louis XVI during the Terror can be seen as underlying and explaining the kind of obsessive sense of guilt and loss that Oswald, more than Corinne, is portrayed as feeling, although both characters are depicted in the novel as having lost their fathers, whom they loved very much. As the narrator observes near the beginning of the novel, "Indeed, how is it ever possible to replace that affection born with us, the natural empathy of blood relations, the friendship that heaven compounds to unite a child and his father?" (17).

Corinne does attempt, however, to replace both the father and the king, and to propose meaningful alternatives to traditional patriarchal and aristocratic figures of power. In the public domain, Corinne first emerges as an alternative king in the key scene of her crowning as a poet, with its unmistakable overtones of the crowning of Staël's archenemy Napoleon. Like him, Corinne has aspirations to heroic stature and glory, and is adored by the people. Such aspirations strike a remarkably modern note. For in her role as substitute king, Corinne not only promotes the value of women; she also acts to grant women, if only symbolically and indirectly, the political powers of men. One is reminded of a contemporary example, Monique Wittig's "guérillères," who are not content merely to be lovers and nurturers but strive to perform as rulers and fighters as well.[21] The importance of Corinne's role in this regard as an alternative to patriarchal power cannot be overemphasized. For although Staël ultimately fails to valorize the notion of a female alternative to male power in society or even within the family politically, she does promote that notion symbolically, an important consideration in a period where the political and the symbolic were inextricably linked. In the final analysis, Corinne proposes a far more meaningful alternative to traditional power than do other, male figures depicted or evoked in the novel. Unlike her absolutist, aristocratic lover Oswald, she values cultural diversity and liberation from mere tradition. Although she is Italian and Catholic, she points out to Oswald: "Our principles are liberal, our dogmas are absolute; and yet in practice, our despotic orthodoxy comes to terms with individual circumstances, and your religious freedom requires that its laws be followed without exception" (181). Moreover, she is presented in the novel as an antithesis rather than the female equivalent of Napoleon. She is a peace-loving ruler whose crown is gained for merit, not traditional privilege, whose glory is aesthetic, not military, whose freedom is gained through the powers of the mind and the pen rather than brute force and the sword. She stands as an alternative to Napoleon's absolutist aspirations to royalty and aristocracy as emperor.

In the private domain, Corinne plays an equally significant and modern role as substitute father, for both herself and Oswald. For herself, she replaces the father by assuming, upon his death, the control that a father traditionally exercised over his daughter's life. She succeeds thereby in escaping the rigid patterns that his English upper-class society sought to impose on her. Her rejection of her father's name is symptomatic in this regard of her larger rejection of patriarchal authority, which in *Corinne* marks the aristocracy most visibly, although in reality it similarly characterized the nascent bourgeoisie as well. It is true that she ultimately fails in her attempt to replace the father: revealingly, she adopts the traditional Catholic form of address to a confessor at the end, stating "Father, now that you know my sad destiny, judge me" (418). It is nonetheless her valiant if only transitory success prior to the end that gives her heroic stature.

For Oswald, Corinne replaces the father by assuaging his feelings of filial guilt and loss. In one crucial scene during his illness, she even assumes a male voice by reading aloud to him from his father's spiritual reflections. But whereas she succeeds to some extent in her own life in breaking out of the aristocratic patterns represented by paternal influence, Oswald remains a prisoner of and reactionary adherent to them. It is significant to note in this regard that he, not Corinne, is the chief figure of conflict in the novel, the character who is torn between the competing demands of the old and the new, between allegiance to the aristocratic patriarchal father and the bourgeois substitute father. Revealingly, the novel begins with him in the winter of 1794–1795 at the moment when the Terror had reached its end, when the fate of the Republic, torn between the forces of reaction and revolution, was at issue. And it is he who, by rejecting the alternative to patriarchal authority that she proposes, symbolically kills both her and the Republic, as did the similarly male, absolutist figures of the ancien régime, the Terror, and the Empire. His role as a figurative assassin is underlined in the text. Maija Lehtonen notes that "In her misfortune, Corinne feels as though she has been sentenced to death"; she calls attention to the revealing existence of scaffold images in Staël's novel, concluding, "All these images make Oswald seem like a murderer."[22] If men have killed the republic in the past, Staël suggests, they should in their future efforts to restore it give serious consideration to the alternative models that women like Corinne have to offer.

In conclusion, I have attempted to propose an interpretation of *Corinne* that casts Staël in a more positive feminist role than she has typically been credited with playing. On the basis of the thoroughgoing political nature of the novel that I have been exploring, I would urge that politics along with love provide the keys to interpreting *Corinne*. Corinne must be betrayed because the Revolution was, not just because Oswald preferred Lucile. She must die because the early dreams for the Revolution did, not just because she was the hopeless romantic that some readers might take her to be. Such an interpretation highlights the political significance of a novel whose feminist importance has often been questioned. When only viewed romantically, that novel seems to glorify submission to male control. When the romantic is placed in the larger political context to which it belongs, *Corinne* can be seen to call into question, if not openly reject, paternal models of authority. Through her indirect presentation of key political and class issues surrounding the French Revolution, Staël can today be seen as having promoted a new system of non-aristocratic values in which women had a highly significant, if still largely symbolic, role to play.

PORTRAIT OF THE
ARTIST AS SAPPHO

Joan DeJean

Germaine de Staël's literary production testifies eloquently to her life-long obsession with Sappho.[1] From an early "romance" on the story of Sappho's involvement with the mythical Phaon to the tragedy *Sappho* at the end of her career, Staël at times paid homage to and at times radically revised the plot decreed for her Greek precursor by male writers both ancient and modern. Staël effectively positioned her career under the image of Sappho, much as, after her death, Gérard's painting *Corinne au cap Misène*, sometimes known as *Madame de Staël en Corinne au cap Misène*, presided over Juliette Récamier's salon and Chateaubriand's first readings of the *Mémoires d'outre-tombe*. One editor describes Staël's otherworldly presence in the Récamier salon as a "symbol of glory and its transience . . . hover[ing] over" these readings.[2]

Just what the portrait of Sappho that hovers over so many of Staël's productions represented for her cannot be neatly summed up: throughout her career, Staël created fictions that evolved in tandem with the contemporary tradition of speculation about Sappho. Because Staël produced such a significant body of Sapphic fictions, she belongs to a rather quirky subcategory of French women writers: as if under the influence of a strangely persistent mathematical "law," each century has a single French Sappho, a writer whose involvement with the original woman writer plays a central role in her coming to writing and continues unabated throughout her career. Louise Labé initiated the pattern that was perfected by Madeleine de Scudéry and continued by Germaine de Staël and Renée Viviens. (I would make a case for Marguerite Yourcenar as our century's Sapphic self-incarnation, even though her involvement remained resolutely oblique.)

One of Germaine Necker's first literary efforts, her coming to writing through Sappho, is the naively childish song, "Romance to the tune: We loved each other from childhood." Readers familiar with Ovid's *Heroides*, and in particular with both the eighteenth-century translations of this text so central to the development of French epistolary fiction and the eighteenth-century genre known as the "new heroides," will recognize in Staël's romance the essence of the watered-down version of Ovid promoted in her day. Her initial vision of Sappho is thus a far cry from Ovid's woman consumed by wild passion and raw sexuality. She is a piteous creature, abandoned by women jealous of her talents and by her unfaithful lover, Phaon. It is evident to any reader of Staël's mature fiction that her preoccupation with Sappho takes shape because she recognizes in this Sapphic plot the basic elements of her recurrent vision of female abandonment. If Staël's fascination with Sappho continues unabated throughout her career, however, it is because she is able to develop her rather primitive initial scenario to incorporate elements borrowed from the two main traditions of late eighteenth-century Sapphic speculation, one native French and the other Italian, largely generated under the Napoleonic occupation.

The French tradition is represented most notably by the abbé Barthélemy's 1788 *Voyage du jeune Anacharsis en Grèce*. Although this work's immense contemporary authority seems inconceivable today, the novel is easily the most influential fiction of Sappho in the entire French tradition. The foundation of Barthélemy's influence is his invention—based on a misreading of an ancient chronicle, the Parian marble—of a political Sappho. Ovid's early commentators had already concocted the notion of a voyage to Sicily made by Sappho in a futile effort to make her wayward lover Phaon return to her. Barthélemy accepts the journey to Sicily, but he transforms its motivation from lovesick wandering to political exile: Saphho is banished there along with her coconspirators in an unsuccessful revolt against the dictator Pittacus.

Only a few years after her own initial foray into Sapphic image-

making, in the course of a banquet in Barthélemy's honor, Staël improvised a long poem eulogizing the abbé as the new Homer and asking
him to lend her his "golden lyre" (*Correspondance littéraire*, February
1789). Years would pass, and Staël would herself live the life of an
exile before she took up that lyre to play Sappho to Barthélemy's
Homer and create, first in *Delphine* and then in *Corinne*, fictions that
show the effects of his politicized plot for Sappho. In these fictions she
simultaneously inscribed her rejection of the tradition which, while it
is actually initiated before Barthélemy's politically empowered Sappho, comes to be viewed in the nineteenth century, especially by the
most powerful German philologists of the age, as the antidote to the
dangerous French vision of a seditious Sappho.

The second tradition of Sapphic speculation, which will come to be
identified as Napoleonic, originates with Alessandro Verri's 1780
novel, *Le Avventure di Saffo*.[3] In Verri's first chapter, "Phaon Transformed," Verri exaggerates Phaon's masculinity in order to put a revitalized hero at the center of the Sapphic plot. At the annual games in
Mytilene, Saffo falls in love at first sight when she watches Phaon in
the wrestling contest. What Verri has his reader admire through her
eyes is the sheer beauty of Phaon's body. Surely few, if any, fictional
scenes available in 1780 afforded the novelist the possibility, in which
Verri luxuriates, of narrating the moment at which a handsome young
man "stripped off his garb . . . and appeared perfectly naked, having
only the usual wrestler's girdle." The author then dwells on "the action of his muscles" (39)—all this for the seduction of an adolescent
female. Saffo is so enraptured with this display of male flesh that she is
moved spontaneously to embark on her poetic career and, "framed in
sudden poetic frenzy," she improvises her first poem in his honor (47).
This is the single element in Verri's Sapphic plot that proved most
influential for the century to come: he makes women's writing dependent on Woman's desire for the perfect male body.

The original edition of Verri's novel predates the Napoleonic presence in Italy. No sooner had Italy been brought under French control,
however, than the novelist seized the opportunity to capitalize on his
fiction's potential to find favor with the new regime. In 1797, Verri
reedited his *Saffo* with a dedication to Napoleon's sister Caroline,
whom he calls "our Saffo." In a dedicatory preface, he details the
ideology that he feels will appeal to the new ruling family: "Such a
truth is too well understood by you, fairest Citizen [*Cittadina*], for you

have engraved upon your mind the maxim that was carved in gold letters by her wise parents above the door of our Saffo's study: that work keeps the soul peaceful, just as exercise maintains the health of the body."[4] At the height of French imperialism and the new militarism on which it was founded, the story of Sappho is deployed as an allegedly moral tale worthy of the citizens of the new republic, because it justifies the work ethic and glorifies physical fitness. Furthermore, the syntax of Verri's overblown dedication leads us to read into it more than undeserved praise. Caroline Bonaparte is addressed in both the second and third persons, and that pronominal split allows the reader to see the passage not as a eulogy of a woman who was hardly a Sappho figure in any usual sense of the term, but as an indication of the moral presented by Verri's novel, a warning to "our" true Saffos. Had Saffo followed "parental wisdom," she would have used work to "keep [her] soul peaceful," and therefore would not have been a source of trouble to the patriarchal order. It would be a mistake to dismiss Verri's ingenious self-promotion as simply an attempt to make his fictionalization palatable to the future wife of the Napoleonic general Murat. For Verri is far from unique in his attempt to put a revitalized, masculinized Phaon at the heroic center of Sappho's plot.

This Napoleonic plot was further developed by Lantier in his 1797 *Voyages d'Anténor*, by the fanatical Napoleon loyalist Chaussard in the adaptation of Verri included in his 1801 *Fêtes et courtisanes de la Grèce*, and by the Neapolitan general Imperiale in his 1803 *La Faoniade: Inni ed odi di Saffo*. The authors' lingering over Phaon's young flesh can be seen as a proto-fascist iconography of the male body, a hymn to the male body as a well-oiled machine for the domination of all forces that threaten, in Verri's terms, "the peace of the soul," the ability of each man to play his proper role in the patriarchal order. The writer who makes Phaon the origin of Sappho's poetic gift brings full circle the plan initiated by Ovid: the beautiful young man now inspires, in addition to destroying, her poetic voice.

Despite the fact that Lantier's and Chaussard-Verri's plots closely parallel Barthélemy's in many respects, they contain no mention of Sappho's exile and her political activities. In addition, Sappho also loses the ability to attract a series of rival poet-lovers. In short, any potential for an active plot is denied her in the fictions that allow Phaon to bask in glory at her expense. The logical counterpart of the presentation of Phaon as a locus of "mental peace" and "bodily health" is the promotion of the legend of Sappho's suicide as the dramatic center of her life. The image of Sappho's leap from the White Rock of Leukas first figures in Sappho iconography only in the illustrations to French translations of her poetry in the 1760s. The full exploitation of the scene's dramatic potential begins several decades later outside France in association with the developing Napoleonic tradition, most notably in the aquatints by Henry Tresham illustrating Verri's romance. Tresham joins Verri in celebrating Phaon's physical beauty and in promoting Sappho's consequent emotional and physical disarray by including melodramatic portrayals of her running to the cliff and then leaping from it.

The pictorial representation of the suicide destined to have the greatest impact on the literary tradition was exhibited in the salon of 1801 by Baron Gros, a painter whose ties to Napoleon are well known. Moreover, Gros's *Sapho au cap Leucade* is the first fiction of Sappho whose inspiration is directly traceable to the future Emperor's immediate entourage. After Gros was presented to Joséphine in Genoa, she brought him to Milan to meet Napoleon, who quickly commissioned a painting from him. They then introduced him to General Dessoles, who in turn commissioned the painting of Sappho. The origin of the painting's subject has not been determined, but whether it came from painter or patron, the idea of focusing attention on Sappho at the moment of her suicide and of couching the representation in agitated, dramatic rhetoric was formulated by someone intimately linked to Napoleon.

Both patron and painter were committed to the renewed militarism that was the foundation of the Napoleonic myth. Gros was primarily a military painter; in the 1801 salon in which his *Sapho* was exhibited he was also represented by a more typical canvas, *Bonaparte Crossing the Bridge at Arcola*, a tribute to Napoleon's courage and daring in a 1796 battle that had won for him both the gratitude of the Directory and the loyalty of his troops, helping prepare the coup d'état that had made him Consul in 1799. Thus, in 1801, Gros was already an official maker of Napoleon's superhuman legend, a recorder of the events—such as the crossing of a strategic bridge—that were the foundation of the new patriarchal order. He took time off from these essential tasks to depict a tormented Sappho leaping to her death, even though representations of suicide were violently criticized on moral grounds in Napoleonic France. Gros's gesture suggests that France's new regime may have had a stake in the violent self-destruction of the original woman writer, a conjecture that finds support in the most developed Sapphic fiction of the turn of the century, Germaine de Staël's *Corinne* (1807). In *Corinne*, the battle lines between literary women and the forces of the (Napoleonic) patriarchal order are drawn as nowhere else.

Corinne reinstates, literally with a vengeance, the writer in the Sapphic plot. We first encounter Staël's heroine on the morning she is to be crowned at the capitol as "the most famous woman in Italy, poet, writer, improvisatrice."[5] In the course of this ceremony it becomes clear that Staël wants her heroine to be seen as not only a Sappho figure, but as the direct successor of Sappho, the Sappho of her day. Sonnets of praise are read to her, "a pleasing mixture of images and mythological allusions that could have been addressed from century to century, from Sappho to our day, to all the women celebrated because of their literary talents" (54). By choosing "Corinne" as the name for her heroine, Staël elects a name with Sapphic associations—Korinna was, after Sappho, the most famous Greek woman poet—but a name, unlike Sappho, bound neither to an oeuvre nor to a biography. Before the twentieth-century papyri discoveries, almost nothing remained of Korinna's work, and even today all that is known of her life is the story of her rivalry with Pindar, over whom she was allegedly victorious in poetry contests.

Staël multiplies the resemblances between Corinne and the mid-eighteenth-century French Sappho: both are dark, with unusually expressive eyes; both perform their poetry to musical accompaniment; both give up glory, a circle of admirers, and eventually even their poetic gifts when they fall hopelessly in love with younger men; both are abandoned by their lovers, who sail across the sea to the charms of younger women.[6] In *Corinne*, Staël's personal contribution to that tradition of fictionalization is a modernization of the Sapphic plot to stress its legal and political implications for the "superior woman" of her day.

The reader first encounters *Corinne*'s Phaon when he engages in a fierce battle to rescue the inhabitants of Ancona from a raging fire (4). Staël's presentation of the scene differs, however, in essential ways from the Italian tradition of Phaon the athlete. To begin with, the scene is staged to demonstrate Oswald's courage rather than his physical attributes. Most importantly, Staël's heroine owes nothing of her own self-constitution to this vision of the male in his glory. Indeed, *Corinne* reverses the model established by Napoleonic Sapphic fictions, in which the obscure young woman is irresistibly attracted to the handsome, strong man. Oswald and Corinne only meet when he arrives in Rome. A foreigner totally outside his element, he is caught up in the immense crowd celebrating the coronation of female literary genius, and the unknown young man falls under the spell of the celebrated writer's literary glory. The goal of Staël's reversal of the dominant contemporary plot is to explain its origin by exposing the nature of the threat that the woman writer's exercise of power over the physically vigorous hero constitutes for patriarchal fictions.

Oswald is no sooner "dazzled" by Corinne's brilliance than he pulls back from her, overcome by "a sort of terror at the emotion that was carrying him away." This terror leads him to question the source of his "captivation": "Was [Corinne's] charm the result of magic or of poetic inspiration? Was she Armide or Sapho?" (77). The sentence reads literally "was *it* [*était-ce*] Armide or Sapho?", as though such a powerful female figure could not be essentially human. The equation Staël has her hero voice, between Sappho and Armide, succinctly formulates the definition of the "woman problem" in *Corinne*. In Tasso's *Gerusalemme liberata*, Armida is the seductive princess who uses her charms to lure the crusader knights away from the quest to which they have been assigned. Like an Armide, a female literary genius such as a Sappho or a Corinne employs "poetic inspiration" as a "magic charm" to cast a spell over the defenseless young innocent. Oswald is "captivated," "blinded," "carried away," "subjugated"—all by the glorious spell woven by Corinne at their first encounter.

This same vocabulary of enchantment is indissociably linked to the particular literary domain in which Corinne displays her genius, improvisation. Even today, in all the examples of "improvisatrice" given in the OED, Corinne's official title is attached to words like "bewitching" and "generating enthusiasm," with the sense of being transported outside of oneself that these words imply. This association is already present in Staël's novel, as it undoubtedly was in the Italian context from which she drew both this vocabulary and her sense of its referential context. In all the early references of "improvisatrice" and "improvisation" cited in the Robert and Littré Dictionaries, one author's name predominates: Staël's. The vocabulary of improvisation is in large part her gift, in *Corinne*, to the French language. The inspiration for these neologisms dates from Staël's travels in Italy, where, as Gutwirth notes, she heard some of the legendary improvisatrices.[7] These improvisatrices, like Corinne and like the late eighteenth century's Sappho, are geniuses of a sublime fugitive passion, women who can abandon themselves to the transport of their gift so that their poetic voice issues forth in apparent spontaneity. In *Corinne*, improvisation is the Sapphic language, and the "phobeitai" is the origin of both literary genius and its threat to the patriarchal order. The improvisatrice is transported outside of herself, and she also has the power to sway her audience. Tasso's Armida seduces the crusaders from their predictated course with her beauty. Staël's Sappho figure is a literary enchantress, a Circe who sings an improvisation designed to lure the protector of his country outside the boundaries of his family plot.

Oswald ends his meditation on the origin of Corinne's terrifyingly seductive charm with what initially seems a non sequitur: "O my father . . . if you had known Corinne, what would you have thought of her?" (77). At the beginning of the next chapter, his traveling companion, the comte d'Erfeuil, says to him, equally unexpectedly: "You were made to live in the happy time of the patriarchs" (78). What both young men know instinctively, and what Oswald will spend most of the novel trying to articulate, is the irrevocable unacceptability of the literary sorceress to the representatives of the paternal law. Her menace, however, is easily removed.

The novel builds up to the scene at Cape Miseno, Corinne's most Sapphic moment: from the top of the cliff, she looks down at the sea; dressed in flowing, antique garments and accompanying herself on her lyre, she improvises her last song (348). At this moment, the archetypal turn-of-the-century iconography of Sappho and what was to become the archetypal vision of Staël's heroine (and eventually also of Staël as her heroine) intersect. Gros's 1801 *Sapho* depicts the poet in the moonlight atop Cape Leukas, eyes closed and poised for a passive self-abandonment rather than a leap into the sea, and his choice is ratified by both Staël and the other official Napoleonic court painter to produce a Sapphic canvas, the Baron Gérard, in his *Corinne au cap Misène*. Dramatic lighting, billowing draperies, the lyre in hand—all point to the fact that Miseno is Leukas, just as Sappho is Corinne (is Staël). Nevertheless, after this clifftop pause, Corinne, unlike Sappho, does not leap to her death in the water below. Before she accepts the destruction decreed for her by the patriarchy, she reveals her past in the form of a written document she leaves for Oswald to read.

The text of Corinne's "avowal" is a double reversal of the family romance, the story authorizing and recounting the hero's passage into the social order. She tells of the fictions projected by others onto a young girl in order to exclude her from "the chain of [familial] affection." Staël follows the most recent plot for Sappho's childhood, found in the Italian romances, in which she loses first her mother and then her father when she is no longer a child. After the death of her Italian mother, Corinne's father obliges her to join him in England, where he remarries and has another daughter before his death leaves the budding improvisatrice without parental protection in a country suspicious of the charms of literary women. When we first meet Staël's heroine on the day of her crowning in Rome, we learn that "no one knew her family name" (50). In her story, we learn why she was obliged to abandon her father's name when she became an expatriate from his native land. When she announced her intention of embarking on a literary career, her stepmother, fearful that Corinne's reputation as an "extraordinary person" would affect her chances of "establishing" her own daughter, declared that she "owed it to her family to change her name and to pass for dead" (382–383). So Staël's heroine baptized herself "Corinne" (386), the name that simultaneously signified her birth as a literary woman and her death to the patriarchy.

After he learns of Corinne's past, Oswald attempts to win forgiveness for her so that they can be married. But her stepmother explains that "a person who fled the paternal home, . . . abdicating her rank, her family, the very name of her father" is a permanent source of scandal and can never be readmitted to the social order (459). Oswald persists in his intention of making a new "Lady Nelvil" out of the woman he calls "Corinne Edgermond" (459)—an onomastic impossibility forged by linking the sign of the heroine's existence in the world of literature to the name under which she had refused to be bound to the paternal law. He learns that, by decreeing her stepdaughter's exile from the fatherland and the father's house, Lady Edgermond had simply been following the wishes of the dead father whose spirit holds sway over Oswald's existence, in the form of an incessant voice of guilt recalling him to the destiny from which Corinne threatens to seduce him. Corinne's stepmother reveals that Lord Edgermond had proposed a union between their children to the previous Lord Nelvil. In a letter to Corinne's father, Lord Nelvil had objected to her because of the very qualities that define her literary gift: she "pleases," "captivates," "enchants." Under the power of such a woman, Lord Nelvil theorized, his son would abandon the patriarchal values— "soon he would lose that national spirit, those prejudices that bind us together and make of our nation a body, a free but indissoluble union that can only perish with the last of us"—and finally be lost to the patriarchy. "He would go establish himself in Italy, and this expatriation, if I were still living, would make me die of grief" (467). Since Lord Nelvil is already dead when his son reads this letter, he does not have to carry out this threat. Oswald understands perfectly the blame he is meant to feel for his father's death, and he soon fulfills the wish with which his father closed the letter by marrying the woman his father termed "the true English wife," Corinne's blond, demure, dependent half-sister Lucile (468). *Corinne* explains that the Sappho figure must be kept expatria because she could prevent a dutiful son's passage into his rightful place in the social order.

"Italy alone suits [Corinne]" (467), Lord Nelvil declares, decreeing the country of her exile. He has in mind the contrast his son recognizes immediately upon setting foot on English soil again, between a country where the coronation of the reigning improvisatrice is considered more important than the concern for "prosperity and commerce" that rules the father land (447). Writing in 1791, Lord Nelvil could not have foreseen that, by the time his decree took effect, the Italian political situation would have evolved dramatically. It is easy for the reader to overlook this evolution for, as Balayé points out, the increasingly dominant French presence is mentioned only in passing, and the situation is not developed even at the end of the novel when Oswald returns to Italy in 1803.[8] However, Staël's lack of an overt political context for her romance should not be taken for an omission. Staël began *Corinne* in the summer of 1805, one month after Napoleon, already Emperor of the French, had been crowned King of Italy, and directly upon her return from travels in Napoleonic Italy, where the original improvisatrice had become the Saffo of Verri, Imperiale, and Baron Gros. It is impossible to imagine that Staël, writing from such a vantage point, chose her novel's chronological and geographical situation in innocence of any reference to her archenemy, a man whose opinion of woman's role in the patriarchy, and in particular of a literary woman's complete lack of value in the social order, ratified perfectly that of Lord Nelvil *père*.[9]

Staël makes the ruling improvisatrice of Italy the political Sappho of Barthélemy's dreams, a revolutionary poet who would have merited exile in the occupied state Italy actually was at the time she chose for her novel's action. Gutwirth shows how Corinne's extended improvisations can be read as meditations on Napoleon's annihilation of Republican values (236). Her spontaneous literary outpourings can also be seen as a plea for passive resistance to military oppression. Corinne's first improvisation is a eulogy of the forms of Italian domination across the ages: "Italy, empire of the sun; Italy, mistress of the world; Italy, cradle of literature, I salute you. How many times has the human race submitted to your authority, dependent upon your arms and your fine arts?" (59). Her eulogy of the formerly free Italy is followed by a justification of the durability of Italian influence even more threatening to the social order of Staël's day: "Rome conquered the universe with its genius, and was queen by means of liberty . . . [Italy] continued as queen because of the scepter of thought" (60). Corinne's dominant political value is that of Barthélemy's Sappho: rule by liberty. Staël sets what she portrays as an inherently female reign—Italy was "mistress," "queen"—in resolute opposition to the patriarchal militarism of the Empire that controls the Italy of her day: the cornerstone of the empire of liberation is literary genius.

Staël's awareness of the utopian quality of such political meditation is clear from the contrast between Italy and England that, as we have seen, Oswald makes on returning to his father's house. The daughter of the celebrated Genevan financier and banker Necker surely agreed with Lord Nelvil's son's assessment that "commerce" and "industry" and not "fine arts" would dominate the politics of the dawning nineteenth century. Nevertheless, she devotes Corinne's final improvisation, in her Sapphic pose high above Cape Miseno, to a consideration of the transience of political authority and of the relative unimportance of all human power. Turning her gaze from the "lake of Avernus, an extinct volcano which formerly inspired terror" to the still awe-inspiring Vesuvius, she speculates that, like volcanoes, so do civilizations and governments succeed each other: "The masters of the world, in turn slaves, subjugated nature to console themselves for their own oppression" (349, 351). It is important to remember that Staël's meditation on the fugacity of militaristic oppression, composed in 1806, the year that witnessed many of Napoleon's most spectacular victories, is also the swan song of her heroine's Sapphic gift. When Corinne comes down from the mountain, she begins her final march toward suicide. Staël scripts the scenario of her death so that, like the passive resistance Corinne urges on the citizens of the occupied Eternal City, it contains an element of rebellion against the patriarchal plot.

Oswald spends almost no time with his "true English wife" before his regiment is called up for active duty (undoubtedly against the French, although this is never said), and he sets his private life aside for the good of the English nation, as his father would have wanted. He leaves Lucile with child and under Corinne's spell so that, when their daughter Juliette is born, "the little girl looked more like Corinne: Lucile's imagination had been strongly preoccupied with the memory of her sister during her pregnancy" (542). Oswald returns from the army to find a three-year-old perpetual reminder of his involvement with poetry's fugitive transports. As soon as the peace is signed, he returns to Italy with his family, ostensibly because of his health, but really to figure in Corinne's carefully shaped suicide.

Corinne does not technically take her own life. She is able to control her death to extract from it the maximum amount of punishment for the man who betrayed her, making it for all intents and purposes a suicide. Unlike previous representations of the end of the improvisatrice, Corinne's end is not passive self-abandonment or submission of personal will to the collective Law, but rather a final gesture of independence from the forces of public opinion, an act of self-possession. She thereby fulfills the potential of Staël's reading of the Sapphic plot. Even in Staël's original fiction of Sappho, the romance she composed as a teen-ager, she portrays her suicide as a liberating gesture: "From your unhappy destiny / Sapho you must set yourself free."[10] For the woman abandoned, the goal of suicide is to make her memory more powerful than the woman who has taken her place.

When Staël's heroine meets Oswald and Lucile's daughter and finds that Juliette is, in Oswald's terms, "her miniature" (575), she begins to instruct the child to take over the life she is about to relinquish. Corinne first transmits to her future double her accent in Italian and, as Juliette explains to her father, "she promised to teach me all she knows. She says that she wants me to resemble Corinne" (575). And that she does: Oswald walks by one day during a music lesson and sees his daughter learning to place her arms in Corinne's manner around a miniature lyre. Corinne teaches her double to sing to the lyre's accompaniment. Unlike her teacher, however, Juliette will not improvise: Corinne teaches her the song she played for Oswald on a visit to her villa at Tivoli, and she extracts from her miniature a promise to play the same air for her father every year on the anniversary of that visit.

The subject of the song reveals that, by taking revenge on Oswald-Phaon, Corinne-Sappho is also resisting her ostracism from the social order. The song is identified as a "Scottish air that Corinne had played for Lord Nelvil . . . in front of a painting inspired by Ossian" (576). Corinne interprets the canvas for Oswald while giving a tour of her villa: "Caïrbar's son sleeping on his father's tomb. He has been waiting three days and three nights for the bard who is to pay homage to the memory of the dead. The bard can be seen in the distance . . . ; the shade of the father broods over the clouds" (237–238). Both the date chosen for the recital and the subject of the painting connect the scene of the father's death with the woman writer and her exclusion from the paternal order. The bard who will come to sing the air associated with the father's death is female, the reincarnation of the woman writer ostracized by patriarchal veto. Once a year, Juliette will ensure that no representative of the Paternal Law remains at rest: the only homage the dead father receives is from a bard whose creative genius was so threatening to him that he ordered her exclusion from the genealogy he controlled.

In *Sexe et liberté au siècle des lumières*, Théodore Tarczylo describes diverse manifestations of the fear of depopulation that he uncovers as an increasingly widespread phenomenon in late eighteenth-century France.[11] By 1810, this fear had invaded the very home of the Emperor of the French, to such an extent that he had annulled his marriage to Joséphine, of whose quintessential womanhood he had so proudly boasted in a comparison decidedly unfavorable to Germaine de Staël, because the Empress was unable to reproduce and thereby gain value in the patriarchal order. The annulment was quickly followed by his remarriage to Marie-Louise of Austria and the birth of his first son and heir, the beginning of Napoleon's personal contribution to the campaign against the anti-French forces of depopulation.

This crucial period for the Emperor's posterity, sandwiched between the war in Spain and the disastrous campaign in Russia, was also the time during which Germaine de Staël was putting the final touch to her vast oeuvre, in the form of a series of short plays and a five-act tragedy. Her last work, composed the year that the Emperor finally received an heir, concludes nearly three decades of speculation by Staël on the fate of the original woman writer. *Sapho, drame en cing actes* (1816) marks a return to Staël's *oeuvre de jeunesse* for, like her youthful romance, it is devoted to Sappho's betrayal and suicide.[12] Staël's decision to take up Sappho's plot where Ovid puts an end to it allows her to make a commentary on the relation between woman writer and posterity explored by Ovid, a commentary that evokes the dilemma surrounding maternity at the time of the play's composition. The genre Staël chose for her final Sapphic fiction is subversive, for her *drame* condemns that ideology motivating that family-oriented theatrical tradition. Staël transfers attention from the issue of biological posterity to the question of literary posterity. This is not to say that her last Sappho is no longer a mother. The adoptive daughter scenario familiar from eighteenth-century fictions is repeated here: Cléone, the daughter of her closest friend Diotime, is like a daughter to Sapho, a younger, nonliterary version of the poet, and it is for her that Phaon betrays the poet who had "inflamed his mind" with her brilliance (323). "I want to possess myself myself" [*Je voudrais me posséder moi-même*] (337), Staël's last Sappho declares, and the double reflexive indicates the degree to which Staël views her suicide as an act of self-reclaiming. Yet this Sappho's vision of immortality is no longer centered on a revenge fantasy involving the daughter figure.

What Staël attempts, once again, is to reunite what Ovid had put asunder, the two Sapphos, woman and writer. Staël's Alcée is a fellow poet and erstwhile lover who, even after Sapho rejected him, remained a faithful friend. It is to him that her heroine turns at the end when she seeks a literary executor. Sapho explains in their last conversation that, since the language of poetry "is only understood by a small number of mortals," she is obliged to choose someone who will accept the responsibility of "teaching the centuries to come what Sapho was" (351). Note that she says "what" and not "who": as in *Corinne*, the pronoun indicates that posterity should look at the writing and not for the woman. "You saw me," she says pleadingly to Alcée, "when Apollo conspired in [that involuntary inspiration] behind the hymns that I addressed to Olympus; You saw me! You will tell what I was, and the inhabitants of these countries will preserve the memory of my songs" (290).

In proper post-Revolutionary fashion, Sapho refers to Alcée as her "co-citizen in the fatherland of the arts" when she gives him what amounts to power of attorney over her literary production: "To you alone do I confide my name among the Greeks" (351). Sapho frames her literary testament as though her given name, like Corinne's, had been shrouded in secrecy. Her bequest is only comprehensible if "name" is understood to mean author's name, in the sense of a legally binding signature by means of which an author both assumes responsibility for his or her fiction and claims authorial rights over its transmission. Staël rehearses Sapho's transfer to Alcée of the power to control the publication of her textual legacy in order to signal her awareness that the paternal law would not allow women's writing to circulate in the "patrie des arts" without male protection, without a father's name to guarantee its ideological orthodoxy. Staël may also have intended to indicate her acceptance of the fact that, without male authorization, the plot she had dictated for Sapho would not be passed down to posterity. She did not publish her tragedy in the six years before her death in 1817. In the preface to the work's posthumous first edition, we learn that it was the only one of her plays not even staged for a limited public at her private theater. In view of its meditation on literary property, the manner in which the work was finally presented to other readers had a fine irony: the 1821 (still authoritative) edition of Staël's *Complete Works* is marked "published by her son," as if to confirm Staël's intuition about the circulation of women's writing in the patriarchy.

Staël may have realized that her vision of a pacifist, antinationalistic Sappho would not be retained by the nineteenth century. Despite the fact that, at Coppet, the French and German intellectual traditions intermingled to an unparalleled degree, the nascent nineteenth-century German philological tradition chose as the foundation for its speculation on Sappho the other contemporary French tradition, the imperial fictions of Verri et al. And throughout the German philological tradition, the influence of which is often still dominant today, Sappho would never again be political, never again narratively or sexually active.[13] A myth of Sappho's dispassionateness was established to silence the speculation about female sexuality so threatening to the builders of empires.

TOPOGRAPHICAL SURVEYS: TRAVEL AND TRANSCEDENCE, FRONTIERS

STAËL'S *GERMANY* AND THE BEGINNINGS OF AN AMERICAN NATIONAL LITERATURE

Kurt Mueller-Vollmer

"That which was unconscious truth, becomes, when interpreted and defined in an object, a part of the domain of knowledge,—a new weapon in the magazine of power."—Emerson

When the American edition of Staël's *On Germany* appeared in New York in 1814, only one year after its first publication in London, the name of its author was already well known to the American reading public. Following on the heels of her spectacular successes in England, her book *On Literature Considered in Its Relationship to Social Institutions* and her romantic novel *Corinne* had been well received and were widely discussed in this country. But it was her work *On Germany* which firmly established Staël as one of the principal authors of the period. Until the publication of Emerson's *Nature*, the inaugural text of New England Transcendentalism, in 1836, more than forty articles on Staël, her opinions, her writings, her reputation, and her influence, were published in American journals and literary magazines.[1] In addition, American editions of her major works were issued.[2] She was hailed by the critics as "an extraordinary woman," "a female author of the foremost rank in modern literature," and even "the greatest woman who has written and lived for the public." Moreover, as the *North American Review* stated in 1822, "it would be difficult to find a name that can come into competition with hers since the time of Voltaire and Rousseau."[3] What seemed most striking to the critics was the appeal that her books enjoyed with the non-specialized general reading public. In 1820 one of her reviewers in the *North American Review* remarked: "Few books in modern times, which were not practical nor scientific, nor directly subservient to the comforts of man and the purposes of society have been so eagerly and universally read, and known so far as hers."[4]

In examining more closely the reception of Staël in America between 1814, the publication date of her book *On Germany*, and 1836, when Emerson's essay *Nature* was published, it appears that the importance of *On Germany* for American letters is twofold. For the prominent group of New England intellectuals, among them men like Ticknor, Bancroft, and Edward Everett, who became the intellectual leaders of the powerful overtly nationalistic new cultural movement that was soon to sweep the country, Staël served as the mediator through whom the ideas of German philosophy and humanistic science were to be studied, ideas which were to play a vital part in the formation of an American national consciousness. From her these men were first to learn about the Herderian concept of the intrinsic value of national culture and literature that dominated her book *On Germany*;[5] and it was her understanding of German metaphysics, her views on Kantian and post-Kantian philosophy and on German literature and culture at large from which the American intellectuals were to derive powerful stimuli for the making of an American cultural and literary identity.

If the formation of an American cultural consciousness and the introduction of certain key notions of European romanticism were a first step toward the creation of a national literature in America, New England Transcendentalism must be seen not only as the live representative of romanticism on American soil, but at the same time as the first manifestation of an autochthonous American literature that was now claiming its place among the literatures of the Western nations. Again it was Staël's *On Germany* which was to assume a key role for the rise of New England Transcendentalism and which was thus to become part of the internal history of nineteenth-century American literature. Offering an aesthetic that combined philosophical, moral, and religious with social and poetic-literary concerns, the book itself became a representative of a new type of discourse characteristic of the romantic movement, one that combined theoretical with speculative criticism and that enriched discursive reason with the intuitiveness of poetic creativity. Consequently Staël's *On Germany* was taken by the transcendentalist writers as part and parcel of the new literature, of which Germany had offered a vital specimen and to which they intended to add a specific American variety of their own.

Setting the Stage in 1813: The Politics and Hermeneutics of *On Germany*

"An account of metaphysical systems by a woman is a novelty in the history of the human mind."—*The Edinburgh Review*

The review article of *On Germany* which was carried in prominent place in the October 1813 issue of *The Edinburgh Review*, probably the most influential literary magazine in the Anglo-Saxon world at the time, offers a number of important hermeneutic hints that reveal to us the direction that subsequent readings of Staël's epoch-making work would take.[6] Already the February number had brought a lengthy review of *On Literature* occasioned by the reissue of the book in London the previous year. But for all his praise of the "bold and vigorous attempts to carry the generalizing spirit of true philosophy into the history of literature and manners," the writer remains quite skeptical when it comes to Staël's application of her notions of perfectibility and progress to the areas of literature and culture.[7] The reviewer of *On Germany*, on the other hand, has no reservations with respect to this book's underlying assumptions, its methods, or its philosophy.

In fact the review's author, Sir James Mackintosh (1765–1832), the well-known Scottish writer and co-founder of *The Edinburgh Review*, openly used his prestige to promulgate the book, which he considered a work of epochal significance.[8] First of all, it presents for him an authentic account of the quiet revolution that had taken place in Germany, which, in "the course of half a century terminated in bestowing" on that country "a literature, perhaps the most characteristic posessed by an European nation."[9] Before that time Germany had remained essentially a nation without a literature; it had been without that "exclusive mental possession" which became the essential prerequisite for the new ideology of nationalism and national culture. Or, as Mackintosh put it, "poetry and eloquence may and in some measure, must be national."[10] The story of the creation in modern times of a national literature, which *The Edinburgh Review* saw exhibited in Staël's book, was to be eagerly absorbed by the American intellectuals who would soon begin to acquaint themselves first with the book and then with its subject matter. It was largely because of Mackintosh's review that they did so along the path laid out by Staël. From this review the Americans derived political, philosophical, and aesthetic impulses for their own endeavors. When it came to creating a national literature, they learned that it was possible for a nation to forego the stages of naive childhood and adolescence and to begin this creation from a state of maturity, that is, from one of enlightenment and of reflection. What Mackintosh, in summarizing Staël's central thesis, thus found remarkable about German literature was precisely that it had its birth in our "own enlightened age," when "the imagination and sensibility of an infant poetry were singularly blended with the refinement of philosophy."[11]

A similar motivation is felt by the reviewer to underlie Staël's *Germany* itself; for him "it is the work of the genius of the philosophical and poetic traveler," in which a fusion of the philosophical and the poetic spirit has led to a new intuitive power, whose application "to the varied mass called a Nation," he finds "one of the most rare efforts of the human intellect."[12] Mackintosh's recourse to this new intuitive power and its recently discovered object, the nation, gives testimony to the hermeneutic turn that has taken place in Staël's *On Germany*. Before any of the ground-breaking works by Herder, the Schlegels, Humboldt, and Staël had appeared, this peculiar object called "a nation" did not lie within the horizon of the public's perception. The idea of the uniqueness and the individuality of nations, their spirit and their culture, was entirely new, as was the need to grasp their peculiar essence by special intellectual intuition. In her book *On Literature* Staël still attempted to comprehend the diversity of cultures by applying philosophical generalizations to national particulars. In *On Germany*, on the other hand, an intuitive idea of the new object, the nation, lies at the heart of her deliberations. Comparing the review of *On Literature* with that of *On Germany*, which both appeared in the same journal during the same year, we can detect the watershed that separates the rationalist hermeneutics of the Enlightenment from the intuitively informed understanding of the romantics that was now beginning to assert itself in the Anglo-Saxon world. The reception of

Staël's work would find its completion within the confines of this new romantic hermeneutics.[13]

There are specific cues in Mackintosh's review that point the way for the subsequent reception of *On Germany* in America. Despite his lavish praise for each of the four parts of the book, it is apparent that it is really the third part which the reviewer finds "the most singular," as it is an "account of metaphysical systems by a woman," which he considers in itself "a novelty in the history of the human mind."[14] He finds most important her manner of treating German philosophy not from a traditional technical point of view, but by judging it as a "contribution rather to the history of human nature." Hence she is concerned with "the source, spirit, and the moral influence of metaphysical opinions more than their truth or falsehoods." If formulations like these seem to anticipate the direction into which the New England Transcendentalists' philosophical interests would soon take them, we can also find statements that already lend themselves to a reading that seems to be embodying the Transcendentalist position *in nuce*: "There are certain facts in human nature, derived either from immediate consciousness or unvarying observations, which are more certain than the conclusions of any abstract reasoning, and which metaphysical theories are destined only to explain."[15] In the same vein, what the reviewer of *On Germany*, in following Staël, finds most remarkable about recent German philosophy is that regardless of different thinkers and approaches, it always displayed "the general tendency . . . to consider thought, not as the product of objects, or as one of the classes of phenomena, but as an agent which exhibits the appearance of the outward world, and which regulates those operations which it seems only to represent."[16] It was precisely the search for this hidden power of the human mind which would motivate and guide the New England Transcendentalists' reading of Kantian and post-Kantian idealist philosophy.[17]

The review article concludes with a discussion of part 4 of Staël's work, which is perceived as the culmination of the entire enterprise for its treatment of "the state of religion" and of "the nature of all those disinterested and exalted sentiments which are here comprehended under the name of Enthusiasm."[18] There Staël is shown finally to develop her own philosophy, which served as the basis for her assessment of Germany and its culture. Not surprisingly her concept of enthusiasm would find acceptance later among the Transcendentalists because it stood for that gratuitous spiritual and spontaneous activity by which in her eyes individuals would find fulfillment of their humanity, an idea close to the heart of the New England writers.

It makes sense, therefore, that the author of the review article would read the concluding part of *On Germany* as a chapter in the history of an ongoing conflict in Western thought between a selfish, utilitarian, hedonistic outlook on morality and human nature and the belief in the spontaneity of our moral feelings and actions independent from considerations of utility and self-love. Mackintosh, in thus describing "the struggle between prudence and enthusiasm, which pervades human life," still hoped for a reconciliation between these two positions, which would save an important part of English philosophy from the wrath that Staël had unleashed in her book. But in America, one avid reader of the review, Ralph Waldo Emerson, would side with Staël's enthusiasm on this issue and reject the utilitarian view of morality.[19] It is at this junction that the English and the American reception of *On Germany* part company.[20] During the Revolutionary War and afterward the literary interests and perspectives of the educated American reading public coincided with those of England, and it understood itself as "part and parcel of the British tradition."[21] When the British began discovering German literature during the latter half of the eighteenth century, the Americans followed suit and, like the British, showed their predilection for authors of the Storm and Stress and sentimental schools, such as Buerger, Gessner, and Kotzebue. During this phase the reception of German literature took place entirely from the British cultural perspective. The appearance of Staël's book *On Germany* in America in 1814 marked the decisive break. No longer was the American preoccupation with German letters "part and parcel" of the British intellectual realm, even though it was often a question of the same books and authors. Paradoxically, then, this work would circumscribe for the American writers and literati the orbit within which they would advance their own aesthetic program and create their own peculiar discourse. But before we can focus on the literary and discursive side of this process, as it can be observed in Emerson's *Nature*, the hermeneutic horizon of the incipient cultural nationalism of the 1820s, within which New England Transcendentalism finds its place, will have to be made visible with the help of some historical specifics.

Toward an American Cultural Identity: Weimar, Coppet, and Boston

"Much is said now-a-days of a national literature. Does it mean anything? . . . Vast forests, lakes, and prairies cannot make great poets. They are to be the scenery of the play, and have much less to do with the poetic character than has been imagined.—Longfellow

For a national literature to come into being two essential prerequisites must be met: first, the establishment of a national consciousness and sense of cultural and political identity among the intellectual elite and the public at large; second, the creation of an aesthetic program and philosophy that results in the production of a literary discourse different from that of previously accepted literary models. In the case of American literature this dual process is intimately connected with Staël's *On Germany* and the uses American readers made of it. For the New England intellectuals who were to formulate the new nationalist credo in the 1820s and 30s, Staël's work served as a guide for the introduction of German philosophy and literature onto the American scene. The experience of German culture in turn functioned as a catalyst for developing the intellectuals' sense of cultural identity and mission.

On the strength of Staël's high praise in *On Germany* of the Protestant German universities, which she considered superior to those of any other country, including England, a first group of young American intellectuals decided in 1815–16 to pursue their academic education in Germany (there were no Ph.D. degree-granting institutions in America until the second half of the nineteenth century). Once there, Edward Everett, George Ticknor, and George Bancroft saw in Staël's book an indispensable guide for the study of German civilization.[22]

Thus, when asked by his friends in America about the state of German culture, George Ticknor in his return letters relied mostly on Staël and what she had to say about the matter. To Thomas Jefferson he complained from Goettingen in October 1816 that German literature had not entered "into the system of our education, nor, until Madame de Staël's book came upon us, was its history or condition talked about or thought of." Echoing Staël's thesis he characterized this liter-

ature to Jefferson as having "all the freshness and faithfulness of poetry, of the early ages, while words are the representations of sensible
objects and simple feeling, rather than abstractions and generalities,
and yet being written so late that it has enough of the modern refinement and regularity."[23] Edward T. Channing in Boston is given the
advice that "as to the peculiar character—of German metaphysics,
you get all the information necessary from Madame de Staël."[24] To
Charles S. Davies Ticknor sent a brief outline of the history of German
letters, which he patterned after Staël's treatment. To Channing again
Ticknor emphasized the national character of German literature in
words that both echo Staël's thesis and anticipate the possible application of the new national ideology to American literature: "I mean to
show you by foreign proof that the German literature is a peculiar
national literature, which, like the miraculous creation of Deucalion,
has sprung directly from their own soil, and is so intimately connected
with their character, that it is very difficult for a stranger to understand it."[25]

The University of Goettingen at that time was dominated by
Herder's students and followers—such as Eichhorn, Heeren, and Bou-
terwek, the favorite teachers of the American students—who, like
Staël, who also admired Herder, expanded on the virtues of the newly
discovered idea of a national literature and national culture. Soon the
entire group of "New Americans" at Goettingen, as Goethe began
referring to them, would expound a similar philosophy—first with
respect to German literature and thought, and eventually with regard
to their own peculiar American national culture.

An example of how effectively Staël's sociological and historical categories asserted themselves among this group of Americans can be
gathered from none other than George Bancroft, who with his nationalistic *History of the United States* (1834) would become the father of
American historiography.[26] Between 1827 and 1829 he would publish
in Philadelphia a series of articles, later combined into a single study,
which constituted the first history of German literature and thought
written in America. By tracing the rise of modern German culture
from the spirit of the Protestant Reformation and by explaining the
peculiar character of German literary history from the lack of a political capital that would have provided a natural center for the cultural
and intellectual life of the German nation, Bancroft continued to elaborate the ideas first advanced by Staël in her treatment of the same

topic. In fact, Bancroft's little book, which climaxes in his treatment of classical Weimar culture, may be read as a peculiarly American version of *On Germany* in its own right.[27]

Upon their return from Europe, Everett, Bancroft, Ticknor, and those who were to follow in their footsteps became the propagators of the new cultural program that was aimed at developing a cultural identity peculiar to America, while at the same time they were absorbing from and critically distancing themselves from European models. This was a period when the United States was experiencing rapid development and expansion in demographics, trade, and commerce. The first transatlantic voyage in 1819 by the steamboat "Savannah," built in New York, and the introduction of the first locomotive in 1828 marked the beginnings of industrialization. During this time the news media became an important instrument for spreading new ideas and for influencing public opinion, a fact that the "New Americans" soon began to appreciate. In 1820 Edward Everett took over as the editor in chief of the *North American Review*, whose policy it was "to foster American genius, and by independent literary criticism, instruct and guide the public taste."[28] Within two years he succeeded in increasing the number of subscribers from a mere five hundred to thirty-five hundred and in transforming the review from a provincial periodical into a publication of national prestige and prominence. Throughout the 1820s and 1830s the *North American Review* was considered the most important literary magazine in America. Everett wrote to Henry Clay about the successes of his editorship: "You do not perhaps know the importance of the *North American Review* as a means of influencing public opinion. I believe I may say there is not a social library, reading-room, library club, mess-room, or public institution in any degree connected with political learning which it does not reach."[29]

The *North American Review* became the chief organ through which the group of "New Americans" was able to propagate their ideas effectively and successfully. It was here that numerous important articles on Staël appeared, along with some of the epoch-making contributions by the New Americans on German literature and philosophy in the 1820s.[30] It was here also that the public could read the same message over again, in the words of Edward Everett, "that literature must grow out of differences of country, of habits, of institutions."[31] That same message was brought home to Harvard by him and E. T. Channing to their students Emerson and Thoreau, who had to learn from their teachers that there was no royal road to the "universal mind," except by passing first "through the discipline or instruction of particular facts" of their own time which alone would make them proponents of their national culture.[32]

When the young German emigré intellectual Francis Lieber, a personal friend and student of Barthold Niebur and Wilhelm von Humboldt, came to Boston in 1824, he joined the circle of intellectuals surrounding the *North American Review* and with their help successfully embarked on a publishing venture of major significance for American cultural history. Between 1828 and 1832 Lieber published in thirteen volumes the first American encyclopaedia, the *Encyclopaedia Americana*.[33] In numerous articles the work informed its readers about America's political and legal system, its young culture, and its history, and conveyed to them the relevant facts concerning the culture and history of the European nations. Most pertinent for our purpose, the work contained numerous articles on the history of German literature, its major authors, such as Goethe, Schiller, and Jean Paul, and on German philosophy and theology and its major representatives from Herder, Kant, and Fichte to Hegel, Schelling, and Schleiermacher. For the Transcendentalists, who once having read Staël's *On Germany* were eager to learn more specific facts about German culture or their favorite authors, the *Encyclopaedia Americana* provided a unique source of information.

The keen interest among intellectuals and the general reading public in Staël's *On Germany* began in 1814 and reached a peak in the 1820s and again in the 1830s, culminating in the early 1840s in the Transcendentalists' exhortation of a specific canon of German works of literature, philosophy, and theology. Practically all the Transcendentalists received their initiation to things German—literature and thought—through *On Germany*. This includes Ralph Waldo Emerson, Margaret Fuller, James Freeman Clarke, and Charles Timothy Brooks, as well as George H. Calvert, George Ripley, John S. Dwight, Theodore Parker and Henry W. Longfellow.[34] What attracted the New England Transcendentalists to Staël's treatment of German literature and metaphysics in *On Germany* was undoubtedly her interpretation of its principal ideas and tendencies as an outgrowth of the Protestant spirit; therefore, its core message was close to the hearts and souls of these New Englanders, for by and large they belonged to that first generation of intellectuals who had begun to emancipate themselves from the stifling bondage of New England's fundamentalist Puritan heritage. In Staël they sensed a spirituality kindred to their own, a sentiment for "the Infinite" for which they themselves yearned, and in her book *On Germany* they discovered a frame of reference and a language with which they could sympathize and identify. It helped them discover their own spirituality and develop their aesthetic program as it moved them to articulate a literary discourse of their own.

It seems curious that the important role Staël played in the nationalization process of American culture and literature has escaped the attention of cultural and literary historians for so long. A leitmotif for this long neglect can be found as early as 1823 in an article printed in the *North American Review*: "If Madame de Staël was received with great attention in the higher circles of German society," we read, "the scholars of that country, who wield the sceptre of criticism, have never looked upon her with an eye of favor."[35]

This opinion, which was widespread in Germany until very recently, is still shared by most American scholars.[36] Henry A. Pochmann, who wrote what is considered the definitive work on *German Culture in America*, as well as René Wellek in his studies on the Transcendentalists' preoccupation with Kantian and idealist philosophy, have effectively perpetuated the prejudicial view that Staël spread nothing but "misconceptions and misconstructions" of German literature and philosophy in America.[37] Judging her book solely from the inappropriate viewpoint of twentieth-century positivist-historicist scholarship, one must not only fail to perceive its peculiar literary and philosophical character, but also become blind to its momentous impact on American literary and intellectual history.

Staël and the Discourse of Emerson's *Nature*

"Every scripture is to be interpreted by the same spirit which gave it forth,—is the fundamental law of criticism. A life in harmony with nature, the love of truth and of virtue, will purge the eyes to understand her text."—Emerson

In William Channing's well-known definition of Transcendentalism in the memorial volume for Margaret Fuller, Staël is listed together with Kant, Fichte, Schelling, Novalis, Coleridge, and Carlyle as one of the "masters" of the movement.[38] In his essay "Thoughts on Modern Literature," published in *The Dial* in 1840, and elsewhere in his diaries, Emerson associates Staël with what he considered the most characteristic feature of modern poetry and literature, namely its articulation of "the feeling of the infinite." In one of his diary entries he notes laconically: "De Staël, Goethe, and all the Germans, Chateaubriand and Manzoni have the feeling of the infinite." He credits her for having imported from Germany into France this precious feeling, which after having made its appearance in England in Coleridge, Wordsworth, Byron and Shelley, now "finds a most genial climate in the American mind."[39]

For the Transcendentalists, then, Staël was one of the representatives of that modern literature of which they themselves wanted to be a part. But it was certainly not only the work, it was the person as well, or rather the myth of that person, which became important. Margaret Fuller saw in Staël a role model for her own career as a woman writer and for her conduct of life. As the intellectual leader of the Transcendentalist Club and first editor of the movement's journal, *The Dial*, she was referred to by Emerson and his friends, not by accident, as "Corinna," the namesake of Staël's heroine.[40]

Through Staël, whose works she discovered as a sixteen-year-old, Margaret Fuller was enticed to the study of German and German letters.[41] It was the canon of German writers she had learned from Staël, with its curious absence of names like Kleist and Eichendorf, which was accepted by the Transcendentalists, and which they in turn passed on to the rest of the country. Fuller's own literary aesthetics, too, may justifiably be called Staëlian, if statements like the following are indicative: "What I mean by the muse is that unimpeded charm of the intuitive powers, which a perfectly truthful adherence to every admonition of the high instincts would bring to a finely organized human being."[42]

Yet as much positive historical evidence as one might want to produce as testimony of Staël's importance for the New England Transcendentalists, this does very little for solving the hermeneutic problem of establishing her discursive presence within the Transcendentalists' literary corpus itself. Only a close textual examination can lead us toward this goal. In this final section, therefore, Emerson's *Nature* will serve as an exemplary text to help in the elaboration of the problem and to open the necessary perspective from which to view and analyze its discursive structure. Customarily there have been two opposing opinions among critics regarding Emerson's status as a writer. One holds Emerson to be an original author of truly American genius. The scholarship resulting from this attitude, however, has been singularly monadic in its outlook regardless of the methodology or professed orientation of the critic. Adherents of the second opinion, who deny Emerson's originality as a writer and a thinker, see in him the mere eclectic who derived his ideas ready-made from European sources and whose "uniqueness" rests on his literary style at best.[43] For the problem at hand, however, both positions are equally irrelevant, because they ignore the peculiar status of the Emersonian texts as part of the literary corpus of European romanticism. Emerson's alleged relationship to European sources cannot be treated differently from the relationship in which Novalis and Coleridge find themselves with Kant, Fichte, and Schelling, or in which Staël stands with the theorists and poets of German romanticism. Consequently the interpreter of Emerson's inaugural text *Nature* must view this text as belonging to a literary province located within the discourse of European romanticism.

Those who have denied Emerson's status as an original writer claim that both inspiration and ideas for his book came to him from Carlyle's essay "Novalis." Pochmann believes that except for the alleged "home-spun phrases and figures," Emerson's work "contains few ideas that have not their counterpart in Carlyle's words on Novalis or in the quotations from Novalis that are adduced for illustrative purposes."[44] If one believes that Emerson's text can be reduced to an amalgam of ready-made "ideas" and "concepts," it can indeed be shown that many of these have their equivalent in Carlyle and in the Novalis text from which he quotes. But in that case one may point out another, earlier text with which Emerson was equally familiar and which contains the same "ideas." It is the chapter in *On Germany* entitled "On the Contemplation of Nature," in which Staël introduces the work and thought of Novalis and utilizes, as Carlyle would after her, examples from Novalis's *Apprentices at Sais*. But here the comparison with Carlyle's essay on Novalis comes to an end. For in *On Germany* the nature chapter occupies a central place, with the section on Novalis constituting a turning point in her argument. It belongs to the fourth and final part of the work, called "Religion and Enthusiasm," where the author switches from her discussion of German culture to an exposition of her own philosophy. At this moment Staël's own discourse, which had spoken to the reader until now only through its subject matter, comes to the fore and establishes itself as the driving force behind the enterprise. This coming-to-the-fore occurs precisely in the Novalis section of the chapter. There we witness the formation of the same romantic discourse within whose confines Emerson's *Nature* will find its place. If, therefore, Emerson's text is to serve our investigation in an exemplary fashion, this calls for a procedure that exposes the relationship of reciprocity between its discursive composition and that of the "nature" chapter in *On Germany*.

Returning, however, for a moment to Carlyle: he too was a student of Staël's as regards German literature and philosophy. The initial inspiration for his peculiarly religious and moralistic version of transcendentalism, which he believed to have found in the German writers, he definitely owed to Staël's *On Germany*. He followed closely in the path of the Anglo-Saxon Staël reception first laid out by Mackintosh in 1813. In 1830 he published an English translation of Jean Paul Richter's voluminous review of *On Germany* in which he praised this work "as the precursor, if not the parent, of whatever acquaintance with German literature exists among us."[45] In his essay on Novalis Carlyle merely reaffirms some of the key notions of romantic philosophy which were espoused first in *On Germany* over fifteen years earlier: among them the all important belief in living nature as *natura naturans* and in the hidden correspondence between nature and mind. In Carlyle's formulation: "The invisible world is near us: or rather it is here, in us and about us. . . . Nature is no longer dead, hostile matter, but the veil and mysterious Garment of the Unseen; as it were, the Voice with which the Deity proclaims himself in man."[46]

Because *On Germany* was taken by the Transcendentalists as part of their own literary orbit, it is not surprising that they would find an abundance of statements in it that conformed with their own aesthetics and metaphysics. Emerson's often maligned and misunderstood views on Kant find their source in the equally maligned and misunderstood interpretation of Kant offered in *On Germany*: "Kant wanted to reestablish the original truths of the spontaneous activities of our soul, of the moral conscience, and of the ideal in the arts."[47] Both Staël and Emerson believed that at the core of Kant's philosophy lay an intuitive feeling (sentiment) that made him reject all doubts of skepticism. In following Staël's terminology Emerson even used the term "imperative forms of the mind," with which she had rendered the Kantian *Kategorien* and *Formen der Anschauung* as "formes imperatives de l'esprit."[48] Emerson also adopted from *On Germany* the famous Leibnizean pun directed against Locke's sensationalist idea of the mind: "There is nothing in the understanding which was not previously in the sense—except the understanding itself."[49] This phrase, which pleased Emerson so much, had been rightly seen by Staël as a nucleus from which German idealist thought would later evolve. Her characterization of German philosophy in its transcendental orientation could well serve as a maxim for Emerson's own interest in German thought: "What is truly admirable in German philosophy," Staël writes, "is that it undertakes an examination of ourselves and reaches to the very origin of our will, to that unknown source from which flows our life."[50]

The significance of the concept of the infinite for romantic aesthetics Emerson first learned from *On Germany*, namely, that its application to art and literature alone would give birth to beauty, and that this beauty was nothing but the "realized image of our soul's representations."[51] Last, but not least, it was Staël's notion of "enthusiasm" (to which Mackintosh had already paid his respects), which seems to circumscribe the very core of the Transcendentalist beliefs, precisely because it represents the attempt to fuse moral, aesthetic, religious, and metaphysical ideals into a single attitude: "Enthusiasm rallies itself to the harmony of the Universe, it is love of the beautiful, elevation of the soul, the delight in unselfishness all united into one and the same feeling."[52] Her retranslation of the term enthusiasm from its Greek roots as "God within us" expressed the idea of the divinity of human nature which is in quintessential harmony with the Transcendentalists' own creed.

If one were to trace the formation of Emerson's thought from his early student days to the time of his first literary and critical productions, focusing on his preoccupation with Staël would constitute an important part of that task.[53] The Staëlian presence in the *Nature* book itself, therefore, comes at the end of a long process. There the reader will encounter both obvious as well as unobtrusive, hidden instances of intertextuality. Obvious but relatively unimportant seems the statement: "Architecture is called 'frozen music' by de Staël and Goethe," for which we find preformulations in Emerson's diaries.[54] Less obvious but more important are some other instances of intertextuality that occur at strategic places in the text. In part 3 of *On Germany* Staël had written: "Almost all axioms of physics correspond to maxims of morals."[55] For this Staëlian Urtext, which is one of her many formulations for the romantic theory of correspondence between mind and nature, we can find several mutational offsprings in Emerson's diaries, in which the name Staël is given, as well as in the *Nature* book itself where the same or similar passages occur without reference to a name.[56] In the reworkings and emendations of a Staëlian Urtext we can thus witness the formative process that is characteristic of the Emersonian Transcendentalist discourse. This process can best be described as one of accrual, that is, elements from one literary text are deconstituted and reconstituted to form an integral part of a new text, thereby assuming an added meaning. In the chapter "Language" we read: "Parts of speech are metaphors because the whole of nature is a metaphor of the human mind."[57] A counterpart may be found in Staël's statement concerning the "grandeur of poetry" which makes us perceive "the entire universe as a symbol for the emotions of our soul."[58]

Emerson's passage continues by evoking once more the previous Staëlian Urtext: "The laws of moral nature answer to those of matter as face to face in a glass," to which the words are added: "The visible world and the relation of its parts, is the dial plate of the invisible."[59] Four years later, of course, the first issue of *The Dial* would appear, the mouthpiece of the Transcendentalist movement.

If Emerson's *Nature* book is part of European romanticism, it must be shown that its discursive characteristic, which I described as a process of accrual, can be found in other literary texts as well. This is indeed the case. Emerson's *Nature* text has its precise equivalent in the "nature" chapter of *On Germany*. His text stands in the same relation to the Staëlian text as does the latter to the one found in the German poet Novalis's *Apprentices at Saïs*.

In Staël's treatment of the German poets in part 2 of *On Germany*, the name of Novalis was conspicuously absent. It is only in the pivotal chapter of the concluding part 4 that this archpoet of German romanticism makes his appearance, a strategic move of great importance to help the reader grasp the true character and inner logic of her book. Initially and on the surface the chapter seems to follow the precedent set by her in the previous literary chapters of part 2, namely to vary factual information with general observations and textual examples.

But the chapter's real topic is the idea of nature and its correspondence with the human soul, which she introduces first in her treatment of Germany's mystical theologians—who like Jakob Boehme perceived in nature "the corporal image of the Godhead" and whom she considers as precursors of Novalis and the entire school of Nature philosophy. Without apparent rupture her discussion of Novalis leads into a segment of text that is presented to the reader as an excerpt from that poet's work *The Apprentices at Saïs*. A brief consultation of Novalis's work shows that the excerpt is taken from its principal section entitled "Nature." The excerpt concludes with an alleged quote: "One must, in order to know nature, become one with her. A poetic and inner-directed existence, a saintly and religious soul, all the strength and all the vital forces of our human existence are necessary to understand her, and the true observer is he who knows how to uncover the analogy of that nature with man, and that of man with the heavens." ("Il faut, pour connoître la nature, devenir un avec elle. Une vie poétique et recuellie, une âme sainte et religieuse, toute la force et toute la fleur de l'existence humaine, sont nécessaires pour la comprendre, et le véritable observateur est celui qui sait découvrir l'analogie de cette nature avec l'homme, et celle de l'homme avec la nature.")[60]

Everything in these formulations will later enter the Transcendentalists' credo: namely the idea that true knowledge of nature can only be obtained through the experience of unity with nature, which in turn requires a conduct of one's life that is poetic and contemplative, and an attitude of the soul that is saintly and religious. Only then will one be able to uncover the analogy between nature and human life and thus encounter the divine in both man and nature. Yet if we search in Novalis's text for the German version of this Transcendentalist credo, we do not find it there. Instead what we discover is that Staël has substituted her own formulations as conclusion of the Novalis text and has placed her own statement within its quotation marks. To those who are familiar with Novalis's *Apprentices at Saïs* this concluding Staëlian statement could well be read as an interpretation of Novalis's position as it is unfolded only in the remainder of the work. But the alleged Novalis passage also expresses one of the favorite notions of Staël's own philosophy, which she is about to develop fully in the concluding portion of her book. The critical edition of *On Germany* has preserved for us the different stages of the reworking of Novalis's text. Whereas a first stage can still be taken as a legitimate attempt at translation, despite the liberties taken with the original, an intermediary phase already transforms key terms and phrases of the Urtext.[61] In the final phase the attempt at translation is abandoned altogether in favor of a re-creation of Novalis's text through the medium of Staël's own discourse.[62] Hence that part of the concluding statement that is entirely Staël's functions as an anticipation and foreshadowing of other, similar formulations of the theory of correspondence in the concluding portion of the work, formulations such as these: "The true final causes of nature are its relations with our soul and our immortal destiny."[63]

In Emerson's *Nature*, characteristically, Staëlian statements undergo a similar process of deconstitution and reconstruction, or accrual, as does the Novalis text in Staël's book. It is characteristic of this process in each case that it is guided by a specific version of the correspondence metaphor, which allows both authors to incorporate heterotextual elements into a new discursive context. From the larger perspective of romantic discourse this means that this metaphor is extended beyond the limits of the individual work: each author is able to substitute his or her own textual recreation of it at strategic places in their work. These specific transformations point at and are manifestations of the interdependency among individual works of romantic literature, regardless of their respective national or linguistic affiliation.

To investigate more fully than I have attempted here Staël's importance for the rise of American literature and American intellectual life during the first half of the nineteenth century, further study will be required, and other writers of the Transcendentalist movement and their literary descendants ought to be considered.[64] That this importance extended beyond the sphere of metaphysical and aesthetic theorizing and speculation and translated into a Staëlian presence within the process of literary production itself, my preceding analyses have clearly shown. Staël's *On Germany* by presenting for the first time in modern history another contempory culture in its otherness, and by providing the horizon and cultural space for its encounter, opened up the possibilities for that process of renewal and self-realization for the writers of the Emersonian generation which led them to assume their rightful place among the community of national literatures that is known to us today as romanticism.

STAËL: LIBERAL POLITICAL THINKER

Susan Tenenbaum

Eve Sourian and Charlotte Hogsett both make the case for taking Staël seriously as a political thinker. I am very sympathic to this claim, for I consider Staël to be a formidable political theorist whose contributions to the development of continental liberal thought have been for too long overshadowed by her literary accomplishments. Sourian brings to the surface the concealed political dimension of the novel *Delphine*, while Hogsett addresses intriguing questions of gender and politics in the *Considerations*. Both scholars underscore the importance of Staël's parents to the development of her political perspectives: Sourian places much emphasis on her relationship to her mother, while Hogsett focuses on her relationship to her father. I concur in the view that Staël's identity as a "Necker" had a profound impact on her political thought, yet raise the concern that too narrow a focus on her family relationships limits our perception of the complexity of Staël's thought as it drew nourishment from the manifold intellectual currents of her day. It is, of course, her engagement with these broader traditions upon which Staël's reputation as a political theorist must ultimately rest. What did she have to say about the nature of political change? About political legitimacy? About institutional forms and social dynamics? The ways she addressed these questions significantly altered the course of continental liberal thought.

In her analysis of *Delphine*, Sourian argues that "the novel is placed under the sign of Mme Necker." She holds that the novel's political content is powerfully shaped by Staël's hostility towards her mother, citing their opposing views on such issues as political liberty, the social equality of women, and divorce. I would suggest, however, that this focus on mother-daughter tensions leads to an overstatement of the intellectual disagreement between them. Sourian contrasts, for example, Staël as a champion of liberty with Mme Necker, who railed against liberty's anarchical social consequences. To be sure, the two thinkers differed in their estimation of liberty as a political value, yet a closer analysis of Staël's concept of liberty reveals affinities with her mother's position. Staël's conception of political liberty was formal and juridical; it related to the retrenchment of state power as a consequence of individual rights. This enlargement of the "private" sphere in a liberal state raised, in turn, significant problems of social control: how, in light of the retrenchment of the state as a moral and disciplinary force, is liberty to be prevented from degenerating into license? Staël devoted her intellectual life to answering this question—thus she argued on behalf of a propertied franchise (landed property being identified with social peace and stability), paid vigilant attention to the role of literature as an instrument of socialization, called for civility in manners, and decried the climate of egotism that followed in the wake of the Revolution. In her attentiveness to the problem of social order posed by the priority of liberty, Staël followed the lead of her mother.

Sourian similarly highlights the contrasting positions of Staël and her mother on the subject of woman's social role: the daughter championing woman's independence and right to self-fulfillment; the mother restricting woman to a subordinate role within the patriarchal family. Again, this interpretive framework allows only a first cut into a topic which yields greater complexities as the scope of inquiry is broadened. Staël's position on the role of woman in the post-Revolutionary liberal state contained deep tensions. On the one hand, her preoccupation with the issues of social control led her to champion a cult of domesticity, ascribing to woman a pivotal socializing role through the cultivation of homely virtues. This ideal is represented, in *Corinne*, by Lucile Edgermond, the Englishwoman who typifies the feminine sensibilities and domestic virtues that defined the parameters and nourished the privatized spirit of the modern liberal state. Strikingly, it is the model of woman framed by Rousseau and passed on by her mother that Staël adapts to her own political ends. On the other hand, Staël draws on the meritocratic principles of liberalism to uphold the claims of the exceptional woman—a Corinne or a Delphine—whose heightened sensibilities and/or creative energies overflow the bounds of domesticity to challenge the social conventions requisite to a stable society. This tension between woman's socializing and dissident roles is forcefully presented by Staël, but never resolved.[1]

In Hogsett's essay, Staël's relation to her father forms part of a wider analysis of the *Considerations* which takes as its focus a male/female, writing/speaking dichotomy. While this dichotomy yields considerable interpretive insights, it similarly fails to allow for the complex nature of Staël's political enterprise. Hogsett's discussion of the authorship metaphor provides an illustrative case. The metaphor is invoked by Staël to explain the failure of the Constituent Assembly to consolidate the gains of the Revolution; specifically, she denounces the innovative initiatives of the Assembly as evidence of a "manie de vanité presque littéraire" (an "almost literary obsession with vanity"). Hogsett cites this passage as evidence that Staël ascribed a "literary cause" to the Revolution, and assimilates this analysis into an interpretive framework which identifies the masculine with authorship and the written word. This very suggestive reading, however, takes no account of the broader stream of political discourse within which Staël situated herself. Specifically, the condemnation of the revolutionary leadership for its prideful disregard of prevailing political institutions and practices was a theme first articulated by conservative opponents of the Revolution and communicated through a broad range of metaphors. Edmund Burke fired the initial volley by describing revolutionary leaders as "children who are prompt to rashly hack their aged parents to pieces," and by denouncing the propensity of the French to change governments as easily as they change their clothes.[2] This theme was further developed by the French conservative Joseph de Maistre, who condemned the writing of constitutions as an act of political hubris:

> Thus he who believes himself able by writing alone to establish a clear and lasting doctrine is a great fool. If he really possessed the seeds of truth, he could never believe that a little black liquid and a pen could germinate them in the world. . . . As for whoever undertakes writing laws or civil constitutions in the belief that he

can give them adequate conviction and stability because he has written them, he disgraces himself.[3]

Staël's use of the authorship metaphor may be viewed as an attempt to legitimate such claims for the purpose of appeasing the politically powerful conservative faction under the Restoration. Staël's role as a political conciliator and consensus-builder is revealed by this reading, which reaches beyond a gender/genre interpretation to situate the metaphor in the intellectual space defined by the politics of Staël's day.

The writing/speaking dichotomy poses further problems when applied to Staël's treatment of the English constitution. Hogsett's analysis fails to lay stress upon the unwritten character of the English constitution, a fact which considerably complicates its placement in the "masculine sphere." Indeed the role of the English constitution in Staël's political thought cannot be understood apart from the broader French debate over codified and uncodified constitutions, and the French tradition of Anglophilia shaped by Montesquieu to which both Necker and his daughter were heir.

On the other hand, I agree with Hogsett that the writing/speaking dichotomy contributes much to the understanding of Staël's role as *salonnière*. Staël was indeed acutely aware of the "softening" effect of the *salonnière*'s discourse and of the conciliatory qualities conveyed by her "dialogic" cast of mind. Yet Staël also recognized the potential of the spoken word for inflaming the passions and heightening partisan spirit. She was painfully aware that as the stridency of male speech increased, the *salonnière*'s *douceur* proved least effective when it was most needed. Because dominion over the realm of conversation was of limited efficacy during periods of revolutionary upheaval, Staël marshalled a second argument to support her claims as a political conciliator. Ironically, it rested on her *exclusion* from the realm of citizenship. Denied the opportunity for direct participation in the political sphere because of her sex, she proclaimed herself an ideally neutral political arbiter, "As for myself, who have nothing either to fear or to hope for from a political career, I thought that this independence gave me the duty of expressing the opinions I deemed useful."[4]

On the broader issue of Staël's creativity, I agree with Hogsett that she was no mere apologist for Necker. Staël moved beyond her father to construct a sweeping interpretive framework for the French Revolution which served as the foundation for the liberal school of Restoration historiographers. And she moved beyond Necker in the scope of her theoretical enterprise: her project was nothing less than the construction of a political society that was both "modern" and "free." Her pioneering attempt to define the contours of a post-Revolutionary liberal state merits Staël an honored place in the history of liberal thought.

TWO VIEWS OF THE
CONSIDERATIONS ON
THE FRENCH REVOLUTION

Beatrice Fink

In spite of their differences in approach and content, Charlotte Hogsett's and Michel Delon's essays have certain elements in common. To begin with, obviously, they both deal with Germaine de Staël's *Considerations*, that is to say, a nonfictional, unfinished text drafted in the final years of the author's life when she was able to view the events of the Revolutionary era from a distance. Without going into my own reading of Staël's text, two points seem essential:

1. The *Considerations* is an outgrowth of the author's original intention to write a commentary on her father's political acts and works;

2. The only published version of this text available to date is one that has been edited, thus modified, particularly in its latter portions, by the author's son and son-in-law, Auguste de Staël and Victor de Broglie. According to Simone Balayé, the current version is considerably different from the original. There are therefore two additional pens, male pens, that must be accounted for when turning to the *Considerations*.

In addition to their common subject matter, Hogsett's and Delon's presentations are both structured along a binary grid. In Hogsett's case, the grid rests on the opposition and interplay of the spoken and the written, and that of male and female. With Delon, a number of paired elements—circumstance and principle, chance and necessity, the particular and the general, the memorized and the reflexive—are grouped under the overriding polarity of a fixed real ("unicité du réel") and a variable possible ("diversité du possible"). An offshoot of the latter, which Delon terms "l'irréel du passé," the unreal of the past, ties in with Hogsett's remarks on the conditional tense. Both essays, in other words, represent the author's text in terms of displacement, shifts, and slippages, of antithetical tensions.

So much for the two essays' similarities. Now let us examine their specificity.

Staël's overall concern with language is indeed, as Hogsett points out, reflected in the *Considerations*, and one way of expressing this concern is distinguishing between the spoken and the written word, between *parole* and *mot*, if you like. If the distinction is to be made in terms of pros and cons, in order to establish a hierarchy, then stumbling blocks arise. Hogsett is aware of this, since she notes that "Staël views speaking more positively than writing" while on the other hand recognizing the priority of written, that is to say male, language. But where is the line to be drawn between the spoken and the written? Is a pre-crafted but orally delivered speech, one for instance given by a member of the Constituent Assembly, to be labelled spoken, written, or both? Does Necker "speak" through the medium of the Staëlian text? (Hogsett suggests as much when she states "Staël both does and does not let him speak for himself.") If speaking comes under "le talent de causer," that is to say the ability to converse, it is also the linguistic mode of what Staël somewhat disparagingly terms "esprits de salon," drawing room wits, in turn contrasted with the ideologically-charged "hommes à principes."

The linguistic debate—perhaps elements of a theory of language would be a more appropriate appellation—criss-crossing the *Considerations* is, and I am sure that Hogsett would agree, much broader-based than the spoken/written opposition. Given the Revolutionary time frame, it focuses on political language and implicitly asks: what is political literature, and what should it be? The notions of power and communication, as discussed by Frank Bowman in this volume, are central ones. Power and persuasion, the power of persuasion, how does one persuade, what are the relative merits of *opinion* and *parole* (in the *Considerations* "parole" is likened to "raison")—these are the issues raised. While the Revolution consists of deeds, events witnessed at first hand, it is also a verbal revolution, a script: "Ils ont pris les acteurs pour la pièce" (actors were taken for the play).[1] In an article on

Staël and the rhetorical tradition, Aurelio Principato stresses the underlying moral component of language. In the *Considerations*, he notes, the author addresses the problem of linguistic responsibility, linking language and "moeurs."[2] The disarray of language, we are told, generates the breakdown of moral values. In the search for freedom, language is tasked with redeeming a fallen eloquence. As Frank Bowman has noted, Staël views eloquence as a politial instrument badly in need of rehabilitation.

I now turn to the gender component of Hogsett's discussion and its overlap with genre. Again, we are faced with interplay rather than with delineation in the binary construct. This is because Staël herself is *hors catégorie*. She is literally just that, the exceptional, non-categorizable woman, as distinguished from "les femmes." She is multifaceted, at once witness, author, and daughter of an exceptional man, himself one of the prime actors of the Revolution's early stages (the romantic motif of the extraordinary comes to mind). Transcending and transgressing her own model, Staël's multiple roles and corresponding multiple self-images lead her to a double bind. Her role as "conduit" (Hogsett's term) for her father's life and thought, coupled with her wish to create rather than to transcribe, introduce the problematic of filial writing, that of scriptural affiliation. Questioning, at the very least altering, the patrilinear, taking the linguistic initiative away from the father, is in and of itself revolutionary. The displacement is reflected in the shift and broadening of the *Considerations'* initial subject matter. This process, however, is deflected at a further stage when Staël's son and son-in-law, with the assistance of the son's surrogate father, Wilhelm Schlegel, act on the maternal text and, as in the primary case, both do and do not leave the author's language intact. This latter displacement, it is hoped, will itself be displaced by a new and more accurate edition in the near future.

For Delon, two questions underlie the Staëlian grid: what is the author's "global vision" of history, and by what means or devices is this vision projected in the *Considerations*? Delon points out a number of contemporary writers who think along the same lines as Staël: history is patterned and directional, it advances along the double lines of chance and necessity, the singular and the analogous, the particular and the general, the is and the ought or might have been. Its cyclical evolution in stages—"époques"—is, if not goal-oriented or purposive (one hesitates to qualify Staël's historical thinking as teleological), at least value-laden, since the quest for freedom, considered in its nineteenth-century liberal/libertarian form, is privileged. In this context, one contemporary Delon neglects to mention is Benjamin Constant. Not surprisingly, Staël's and Constant's historical thinking have many similarities. Like Staël, Constant views history in terms of stages defining a forward march of mankind (the Staëlian expression is "la marche de l'esprit humain"), and his writings on religion, on "perfectibilité," in fact all of his historical/historicist thought reflect this view.

The most telling point of Delon's essay is the idea that Staël's development of "l'irréel du passé" lies at the heart of her reading/writing of history. Counterpointing historical actualization, what did indeed take place, is historical latency, the curves on the historical graph that remain dotted, the various "possibles," the "rendez-vous manqués." A corrective, revisionist, normative process interweaves with a factual one. Staëlian history thus rests on dialectical confrontation. The ought or might have been, as Delon notes, is not pinned down to the unfulfilled. What is possible is of the future as well as the past (the conditional, Hogsett reminds us, ties in with an implied future). What might have happened or been, but didn't, wasn't, what might take place if, are part and parcel of a text's narrative fabric. In his most recent narratological investigations, Gerald Prince focuses on the "dénarré," the non-happenings inscribed in a novelistic text that constitute a component of its narrative structure, and may be used, inter alia, to isolate patterns and topics. Prince applies the notion to fiction, but it may be extended to nonfictional works, serving, in fact, to uncover a parafictional parameter. That the *Considerations'* "l'irréel du passé," historical latency, revolves primarily though certainly not uniquely around the father, Necker, suggests a conflated reading of Hogsett and Delon.

Finally, and responding to Delon with Delon, the parafictional or unreal inherent in the Staëlian perception of history is stylistically enhanced by metaphorical means. I am referring to Delon's essay on "La Métaphore théâtrale dans les *Considérations*," in which he underlines the recurrence of theatrical imagery and the projection of history as play, in other words, the displacement of reality, of the witnessed, onto a stage, onto the "irréel" of scenic transposition.[3] When Staël writes history, we are indeed crossing the borders.

STAËL AND THE FASCINATION OF SUICIDE: THE EIGHTEENTH-CENTURY BACKGROUND

Gita May

That throughout her life Germaine de Staël was obsessed with the notion of suicide is amply attested to by her literary production. One instance of this constant preoccupation, among others, is the *Reflections on Suicide*, published in January 1813. What has generally been overlooked in this lifelong attachment to the notion of suicide is its eighteenth-century background. To be sure, suicide has long been identified with the romantic *mal du siècle* and traced to Goethe's *Werther*. The romantic celebration of acts of voluntary death marks a high point of nineteenth-century lyricism. But what has not been sufficiently underscored is what Staël's own approach to voluntary death owes to the Enlightenment, to which she was both personally and ideologically linked, and to Rousseau, whose works had a particularly strong impact on her thought and sensibility.

The legitimacy of voluntary death was extensively debated by the *philosophes* of the Enlightenment, although, as John McManners, in *Death and the Enlightenment*, reminds us, under the Old Regime suicide was viewed as an offense against God, as well as a crime against society. A royal ordinance prescribed that the corpse be tried, and on conviction, be publicly exposed and hung by the feet, then buried in an unmarked grave, or burned, with the ashes thrown to the winds.[1]

The philosophes inherited a tradition, coming to them from classical antiquity through Montaigne and Charron, which argued that suicide was justifiable under certain circumstances.² That such a philosophical stance, which owes a great deal to Stoicism, is essentially anti-Christian suited the purpose of the philosophes, for it provided them with yet another opportunity to combat the teachings of the Church. It was precisely because the Church condemned suicide as a mortal sin that the philosophes were determined to defend it. In their eagerness to discredit Christian and especially Catholic values and to propound a new ideal of earthly fulfillment and individual freedom, they were highly sympathetic to the notion that when life fails to come up to one's expectations one has the right to end it.

In letter 76 from Usbek to his friend Ibben of the *Persian Letters* (1721), Montesquieu's lightheartedly satirical and ironic tone barely masks his indignation against the existing laws:

> European laws are merciless against those who take their own lives. They are made to die, so to speak, a second time. They are infamously dragged through the streets; they are covered with ignominy; their possessions are confiscated. It seems to me, Ibben, that such laws are quite unjust. When I am overwhelmed with grief, misfortune, scorn, why should they want to prevent me from putting an end to my troubles; and why cruelly deprive me of a remedy that lies in my own hands?³

Neither should we overlook the fact that it is in the *Persian Letters* that we find one of the earliest instances of a woman committing suicide as a supreme act of rebellion against male oppression and enslavement and as a proud affirmation of her right to individual freedom. Roxane, the favorite but profoundly unhappy concubine of Usbek, takes her own life in an ultimate act of defiance, and it is no coincidence that the *Persian Letters* ends with her wrathful letter to Usbek as the poison she has taken is already coursing through her veins: "How could you have thought that I was naive enough to imagine that I was put in the world only to adore your whims? That while you pampered yourself with everything, you should have the right to mortify all my desires? No! I might have lived in servitude, but I have always been free."⁴

One does not find in Voltaire's work the same kind of direct pleading in favor of suicide. Nevertheless, he seems to vindicate the notion of voluntary death, if only more ambiguously and indirectly, by underscoring the absurdity rather than the tragedy of existence and the vanity of all human projects. In response to the blithely reassuring cliché that "Malheur est bon à quelque chose" (in free translation: "Misfortune has its uses"), the unpalatable conclusion to *The Ingenuous One* is "Malheur n'est bon à rien" ("Misfortune is useless").

Diderot, for his part, identified with Socrates and found in the latter's voluntary drinking of the hemlock a great source of inspiration in facing his own tribulations. He especially admired Socrates' determination to hold on to what he believed to be the truth, despite the charges of impiety that would ultimately lead to his trial, conviction, and death. The republican ideal, increasingly invoked as the eighteenth century advanced, provided at least one hero, Cato the Younger, who committed suicide as an act of protest against Caesar. Diderot and Rousseau, in particular, were great admirers of the ancient Stoics, and for them the situation of a man who prefers self-inflicted death to enslavement was a supreme example of patriotism and civic virtue. The philosophers of antiquity had clearly shown that suicide is the best proof of human freedom and a legitimate remedy to certain intolerable situations.

As Roland Mortier has convincingly demonstrated in *La Poétique des ruines en France*, the peculiar appeal of fragmentary monuments of antiquity, especially of Rome, for eighteenth-century writers had a great deal to do with a heightened sense of mortality, both of the individual and of entire cultures and nations.[5] That this theme is prominent in *Corinne* has also been evident to readers of this novel. But here, again, we find a model in the eighteenth century. Diderot was especially sensitive to the esthetic and psychological implications of the contemplation of ruins.

The ruins of an ancient palace or a monument have the capability of inducing in us meditations both pleasurable and melancholy on the transitory nature of individual lives and entire civilizations. Antique ruins are all the more evocative and moving because they so eloquently bespeak the evanescent and transient nature of life. They invite our imagination to dwell on the greatness and accomplishments of the past and to ponder our own inevitable demise.

In one of the most striking passages of the 1767 *Salon*, Diderot defines in terms that are already wholly romantic both in spirit and language the special fascination ruins exert on our imagination and sensibility:

The notions that ruins evoke in me are grand. Everything van-
ishes, everything perishes, everything passes from the scene, only
time remains. How old this world is! I walk between two eter-
nities. Wherever I cast my eyes, everything that surrounds me presages an end and leads me to resign myself to the one that awaits
me. What is an ephemeral existence in comparison with that of
this rock that is crumbling, this vale that is hollowing out, this
forest that is teetering, these masses above my head that are tot-
tering? I see the marble of tombs fall into dust; and I don't want
to die.[6]

These remarks were largely inspired by Hubert Robert, the preeminent
eighteenth-century painter of ruins in France. Robert imbued his pic-
turesque scenes of ancient ruins with a fluid, evocative sense in which
the real and the imaginary are fused in a spontaneous, buoyant style
reminiscent of Fragonard. It was largely while contemplating the
paintings of Robert that Diderot yielded to philosophical and aesthetic
reflections on the fragility of civilization and on human mortality in
general. Neither should the time of these remarks be overlooked. By
the late 1760s the rococo style was distinctly on the wane and being
superseded by the neoclassical revival, while the romantic spirit was
beginning to assert itself.

What matters more to us here is that the meditation on ruins was to
become a kind of set piece for the early romantics. It is no coincidence
that the passage just quoted in Diderot's 1767 *Salon* (also repeated in
Jacques the Fatalist) was to inspire Musset's poem *Souvenir*. In Bernar-
din de Saint-Pierre's *Studies on Nature* (1784), chapter 12 is entitled
Pleasures of the Ruins. And of course we have Volney's *Les Ruines*
(1791) and Chateaubriand's *Letter to Mr. de Fontanes on the Roman
Countryside*. No wonder, therefore, that ruins should also appear as a
significant motif in Staël's *Corinne* and that it should be directly linked
with the theme of death and suicide.

With the rise of *sensibilité*, suicide was once more invoked, but
more as a manifestation of personal disenchantment, disillusion in
love, or melancholia and ennui than as a public and political act.
Rousseau's *La Nouvelle Héloïse* dealt more fully with suicide in this
personal mode, especially with suicide for thwarted love, than any
other eighteenth-century text.

The epistolary form enabled Rousseau to use a rhetoric of argumen-
tation for and against suicide by means of an exchange of letters be-

tween the distraught Saint-Preux, who has learned that his beloved Julie has married the elder Wolmar, and his friend and benefactor, Milord Edouard.[7] Saint-Preux's letter lists the reasons why he has the right to take his own life, beginning with this melancholy disclosure, which will become a leitmotif for the romantics: "Yes, milord, it is true, my soul is oppressed by the weight of life. For a long while, it has been a burden to me: I have lost everything that could endear it to me, troubles are the only thing left to me. But I am told that I am not allowed to dispose of it without the permission of the One who gave it to me."[8]

Saint-Preux realizes, however, that a defense of suicide in terms of unhappiness in love would be a morally indefensible one. What follows, therefore, is a closely reasoned apologia for suicide which aims at dealing with the issue in objective and rational terms and which refers to ancient as well as Christian sources in order to reconcile voluntary death with the tenets of Christian morality. "You want us to reason; well then, let's reason. You want us to give the discussion the proper perspective its importance demands; I agree. Let's seek the truth peacefully, calmly."[9]

Saint-Preux's "objective" arguments in favor of the legitimacy of suicide are, however, countered, point by point, by Milord Edouard, who finally appeals to his friend's responsibility toward his less fortunate fellow human beings and to an ethic of moral and social commitment transcending selfishly personal happiness in light of which living becomes a duty: "Listen to me, young fool; you are dear to me, I deplore your errors. If you still have in your heart the slightest sentiment of virtue, come to me, let me teach you to love life. Each time you will be tempted to depart it, tell yourself: 'Let me do one more good deed before dying.'"[10]

The twenty-two-year-old Germaine Necker, carried away by her enthusiasm for Rousseau, makes it clear in the *Letters on the Writings and Character of J. J. Rousseau* (1788) that she considers Saint-Preux's letter superior to that of Milord Edouard: "What beautiful letters for and against suicide! what powerful metaphysical and philosophical arguments! The letter that condemns suicide is inferior to the one that justifies it."[11] Furthermore at that time she believed not only that Rousseau himself sided with Saint-Preux in the latter's defense of suicide, but that he had taken his own life. In support of her theory she cites reasons of a sentimental as well as psychological nature, at the same time as she places much of the blame on Thérèse Levasseur: "But who could have prompted Rousseau to commit such an act? It was, I have been told, because he became convinced of having been betrayed by the woman who alone had retained his confidence and had made herself indispensable by detaching him from all his other relationships."[12]

Staël's later and more sober *Reflections on Suicide* (1813) is a revealing yet baffling text in many ways. Written as the Napoleonic era was about to disintegrate, it reflects the author's own personal turmoils and her bitter experience with the political upheaval of the Revolution and its aftermath. It essentially utilizes Rousseau's pro and con arguments, but it is obvious from the outset that the author is, at least seemingly, repudiating her earlier sympathetic notions regarding voluntary death, as set forth in her *Letters on the Writing and Character of J. J. Rousseau* of 1788 and her *On the Influence of the Passions on the Happiness of Individuals and Nations* of 1796. Here she tries very hard to marshal every conceivable argument against self-destruction. It is worth noting, however, that instead of clearly and openly acknowledging this apparent reversal in the introduction to her essay, she discreetly relegates it to a footnote: "I have praised the act of suicide in my work *On the Influence of the Passions*, and I have always regretted this thoughtless remark. I was then in the full pride and vivacity of early youth; but why would one want to live if not in the hope of improving oneself?"[13]

In this curiously ambivalent text we see a most earnest attempt to reach a compromise between the message of the philosophes, with its acceptance of self-interest and earthly happiness as a basis of human conduct, and Christian morality, which stresses spiritual and otherworldly values: "The eighteenth-century *philosophes* have rested morality on the positive advantages it can provide one in this world, and have viewed it as enlightened self-interest. Christians have transposed the source of our greatest satisfactions in the depths of our souls."[14] While the philosophes as well as Rousseau held that suicide is acceptable under certain circumstances, whether for compelling personal or ideological reasons, Christian ethics unequivocally forbids it. On the whole, however, in this work Staël tends to incline toward the Christian notion that a quietly resolute acceptance of one's fate, no matter how harsh and hopeless, is the best proof of superior moral character. Among the remarkable individuals cited as worthy of our admiration for the way in which they steadfastly and unflinchingly faced an unjust death is none other than Louis XVI, who is extolled as a martyr following in the footsteps of the saints and of Jesus Christ himself.[15]

Among such early romantics as Rousseau, Goethe (in *The Sorrows of Young Werther*), and others, suicide, whether it be personal or ideological or a combination of both, was treated as a man's prerogative. With Germaine de Staël, suicide becomes a legitimate right for the woman of superior intellect and sensibility who for various reasons may find life intolerable. No wonder, therefore, that her two major heroines, Delphine and Corinne, should confront this option in terms not unlike those invoked by Rousseau in *La Nouvelle Héloïse*.

It might be worth recalling that in the original ending to *Delphine*, the heroine poisons herself. This suicide aroused such vociferous criticism that Staël offered an alternate conclusion for the novel, wherein the heroine's death is more in keeping with sentimental and novelistic conventions (she dies of a broken heart). Corinne's death, although not by her own hand, also falls into the category of *liebestod*.[16]

This brings us to the theme of Sappho, which is directly related to that of suicide. That Corinne is a reincarnation of Sappho has already been noted by a number of critics (see the essay by Joan DeJean, *supra*). Whereas Delphine stands out as a conversationalist and letter writer, Corinne is not only a writer, but also a poetess and lyric improviser of genius. She is the inheritor of the Sapphic tradition. In modernizing the theme of Sappho Staël obviously wanted to stress the tragic fate that awaits the woman of genius in a patriarchal society unwilling to accept members of the "second sex" endowed with superior talents. Oswald, Corinne's pusillanimous lover, eventually marries Lucile, a proper, demure young lady.

Corinne does not take her own life, but her death is practically self-willed. Yet Corinne, like her creator and Sappho herself, conveys the message that the poetess, although doomed in a society bent upon male domination and political power, can transform her own downfall into a moral and esthetic triumph. No wonder, therefore, that the theme of suicide and the Sapphic theme should become inextricably intertwined. It does not matter that the story of Sappho falling in love with Phaon and committing suicide by leaping from a cliff is most probably the kind of fictional stuff of which myths are made. In this legend Staël found the message she needed to justify her own political and artistic stance through her heroine Corinne: the artist, and especially the woman who has consecrated her life to freedom of artistic expression, must be willing to accept peril and defiance as part of her fate, including death, either self-inflicted or imposed from without. Staël's 1811 play entitled *Sappho*, patterned after the model established in *Corinne*, reenacts the same leitmotif. Thus suicide achieves both a moral and an esthetic apotheosis. It becomes an act of supreme rebellion and defiance by the artist in a society that is hostile or indifferent at best to the individual that refuses to conform to a preestablished mold.

Staël's choice of Sappho as a symbol is also revealing in another way. Hardly ever do we see Staël think in terms of the political and social struggle for the equality of sexes, or identify her own cause with that of more ordinary women: for instance the middle-class wife and mother, or the more lowly housemaid or servant. One is indeed hard put to find any instance of Staël taking advantage of her fame, controversial though it was, in order to protest against the lot of women in general or to advocate better education and more equitable laws for the countless members of her sex who could not claim any special distinction of birth, rank, or achievement. Germaine de Staël was no Mary Wollstonecraft.

In all her works and throughout her lifetime, Staël continued to plead tirelessly her own case. In her romantic narcissism, she could only envision herself in the tragic but also highly flattering role of Corinne (alias Sappho), the improviser of genius who seals her doom by entrancing the multitudes on her lyre. This highly theatrical pose suited her purpose. A certain amount of indulgent self-worship was of course not alien to the romantics in general, and it would be unfair to take Staël to task for assuming a self-aggrandizing posture so common to her contemporary male counterparts. But this flattering self-dramatizing stance somewhat diminishes, if not her status as a writer, at least her effectiveness and credibility as a woman who otherwise courageously fought her own battle for personal emancipation and literary recognition. She movingly wrote on behalf of the superior woman whose exceptional gifts mark her for unhappiness in a society hostile to individuals of superior talent. But in this respect, Corinne's lamentation does not differ markedly from that of the paradigmatic romantic hero, whether he be Chatterton or Byron.

One can perhaps express the regret that Staël did not feel moved by the urge to speak out for her less educated or less articulate sisters and generally remained aloof from them throughout her turbulent life. To be sure, she viewed the woman of genius as more vulnerable than her male counterpart, but her plea, urgent and moving though it was, remained limited to that special, particular case, which happened to be her own.

Staël's involvement in revolutionary politics also reveals the same kind of ambivalence regarding the "woman question." Unlike such bold advocates of women's full participation as citizens in a republican form of government as Olympe de Gouge, Etta Palm d'Alders, or Mary Wollstonecraft, she did not speak out for the full political rights of women. But her ambiguous attitude in this respect does not differ markedly from that of other notable women of the Revolutionary era who like her had been profoundly influenced by the Enlightenment thinkers and especially by Rousseau. The name of Madame Roland, for instance, comes readily to mind.[17]

One is strongly tempted to muse on the personal, psychological, and cultural reasons why Staël did not play a more aggressive and fearless role in denouncing the progressive elimination of women from public life and political involvement because of their alleged physiological and intellectual limitations. In the last analysis, she could never quite bring herself to give up the enticing image of the kind of vulnerable, dependent, self-effacing womanhood that finds total fulfillment in marriage and motherhood, an image so compellingly depicted by Rousseau in *La Nouvelle Héloïse* and *L'Emile*.[18]

GERMAINE DE STAËL
AMONG THE ROMANTICS

Isabelle Naginski

Germaine de Staël has often been called "mistress to an age,"[1] an honorary title which defines her as an historical figure and stresses the public role she played in the Revolutionary and Napoleonic eras. For two romantic writers, however, Sainte-Beuve and George Sand, it was Staël the writer rather than the *femme du monde* who presented the most inspiring model. They saw her predominantly as a literary figure, and looked upon her not so much as the emblematic public figure of a generation but as a voice of transition in the unfolding of the French literary canon from the eighteenth century of lights to their own nineteenth century of shadows. As a representative of preromanticism, Staël was a writer caught between two ages and two sensibilities. Her situation, like that of her fellow writer, Chateaubriand, epitomized what *Mémoires d'outre-tombe* termed "la confluence," a spatial metaphor to denote the drama of a person caught between two very different chronologies:

I found myself between two centuries, as if I were at the confluence of two rivers *(comme au confluent de deux fleuves)*; I plunged into their troubled waters, moving away with regret from the ancient shore where I had been born, swimming with hope toward an unknown shore.[2]

From a literary point of view, the "ancient shore" Staël's illustrious contemporary refers to is classicism. Both writers bathed at its shores, as their common allegiance to an ethos resonating with classical values makes clear. In her article, Joan DeJean shows how Staël was able to reshape the classical myth of Sappho and make manifest its feminist potential, so that it would embody some of her most obsessive ideas regarding the woman of genius. By contrast, Staël's "unknown shore" is romanticism, and it is here that her impact on Sainte-Beuve and especially on George Sand can be felt with the most vigor. In her essay on the theme of suicide, Margaret Higonnet argues for the modernity of Staël's vision and for its lasting impact on our modern sensibility. Since my task is to respond to both of these articles, I will first direct my comments to the question of suicide as treated in Higonnet's essay, and then address the theme of Sappho. In so doing, I hope to show the crucial role *Corinne* played, with its Sapphic and suicidal heroine, in the arena of the romantic imagination.

Suicide in Staël

Suicide has long been a privileged literary topos. The neoclassical tragedians perceived it as the best strategy for the transformation of Pascal's "moi haïssable" into a "moi admirable," whereby a character's personal failings could be redeemed through the ultimate sacrifice of one's life. The example of Phèdre is significant in this respect, her suicide metamorphosing her from a character in the throes of a condemnable passion into a heroine finally able to take control of her destiny. Suicide is seen as an ennobling act. While there are elements of this elevating effect of suicide in the writings of Staël, her emphasis lies elsewhere. She is not so much concerned to map the transformation from weakness to strength as she is to delineate the specific character of feminine suicide. And in her theoretical writings, she accomplishes precisely that, claiming that female suicide was binary, envisaged either as a sacrificial act inspired by virtue or as the ultimate punishment of a faithless lover.[3] In her preromantic fictions, heroines such as Sapho and Corinne manage to incorporate both systems of meaning in their suicides—vengeance lurks beneath the heroic surface of self-sacrifice. Staël, then, did not so much place suicide on the literary map (since it had always been there), as she redefined the raison d'être of a suicide *au féminin*. Her fictions portray a very different kind of tragic figure from a classical heroine, because they insist directly on a link between gender and the psychology of suicide.

Furthermore, to return for just a moment to the image of Chateaubriand's twin rivers, there is no doubt that Staël's comments on suicide flow in two separate riverbeds, thus constituting a double and somewhat contradictory discourse about the same subject. On the one hand, her *Reflections on Suicide* come out of the philosophical tradition of the "Century of Lights," which argued against suicide. On the other, in contradistinction to her philosophical voice presenting the case in favor of life, Staël's *cris de coeur* betray a preromantic novelist fascinated with self-inflicted death. The valorization of suicide is overwhelmingly present in her fictions, where virtually all her heroines kill themselves, thus proving the critic Bédé right when he remarked that Staël always secretly reserved a place for suicide in her heart.[4] Staël had come into contact with writers of her own generation who only considered male suicide to be worthy of philosophical enquiry. She had praised what she considered to be the German suicide novel par excellence, *Werther*. And she had perceptively discerned that Rousseau was an apologist for suicide in *La Nouvelle Héloïse*. Her contribution was to bestow the same privilege to women.

Suicide per se is not, of course, a bearer of meaning. It is an empty space which can be filled with several, sometimes antithetical, meanings. Higonnet demonstrates the powerful desire for "self-construction" that lies at the basis of the Staëlian suicide, just as DeJean identifies the Sapphic leap rescripted in *Corinne* as a manifestation of the individual's affirmation of "self-control."

The emphasis of "self-construction" and "self-control" is important because it valorizes precisely that aspect of Staël's oeuvre which Jean Starobinski, in his famous article "Suicide et mélancolie chez Madame de Staël," demeans in his biased assessment of the writer. As Higonnet makes clear, Starobinski is first of all guilty of an autobiographical fallacy, collapsing the woman writer with her female characters. He refuses to see in Staël's use of suicide the *mise en écriture* of a certain intellectual obsession, the exploitation of her melancholia as a most fertile source of literary inspiration. Furthermore, Starobinski situates the conflict between the "richness of faculties" and "a radical lack" entirely within the psyche. Staël herself, in fact, sees the conflict very differently. In her *Reflections on Suicide*, she defined happiness as the "possessing [of] a destiny which bears some relation to our faculties" (177). The word "destinée" suggests a person's psychological *and* social life, where Starobinski only wants to see an inner "manque" (lack). Starobinski interprets this passage in a strictly Freudian light by suggesting that, lacking a phallus, woman is also lacking an element fundamental to psychic wholeness. But Staël's definition of happiness requires an equilibrium between one's abilities and one's possibilities, and her fictions pinpoint precisely that lack of equilibrium in her heroines' lives, thereby laying bare the tragic imbalance between their "genius" and the absence of a social space where that talent can be expressed. The *décalage* made manifest by Staël's analysis of happiness and suicide prefigures what the romantics will soon call the *mal du siècle*. Through her depiction of the issue in her fictions, Staël emphasizes her primary concern with the ways in which the model applies to women, and particularly to women of genius. For Delphine, Corinne, Mirza, Zulma, Pauline, Adélaïde, Sapho, the "manque" is not restricted to the psychological flaw Starobinski insists upon, but rather denounces the catastrophic situation of the exceptional woman. In the earlier *On the Influence of the Passions* Staël had already articulated her position:

> By examining the small number of women who have a true claim to glory, we will see that this striving of their nature has always been at the expense of their happiness. After having put into song the sweetest lessons of ethics and philosophy, Sappho hurled herself from the top of the rock of Leucas. . . . women are forced to think that, for the sake of glory, they have to give up the happiness and tranquillity which constitute the destiny of their sex.[5]

The inevitable tension between fame and the pursuit of happiness in the lives of women—between the female public persona and the private self—is an obsessive theme in Staël's oeuvre. Its recurrence helps to delineate what, in Charles Mauron's psycho-critical perspective, we would call the personal unconscious of the author. Suicide clearly stands out for Staël as one of the few options available for the woman of genius. And the tragedy such a decision embodies is exemplified for her in the story of Sappho. The philosophical problem and the classical myth are thus intimately linked. A discussion of suicide in Staël's works inexorably leads the reader to the writer's figuration of Sappho.

The Sappho Myth

Staël probed the myth of Sappho repeatedly in her works, not only in her play, *Sappho*, but also in *Delphine* (which originally ended with a suicide), and in *Corinne*, a text which DeJean calls "the most developed Sapphic fiction of the turn of the [eighteenth] century."[6] Taking DeJean's discussion of the Sappho myth as it is expressed in *Corinne* as a springboard, I want to concentrate here on the novel's impact in the romantic arena. The novel which bears most strongly the stamp of Staël's Sapphic heroine one generation later is George Sand's *Lélia*.

Victor Hugo once defined the battle of Waterloo as "le gond du dix-neuvième siècle" ("the hinge of the nineteenth century"). Exploiting the same image, one could, I think, claim that *Corinne* is one of the "hinges" of French romanticism. Some thirty years after the novel's publication, Lélia's voice, echoing Staël's heroine, claimed that women's spheres continued to be constricted, reducing half the population to despair: "Cursed be that fierce half of the human race [the masculine half] which, in order to appropriate the other half, has only given it the option of enslavement or suicide."[7] George Sand's heroine, one of Corinne's most illustrious descendants, first made her appearance on the literary scene in 1833. It is noteworthy that the *Lélia* of 1833 bears the stamp of *Corinne* much less than the second, completely rewritten version of 1839. Significantly, between 1833 and 1839—that is, between the first and second redactions of Sand's novel—Sainte-Beuve published two important pieces about Staël: a long study in *La Revue des deux mondes* in 1835; and an introduction to *Corinne* in 1839. Sand, one of the writers at *La Revue des deux mondes* and a close friend of Sainte-Beuve, could not have let those texts pass by unnoticed, and they may well have played a role in the "Corinnization" of Lélia.[8]

Both Sainte-Beuve and Sand stressed the kinship which linked the two women writers, as well as the poor treatment the two *écrivaines* had received at the hands of the critics. Sainte-Beuve mused: "Have we not witnessed in our day a similar unleashing of abuse [on the part of the critics] . . . against the most eminent woman in literature to emerge since the author of *Delphine*?"[9] Sand herself concurred. In a June 1836 letter to Charles Didier, she wrote: "The proud Madame de Staël with her *salon* at Coppet was insulted just as much as I was in the press."[10] It was inevitable that the press of the day should have associated Staël and Sand, often with malicious intent. One such journalist was Etienne de Jouy. Insisting with phallocratic authority on what he perceived to be the indissoluble link between the occupation of writer and the male gender, he mocked the woman writer as a sexual anomaly. In the satirical verses he addressed to Sand, the *vaudevilliste* emphasized her *parenté* with Staël:

> Are you a man, a woman, are you an angel, a demon?
> What is your gender, sublime and equivocal being?
> Sand, are you a son of the heavens or a daughter of the abyss?
> Are you Sappho, de Staël, Jean-Jacques or Byron?[11]

Jouy accentuates the fantastical, almost monstrous, nature of the woman of genius. But his nonchalant association of Sand with two great women writers of the past fails to highlight the crucial link between them. Their bond is to be found not in any supposed freakishness but in a shared desire to break the unwritten rule discouraging the literary creation of exceptional female characters. Even Sappho, in the few fragments that have survived to us, portrayed young poets in the feminine.

Redeemed as a fictional prototype for the woman of genius, the Greek poet was reborn in the two sister-characters of Corinne and Lélia. Up until the late 1830s, Sand tended to use male models as prototypes for her characters, both male and female. The Lélia of 1833, for example, who was the first character to express the romantic *mal du siècle* in the feminine, took her cue from three preromantic brothers, Werther, Obermann, and René. In the text of 1839, however, Sand's altered figuration of Lélia makes clear that she had finally discovered in the Staëlian character a female model for her heroine to emulate. Because the original portrayal of Lélia lacked a sense of coherence, Sand sought a focus that would organize the scintillating but somewhat disorderly discourse which characterized her heroine. This consistency of character was achieved in part by "Corinnizing" Lélia. As Marie-Jacques Hoog has demonstrated, the Lélia of 1839 emerged as a much more coherent heroine, because she was presented as an *improvisatrice* and as a frustrated poet who could not find her place in the world.[12] *Corinne* thus provided a central key for Sand's new heroine, who no longer needed to vent her rage in nihilistic attacks on

society and on the human condition without providing any clear indication of the cause of her fury. Her lamentations now focused on her
lack of poetic power in the existing social order.

A feminized cast of classical characters provided Sand with an orga-
nizational principle for her *Lélia* of 1839, as the numerous allusions to
mythological feminine divinities and priestesses—nymphs, bacchants,
pythias, sibyls—attest. But the novelist was no less inspired by an intermediary figure that bridged the gap between the classical and the
romantic—and that mediator was Corinne. Take as an example a crucial scene in which Lélia sings in public for the last time, as she is about
to take her final religious vows. The passage provides an insight into
the synthetic imagery of Sand's fictional universe—in which the figure
of Corinne makes possible a fusion of pagan and Christian motifs:

> It was the last time that Lélia's magnificent voice, endowed by her
> genius with an invincible power, was heard. Half-kneeling before
> her harp, her eyes moist, her face inspired, more beautiful than
> ever in her white veil . . . she made a profound impression on all
> those who saw her. Everyone was reminded of Saint Cecilia [pa-
> tron saint of music] and of *Corinne*. (*Lélia* 2:79; emphasis mine)

The Lélia of 1833 only meditated and denounced the world in long
prose monologues. The new Lélia presents herself as a *cantatrice*, thus
prefiguring the future heroine of *Consuelo*, and as an *improvisatrice*,
taking off on the wings of inspiration. The figure of Corinne, improvising on her lyre on the Cap Misène, lies in palimpsest beneath the
figure of Lélia singing her variation of *Super flumina Babylonis*. Her
choice of psalm emphasizes the mood of melancholia which inspires
her. Like Corinne's remark that "only knowledge of things divine remains, while all images of the world are troubled," Lélia's canto
stresses her imminent departure into a higher realm, "divorced from
human society."[13]

The endings of the two versions of Sand's novel further clarify the
presence of *Corinne* in the later text. In the 1833 redaction, Lélia was
strangled by the mad priest Magnus, her death symbolically expressing the silencing of the feminine voice. Furthermore, the 1833 *Lélia*
also clearly betrayed the modish stamp of freneticism. As Sand reminds us in *Histoire de ma vie*, frenetic literature was in full swing in

the early 1830s, with its predilection for unearthing "des sujets dégoutants": "Even talented people were enslaved by fashion, and dressed in bizarre and flashy costumes, they rushed into the fray. I was tempted to act like the others . . . and I searched for oddities that I would never have been able to carry off."[14]

The ending of the 1839 version of *Lélia*, however, was completely reconceptualized. Sand composed an entirely new chapter, "Délire," which presents Lélia delivering her last oral improvisation—at once a Sandian version of Corinne's poetic declamation on the Cap Misène and an echo of the Staëlian Sapho's last speech as she sits on her rock before leaping to her death. Like Sapho, Lélia has "a bizarre imagination which seeks misfortune."[15] Like Corinne, she is "a daughter of the sun, afflicted by secret sorrows" (*Corinne* 355). Lélia begins her improvisation:

> There are hours during the night when I feel oppressed by an unbearable pain. . . . All of nature weighs down on me, and I drag myself, broken and loaded down by the burden of life, like a dwarf who would be forced to carry a giant. . . . it is then that the poetic and tender fervor which is in me turns to dread and reproach. (*Lélia* 2:157)

This last phrase echoes Sapho's words: "[My genius] only serves to lay bare the torments of [my] soul," and Corinne's comment: "[M]y genius, if it still exists, makes itself felt only through the vigor of my suffering" (*Corinne* 538). Lélia continues:

> I am in conflict with everything and my soul cries out in the heart of creation like the string of a sacred instrument which has snapped in the middle of its triumphant melodies. . . . I am a grieved sibyl; I am the spirit of ancient times, locked in a brain which rebels against divine inspiration, a broken lyre, a muted instrument. . . . I am a priestess of death and feel that I have already been a Pythia. . . . I am floating in the darkness. (*Lélia* 2:157–158)

Lélia's self-association with the Greek and Roman priestesses of divine prophesy is significant, as it highlights her allegiance to a higher sphere of existence. The images of the broken lyre and the muted musical instrument are metaphors for the broken female word. As an uncompliant Pythia, Lélia struggles to speak her own words, rather than to deliver the phallocratic divine oracle. Conflict ensues—her mental faculties refuse to be reduced to a mere receptacle for the "divine inspiration" of male origin. Lélia's rebellious brain links her to that other recalcitrant sibyl, Corinne:

> Does not fate pursue exalted souls, poets whose imagination stems from the power to love and to suffer? . . . I know not what force independent of will hurls genius down into misfortune. . . . When our minds rise up to the loftiest thoughts, we feel, as atop some tall building, a dizziness that muddles all the objects we lay eyes on.[16]

Lélia's image of floating in the dark is transmuted here into Corinne's sense of vertigo. Both describe a similar state of disarray. The "dizziness" expresses the fall from grace that affects a woman poet in her fruitless search for earthly happiness. The "darkness" is a metaphor for the increasing disharmony between the self and society. The two texts thus highlight the despair of the woman artist as she seeks for an authentic voice in a world where such a quest can only lead to an impasse. Both Staël and Sand are increasingly aware of the alienation of the woman of genius in a world that refuses to take her at her word.

By making Lélia into a rebellious woman poet, Sand created a nineteenth-century incarnation of the Greek priestess, and at the same time emphasized her heroine's poetic lineage with Staël's Corinne. By being situated in a long line of defiant sibyls, the romantic heroine became the most recent embodiment of the doomed feminine search for the appropriation of the Word:

> For ten thousand years I have cried out into the infinite: Truth, truth! For a thousand years, the infinite has answered me: Desire, desire! Oh, grieved Sibyl, oh, mute Pythia, why don't you smash your head against the rocks of your cave, and mingle with the seafoam your blood smoldering with rage; for you think you once possessed the all-powerful Word and for ten thousand years you have sought it in vain. (*Lélia* 2:159)

Lélia is Sand's rescription of the Sappho myth. Lélia is Corinne's younger sister. The climactic scene takes on an ever-increasing Sapphic tone as Lélia's delirious speech (delivered from the top of a cliff) comes to a close; she rises "as if she were about to throw herself down," poised for the heroic leap, ready to choose the form of suicide favored by classical mythology. Held back by her friend and mentor Trenmor, she collapses: "She fell back against the rock: she had ceased to live." Significantly, a similar incident can be found in *Corinne*, when she falls into a swoon at the end of her improvisation on the Cap Misène and Nelvil has to support her to prevent her from falling (*Corinne* 355).

Sand reworked two forms of Staëlian suicide. Lélia's death is a synthesis of Sapho's leap from the cliffs of Leucas and Corinne's "invisible suicide," in which the heroine kills herself through an act of the will alone. This latter abstract model of suicide hangs over the destinies of many nineteenth-century heroines, it is true. Balzac and Stendhal, as well as Sand, all portray heroines who perform such "invisible suicides." But, unlike Louise de Rênal or Henriette de Mortsauf, who succumb passively to the moral illness brought about by a broken heart, Lélia, like Corinne, transforms her malady into a triumphant victory over the finite realm. Thus the destiny that Sand assigns to her heroine is much more in the direct tradition of Corinne than either Balzac's or Stendhal's feminine characters. Just as Staël's heroine, her heart shattered, had been sufficiently in control of her destiny to orchestrate a fitting death for a poet, so Lélia dies a philosopher's death. Because Sand admired the way in which Corinne exploited the poetic potential of her plight, Lélia's final elegy unmistakably bears the mark of her preromantic model.[17]

Sainte-Beuve finished his 1835 article on Staël with words addressed directly to George Sand:

You [George Sand], whom opinion has already unanimously proclaimed to be the first in literature since Madame de Staël, you must acknowledge . . . in your profound admiration for her, a profound and tender gratitude for all the good she would have wished you and would have bestowed upon you! There will always be in your glory a *primeval knot* [un premier noeud] which links you to hers.[18]

The "noeud" which links the two women writers is only beginning to be given the serious study it deserves. Staël's rescripting of Sappho and her "mise au féminin" of a heroic suicide played an important role in the elaboration of Sand's fictional universe. Further study may well illuminate other such connections between Staël and her romantic disciple. I hope to have suggested some of the areas in which further investigation might be entertained.

CORINNE AS AN
AUTONOMOUS HEROINE

English Showalter, Jr.

A confession: when I first read *Corinne* almost thirty years ago, I didn't like it much. Like many readers, including Doris Kadish, I took Nelvil to be "the chief figure of conflict in the novel"; and like Benjamin Constant, I identified with him. Corinne's love and admiration seemed only what was due to such a hero. Corinne, by contrast, seemed absurdly idealized and quite irrational; in the modern idiom she wanted to "have it all," fame, fortune, and family. When she couldn't have Nelvil, she turned into a crazy woman, an early version of Alex Forrest, that male nightmare played by Glenn Close in *Fatal Attraction*, lurking out there in the dark, seducing the child, tormenting the wife, disrupting the family, and generally making life hell.[1] Needless to say, I have changed my mind since then, but I am not the only reader who has had problems with *Corinne*, and I'd like to explore that situation a little.

Ellen Moers, for example, who wrote some interesting pages on it in *Literary Women*, starts off apologetically, "Let us try to take *Corinne* seriously"; she insists only that "at least a few chapters and scattered passages . . . should be familiar to anyone pretending to an interest in the traditions of women's literature," and she concedes that *Corinne* is "a predecessor of those 'Silly Novels by Lady Novelists' which George Eliot so wittily demolished."[2] As has often been remarked, Staël's novels are not part of the French literary canon, and they do not seem to have had even the status of underground feminist cult favorites until recently. Reading Gide's *L'École des femmes* not long ago, I was struck that the rebellious daughter Geneviève finds her spiritual guides in two English novels, Charlotte Brontë's *Jane Eyre* and George Eliot's *Adam Bede*—not that Gide is a great feminist, but he was surely trying to cite works emblematic of female revolt.[3] That reminded me that Simone de Beauvoir, in her memoirs, remembers discovering her heroines in Louisa May Alcott's *Little Women* and George Eliot's *Adam Bede* (again) and *The Mill on the Floss*, but never mentions *Corinne*, even in *The Second Sex*, where she discusses Staël's life but not her fiction.[4] Yet as Ellen Moers showed, *Corinne* inspired every important woman writer of the nineteenth century, including notably George Eliot, exactly as George Eliot later inspired the young Simone de Beauvoir.

Perhaps others have a ready explanation for this apparent neglect. I am going to propose a partial one, which is for me one of the novel's great originalities and a sign of Staël's genius: Corinne—the heroine, not the book—begins the novel as a free, autonomous woman. To my knowledge, she is really the first such heroine of any significance. The well-known female characters of eighteenth-century novels all faced primarily the problem of negotiating some sort of self-realization through a compromise with a paternal figure or his surrogate. They escaped from it only into prostitution, like Moll and Manon. The closest to a free woman one finds is the young widow, a woman who has by definition passed from father to husband and outlived her mate, and she survives as a menacing figure indeed, like Mme de Merteuil or Mme de La Pommeraye.

Corinne in the first half of the novel is thus an entirely new creation. With no name and no past, but with the exalted status of a national celebrity and creative genius, she is in full control of her social destiny. She is, of course, an idealized character, and her conception owes something to the characters of heroic romances, those mysterious figures of compelling beauty, who turned up in the strangest places, as shepherds and shepherdesses, hermits, slaves, and castaways, and eventually told their life stories which revealed their origins as princes and princesses. Although the details have evolved with society, fantasies of this sort still retain great emotional power and a loyal readership. But Corinne's story, when she finally tells it, will have enough plausibility to turn Staël's work toward the realistic genre of the novel, rather than toward the fantasy or utopian world of romance. The invention of this character, a woman who shapes her own life in a believable world, opened the novel to important new developments as a testing ground for women's destinies.

Now that we have read the writers who came after Staël, however, that very innovation may seem a problem. On the one hand, if *Corinne* is read as a wish-fulfilling romance, the career of female bard seems as archaic as that of shepherdess; but on the other hand, for most readers, the real-world difficulty is not how to deal with success and glory already acquired, but how to escape the confines of a routine existence and achieve, if not fame, at least some degree of fulfillment and control over their own destiny. In other words, to appreciate the "roman" of the beginning increasingly requires the reader to make a certain historical translation, whereas the "histoire de Corinne" of the second half continues to have immediate impact and relevance still today. Staël was writing when the "novel" had not yet been clearly differentiated from the "romance"—a distinction still open to challenge and far easier to make in English than in French, where the old term "roman" survives as the standard name for the new genre. I suspect that to nineteenth-century readers that generic confusion seemed less troubling than it seems today.

Moreover, the genre problem is related to gender problems. I would suggest that the opposition of romance to novel is a possible alternative reading of the line from *On Germany*, "Women try to present themselves as novels, and men as history," which Marie-Claire Vallois quotes in the preface to *Fictions féminines* and which Margaret Higonnet cites in her essay in this volume.[5] I would link it to these lines from *Corinne*: "Reverie is the portion of women, of beings weak and submissive from the day of their birth. Man wants to realize his desires; his habitual courage, his sense of strength set him against his fate if he does not manage to guide it as he would like."[6] The "roman" is a dreamworld, outside of time; the "histoire" is a will imposing itself in time. It is one of Staël's great achievements that she will not let Corinne merely present herself as a "roman" but forces her to reveal her "histoire" as well. But of course, as their juxtaposition makes apparent, either genre is a falsification, a form of inauthenticity; this is one of the ways Staël suggests a problem, not only of society and woman's place in it, but as Marie-Claire Vallois has argued, of language and representation.

Staël's conception of Corinne politicizes a new sphere of existence. I think that Doris Kadish overstates the case at the end when she says, "I hold that Corinne must be betrayed because the republic was, not because Oswald preferred Lucile," but she is surely right to link the two betrayals. Staël has made it clear that the personal, the social, and the political are inextricably interwined. In my view, however, another source of *Corinne*'s power lies in its refusal to make politics a simple binary conflict, especially between a good side and a bad side. What makes Nelvil admirable and desirable, what makes him the man to save the storm-tossed ship, the burning city, and the drowning man— what makes Corinne love him, in short—is inseparable from the sense of duty and honor of patriarchal England. It should be noted that England is a "good" patriarchy, as opposed to the literally unspeakable tyranny of Napoleonic France. Likewise, what makes Italy a feminist utopia for Corinne is inseparable from the weakness of its men and their unsuitability as husbands for Corinne. Moreover, neither Italy nor England is a simple place; Rome, Naples, Venice, and Florence are politically differentiated, as are London, Northumberland, and Scotland.

The patriarchal, like the political, is more complex than a simple contrast between Corinne's spontaneity and directness on the one hand, and patriarchal mediation on the other. The most forceful advocate of the English patriarchy is a woman, Lady Edgermond. Ellen Peel has convincingly argued that ventriloquism is a phenomenon linked to patriarchy, so that its use by Corinne at the end adds an element of ambiguity to the conclusion. But Corinne is half English herself, born of a father as well as a mother. As soon as she meets Nelvil, her openness and candor are compromised, for she does not tell him the secret that she knows from the start, that his father had already rejected her. To be sure, she does not know the full gravity and finality of that decision; but I believe a case could be made that her silence as their love develops already constitutes an indirect revenge on the family, the nation, and the patriarchal system that once rejected her. It is, however, a self-defeating and self-destructive revenge, for her English origins remain an inseparable part of her self.

All these complexities are bound up in the fact that, for the reader, Corinne starts from a position of freedom, and she chooses Nelvil. Her election of him valorizes him for the reader as much as his gaze valorizes her. Staël gives many positions in the novel a full voice, authentic in that she does not use her authorial power to silence them. *Corinne* is a dialogic novel, in the Bakhtinian sense; Italy argues with England, female genius with patriarchal duty, and the author has not rigged the debate so that one side scores a clear victory. We leave the characters with a series of questions and doubts, and we come away with a sense that human destiny is composed of choices. In the novel's world, one cannot have both fame and family, both freedom and love, both domestic tranquility and excitement, and that dilemma, painful as it is, applies to Nelvil as much as to Corinne. This refusal to take sides or to provide facile resolutions, the quality I most misunderstood on that first reading when I took Nelvil as the hero, now seems to me precisely the measure of the novel's enduring greatness.

POLITICS, FEMINISM, AND PATRIARCHY: REREADING *CORINNE*

Nancy K. Miller

What does it mean to reread *Corinne* at the close of the second decade of feminist literary criticism, in the second wave of the feminist movement? As is the case for all questions of rereading, the effort to determine what is "new" requires at the very least the evocation of a history of prior readings. English Showalter has reminded us in this volume that Simone de Beauvoir has her place in that revision. In the section of *The Second Sex* called "The Independent Woman," Beauvoir reflects upon her precursor, a European, female intellectual: "Mme de Staël," Beauvoir writes, "won some resounding victories: she was almost irresistible." I think this "almost" that Beauvoir identifies as the trope of Staël's life is also crucial to the conundrum of *Corinne*. This internal wedge of incomplete fulfillment structures the novel; more specifically, the "almost" serves to mark the ways in which the text's feminism never escapes its fatally dialogic relation with patriarchy's power: at the end of the novel, the dying woman points to the moon-covered cloud which in the novel was earlier associated with paternal irritation at the love between Corinne and Oswald. Faced with the uncanny return of Corinne's dying gesture, Oswald becomes wild with grief: seeing, as if for the first time, the woman he almost—I find myself writing: had.[1]

In Beauvoir's first two references to Staël, Staël is linked with George Sand by their intelligence, their emancipatory struggles, and their distance from the general movements for women's causes. They are also linked, in the chapter on "The Lesbian," as "intellectuals of intrepid spirit" in their enthusiasm for the struggle between the sexes.[2] Beauvoir's reading of the writers' lives deserves an analysis I cannot undertake here, and I want to move out from its framework of heterosexual struggle to raise in textual terms the question of legacy and precursors, a subject implicit in a discussion of new readings, but also a thematic embedded in Staël's novel, as Ellen Peel points out in this volume, in the figures of both Juliette and the young girl who performs Corinne's last words.

Let us begin, then, with the scene of Corinne's "swan song," a scene that has been interpreted by Joan DeJean and Carla Peterson as a defeat of the oral, as the loss of Corinne's unique performance to posterity. To be sure this scene represents a bodily defeat for Corinne— and I mean the body in the broadest possible sense, as the site of what Irigaray calls in *This Sex Which Is Not One* a "first mimesis"—a mode which is not specular, but rhythmic and musical. It is also the representation of an artist's power to write beyond death; this is how, I would suggest, George Sand seems to read it.

As a woman writer preoccupied with the representation of an artist's life, Sand returns interestingly to this moment in her allegory of creativity, *Lélia*. Its heroine, Lélia, described as having the "serious gaze of a long-ago poet," is likened by Trenmor to a type: to the poets Tasso and Dante, and to Shakespeare's "young heroes"—Hamlet, Romeo, and "Juliet half-dead, hiding the poison and the memory of a broken love in her heart. . . . Corinne, dying," Trenmor continues, "must have been plunged into mournful attention when she listened to her last poems being spoken *at the Capitol* by a young girl" (emphasis added). In Sand's *mis*representation, in her transposition of the recital from the academy in Florence to the Capitol in Rome, we have, I think, a woman reader's tribute to the public authority of a female precursor's text. By replacing the last performance at the scene of the first, Sand marks the power of the poet Staël created. Through her revision, Sand enacts the possibility of a different sort of literary community and continuity of women: not the biological simplicity of the father and son rivals of our dominant cultural paradigms but a more complex legacy that, like Corinne's, passes on his values in life to another generation by reading women's writing and taking the measure of their performative acts.

I suggested earlier that I would evoke precursors and legacies by way of identifying new readings, or rather what might be new in these readings. To do this I want to turn now to Ellen Moers's *Literary Women*, which in many ways helped make *Corinne* a "readable" book for an American audience. Moers, we recall, introduced her discussion of the novel by commenting that, "*Corinne* is one of the very few works by women which is trivialized rather than honored by being read as a woman's work." By this she seems to have meant that to read the work as being about "female genius" as opposed to the contemporary reception of the novel as a "celebration of the rights of spiritual genius and intellectual freedom" is seriously to misunderstand Staël's "principal intention," which was to "politicize . . . genius" (182). Madelyn Gutwirth, whose pioneering book on Staël continues to inspire feminist critics, and who has been an enabling precursor in my own work, argues sharply in her unpublished essay "Corinne, or the Appropriation of Allegory" that "what Moers does not seem to recognize is that the novel is claiming the defense of spiritual genius and intellectual freedom as woman's work." Since Moers then goes on to show the impact the novel subsequently had on women writers, we might want to rethink her founding opposition: political vs. woman's work, or in my terms, political vs. feminist. Whatever Staël's intention may have been, her gesture in feminizing genius in a public forum is from a feminist perspective politicizing. To see this, however, would require Moers to take woman as the ground of critique, rather than its metaphor or effect.

Moers makes the claim that *Corinne* is "not in any polemical sense a feminist work." Indeed, she writes, Staël's point "is to show that regional or national or what we call cultural values, determine female destiny even more rigidly than male." She goes on to conclude with a leap directly into the next paragraph: "Oswald's father is quite right. Corinne really is not a proper wife for Nelvil, or for anyone else" (207). Thus despite herself Moers hits on the very piece of Staël's fiction that makes the novel classically, even polemically, feminist. And this is precisely the role of Oswald's father, who embodies patriarchal authority given as a synonym for England. What motivates Moers's apparent non sequitur, then, is that she seems to embrace the logic of the fathers that in woman sees only wife: the rules of propriety that make woman—even a national heroine—finally subject to the laws of patriarchy. In this sense, she reads, we might say, like a man.

At the same time, of course, as Moers maintains, *Corinne* is a novel about the ways in which human lives are shaped by national values. What a feminist analysis that takes the personal and the political, the private and the public together as concatenated scenes of operation can provide, however, is an account of the deeply imbricated nature of these relations.

This is a rather long prelude to some brief remarks about readings produced in the shadow of 1989 designed to raise the question of the political, the canonical, the patriarchal. In that spirit, I want to press Doris Kadish's concluding argument that: "On the basis of the thoroughgoing political nature of the novel that I have been developing, I would urge that politics, not love, is the key to interpreting *Corinne*." What is gained by opposing and then separating affairs of the heart and affairs of state? Kadish herself remarks that "even the surface romantic interest of *Corinne* is not unrelated to the political thrust of the novel" (through why foster a depth/surface opposition?). In a novel which, as Marie-Claire Vallois has demonstrated persuasively, is structured from the title onwards by a fundamental doubleness, two things are likely to be true at the same time. Moreover, to the claim that "the novel seems to glorify submission to male control, but when viewed politically, it can be seen to call into question, if not openly reject, paternal models of authority," I would reply that the entire novel through its representations of masculinity, especially of Lord Nelvil's oppression of his son, works to unsettle the legitimacy of paternal authority. Isn't in fact the framing of Oswald an instance of the strategies of indirection that Kadish sees elsewhere as key to Staël's political writing strategy?

This would seem to be part of what Ellen Peel is getting at in her discussion of "indirect revenge"—which indirectly takes me back to the "swan song" scene. Peel is disturbed by the fact that we never learn the young performer's name. More to the point, perhaps, we never learn Corinne's given first name either.[3] But isn't what finally matters here the continuity between generations: a symbolic representation— to use Kadish's term—of women's performative power?[4] Like the education of Juliette, why not see the possibility of a feminist legacy of women artists as a subversive enterprise within patriarchy? (A point not lost on Lucile.) As Peel herself observes: "Whenever this family feels most nuclear, Corinne will show herself to have been there all along."

Finally, Kadish makes the point via Charlotte Hogsett that while Rousseau, Constant, and Chateaubriand, who write both confessionally and politically, obey the codified rhetorical rules which separate the genres, Staël, like other women writers, flaunts them. In Staël's case, Hogsett notes, "she said she was not going to talk about herself, and yet she seems to do little else." It is perhaps precisely because Staël, in *Corinne* at least, wrote politically and personally at the same time, that the novel, despite its original impact and its current republication, has remained outside the dominant tradition of the French novel.

Which brings me in last place, though of course not least, to Marie-Claire Vallois. In *Fictions féminines,*[5] Vallois brilliantly illuminated the function of the novel's travelogue by showing that when Corinne speaks of Italy, she is speaking of herself; when she performs as tour guide, she is performing autobiographically. Now Vallois makes the provocative suggestion that the tour guide voice in the novel is a manifestation of the maternal *as* voice. If, as Vallois goes on to claim, "for Chateaubriand, writing becomes monumental, but for Staël writing models itself on those ruined monuments that appeal for a voice" [qui font appel à la voix], are we then to take this reading as an anti-Derridean position on voice and writing that would revalorize voice's originary power; a living source engendering a female model of authority?

NOTES

Introduction

1. My terminology here echoes that of Gérard Genette, *Figures II* (Paris: Seuil, 1969). Genette also reminds us of the importance of "gender studies" and space in Bachelard's analyses of the poetic imagination, to which I refer further in this introduction (*Ibid.*, 119).

2. *The Edinburgh Review* 22 (1814): 204, quoted by Kurt Mueller-Vollmer in this volume.

3. Susan Gubar and Sandra Gilbert, *The Madwoman in the Attic: The Woman Writer and the Nineteenth-Century Literary Imagination* (New Haven: Yale University Press, 1979) 83–84.

4. Germaine de Staël, *De l'Allemagne* vol. 3 (Paris: Hachette, 1958–1960) 268 (further references will be indicated in text); and *De l'influence des passions* in *Oeuvres complètes* vol. 3 (Paris: Treuttel & Würtz, 1820) 47. All translations are my own.

5. "The lack of discipline of our young *métèques* only continues a tradition that, although it was introduced in France, has nonetheless remained separate from the true tradition of French literature. One must understand the heterogeneity of Sand, of Staël, and of Rousseau or desist from censuring their heirs; for the latter are but a wave, the last wave, of that Gothic invasion for which Geneva and Coppet opened the way." Charles Maurras quoted by Elaine Marks in her essay "'Sapho 1900': Imaginary Renée Viviens and the Rear of the *belle époque*" (*Yale French Studies* 75 [1988]: 183–184).

6. Lucia Omacini, "Pour une typologie du discours staëlien: les procédés de la persuasion," in *Benjamin Constant, Madame de Staël et le Groupe de*

Coppet (Oxford: Voltaire Foundation; Lausanne: Institut Benjamin Constant, 1982) 387.

7. As for the scriptural dynamics of emancipation, my principal references are Madelyn Gutwirth, *Madame de Staël, Novelist: The Emergence of the Artist as Woman* (Urbana: University of Illinois Press, 1978); and Charlotte Hogsett, who develops the notion of "crossing" in the chapter "A Topography of the Soul," in *The Literary Existence of Germaine de Staël* (Carbondale: Southern Illinois University Press, 1987) 94–131. I also refer to Marie-Claire Vallois's study, *Fictions féminines: Mme de Staël et les voix de la Sibylle* (Stanford: Anma Libri, Stanford French and Italian Studies 49, 1987) on the repressed feminine self-referentiality in fiction, and finally to Nancy Miller's chapter "Performances of the Gaze: Staël's *Corinne, or Italy*," in her *Subject to Change* (New York: Columbia University Press, 1988).

8. Miller takes on Luce Irigaray's discussion on the two mimesises from *Ce sexe qui n'en est pas un* (Paris: Minuit, 1977) 129–130, and translates excerpts from Hélène Cixous's *La Venue à l'écriture* in her *Subject to Change*, 180–181.

9. Simone Balayé has long called for more attention to be paid to this key paragraph on the Count de Stolberg in *On Germany* where Staël explains the two motions upon which the universe is organized: gravity and impetus (5: 76) ("A propos du préromantisme: continuité ou rupture chez Madame de Staël," in *Le Préromantisme: Hypothèque ou hypothèse* [Paris: Klincksieck, 1975] 153–168). Among other sources analyzing Staël's metaphorics of energy and vitality as inseparable from the active resistance to antagonistic forces, see Michel Delon, "La théorie de l'énergie à Coppet" in *Benjamin Constant, Madame de Staël et le Groupe de Coppet* (Oxford: Voltaire Foundation; Lausanne: Institut Benjamin Constant, 1982) 441–451, and Annie Becq, "Politique, esthétique et philosophie de la nature dans le Groupe de Coppet: le concept de l'organisme," in *Le Groupe de Coppet*, actes et documents du deuxième Colloque de Coppet 10–13 juillet 1974 (Geneva: Slatkine; Paris: Champion, 1974) 83–98.

10. M. Kurt Wais, "Le problème de l'unité du Groupe de Coppet," in *Mme de Staël et l'Europe* (Paris: Klincksieck, 1975) 343–344.

11. Paul de Man, *Blindness and Insight* (New York: Oxford University Press, 1971) and Jean Starobinski, *Jean-Jacques Rousseau, la transparence et l'obstacle* (Paris: Gallimard, 1971).

12. Michel Delon, "La métaphore théâtrale dans les *Considérations sur la Révolution française*," in *Le Groupe de Coppet et la Révolution française* (Lausanne: Institut Benjamin Constant, 1988) 163–173.

13. There is a growing interest in Staël's philosophy of language. See Aurelio Principato's essay on "the myth of veracity," "La tradition rhétorique et la crise révolutionnaire: l'attitude de Madame de Staël," in *Le Groupe de Coppet et la Révolution française* (Lausanne: Institut Benjamin Constant, 1989) 107–120.

14. Joan DeJean's "Staël's *Corinne*: The Novel's Other Dilemma," *Stanford French Review* (Spring 1987): 884–902.

15. Elaine Showalter, "Review Essay," *Signs* 1 (Winter 1975): 435, and DeJean, "Staël's *Corinne*," 78.

16. A term created by Naomi Schor to designate "a linguistic act of repetition and difference which hovers between parody and parricide" (*Breaking the Chain* [New York: Columbia University Press, 1985] 12).

Staël and Liberty

1. Germaine de Staël, *Delphine,* ed. Simone Balayé and Lucia Omacini (Geneva: Droz, 1987) book 5: letter 14. All translations from the French are my own (A.G.).

2. See André Maindron's still unpublished thesis, "Fondements psychologiques et transposition littéraire de la peinture de la femme dans le roman français du 19ème siècle, 1789–1830" (University of Nantes, 1985).

3. In the absence of a critical edition as yet, and given the many editions of the book, references will be to volumes, sections, and chapter as pertinent and will be provided in the text.

4. *Des circonstances actuelles qui peuvent terminer la Révolution,* ed. Lucia Omacini (Geneva: Droz, 1979). Further references are given in the text by page number.

5. Germaine de Staël, *De la littérature considerée dans ses rapports avec les institutions sociales,* ed. Paul van Tieghem (Geneva: Droz, 1959) 323.

6. Germaine de Staël, *De l'Allemagne,* ed. Countess Jean de Pange with the assistance of Simone Balayé (Paris: Hachette, 1979) 111. Further references are given in the text by volume number.

Germaine de Staël and Other Possible Scenarios of the Revolution

1. Joseph de Maistre, *Considérations sur la France,* ed. Jean Tulard (Paris: Garnier, 1980) 32. Further references will be given in the text by page number.

2. Germaine de Staël, *Considérations sur la Révolution française,* ed. J. Godechot (Paris: Tallandier, 1983) part 1, chap. 1, p. 63. The critical edition of Staël's manuscript now being prepared may invalidate some of our analyses, in revealing a text different from the one we have worked with. Further references will be given in the text by part, chapter, and page numbers.

3. Book 1, chap. 16 and book 3, chap. 19. On the topology of the session of May 5 and the issue of point of view in the scene, see Michel Delon, "La métaphore théâtrale dans *Les Considérations,*" in *Le Groupe de Coppet et la Révolution française* (Lausanne: Institut Benjamin Constant, 1988) 163–173.

4. See specific anecdotes also in part 3, chapter 9, concerning August 10, 1792: "They came to tell me that all my friends on guard outside the castle had been seized and massacred. I went out at once to learn more" (279).

5. See Jean-Marie Goulemot, *Discours, révolutions et histoire. Représentations de l'histoire et discours sur les révolutions, de l'âge classique aux Lumières* (Paris: UGE, 1975); Karlheinz Bender, *Revolutionen. Die Entstehung des politischen Revolutionsbegriffs in Frankreich zwischen Mittelalter und Aufklärung* (Munich: Fink, 1977); Rolf Reichardt and Hans-Jürgen Lüsebrink, "Révolution à la fin du 18e siècle: Pour une relecture d'un concept-clé du siècle des Lumières," *Mots* 16 (March 1988). Note other references in note 1 of this last article.

6. *Annales patriotiques et littéraires de la France*, 27. 14 Ventôse, Year II (March 4, 1794), quoted by Reichardt and Lüsebrink, "Révolution," 44.

7. Staël is, on this point, close to Volney and to the Ideologues; see M. Raskolnikoff, "Volney et les idéologues: le refus de Rome," *Revue historique* (1982). The Revolution's infiltration by models of antiquity is the subject of Jacques Bouineau's book *Les Toges du pouvoir ou la Révolution de droit antique, 1789–1799* (Toulouse: Ed. Eché, n.d.).

8. See Michel Delon, "La Saint-Barthélemy et la Terreur chez Mme de Staël et les historiens de la Révolution au XIXème siècle," *Romantisme* 31 (1981): 49–62.

9. Staël also refers to that abstract idea of human nature, as is illustrated by the quotation from the first chapter, "the representative government toward which human nature is advancing on every side" (69); also, "the march of human nature that [all friends of liberty] favor by the very nature of things" (6:7: 576).

10. "If hazards of battle, that is, a specific cause, has managed to ruin a state, there was also some general cause which made that state perish in battle" (*Considérations sur les causes de la grandeur des Romains et de leur décadence*, xviii).

11. For the conceptual couple, see Rolf Reichardt, *Reform und Revolution bei Condorcet* (Bonn: Röhr-Scheid, 1973). Necker's dilemmas are similarly expressed in an unreality of the past in 2:18: 231–232.

12. The oriental metaphor recurs in part 4: "oriental courtier" (366); "the despotism of the Orient" (398); "oriental label" (426). A new form of the classical fascination with oriental despotism has been studied by S. Stelling-Michaud, "Le mythe du despotisme oriental," *Schweizer Beiträge zur allgemeinen Geschichte* (1960–1961), and Alain Grosrichard, *Structure du sérail: La fiction du despotisme asiatique dans l'Occident classique* (Paris: Seuil, 1979).

13. In an essay published at the time of the Liberation, Bertrand d'Astorg defines the Terror as a world of the masses and of all possibilities. I have attempted to study the liberating potentialities of Enlightenment in *L'Idée d'énergie au tournant des Lumières, 1770–1820* (Paris: PUF, 1988) 457–461.

14. *Les Confessions, Oeuvres complètes de Rousseau* (Paris: Pléiade, 1959–1969) 1: 43–44. See the reference below to Max Milner's article which compares this page to Chateaubriand's.

15. I developed these observations in "Casanova et le possible," *Europe*

(May 1987) and in "Le nom, la signature," in *La Carmagnole des muses,* ed. J. C. Bonnet (Paris: Colin, 1988).

16. *Mémoires d'outre-tombe,* book 10, chapt. 10. This passage has been brilliantly analyzed by Jean-Luc Steinmetz, "Chateaubriand et ses possibles," *Annales de Bretagne.* Colloque Chateaubriand de Rennes, 1969, and by Max Milner, "Les possibles inaccomplis dans la première partie des *Mémoires d'outre-tombe,*" in *Le Lieu et la formule,* Hommage à Marc Eigeldinger (Neuchâtel: La Baconnière, 1978).

Generative Factors in *Considerations on the French Revolution*

1. This internal conflict is the basic theme of my book, *The Literary Existence of Germaine de Staël* (Carbondale: University of Southern Illinois Press, 1987). In retrospect it has seemed to me that in the pages I devote to the *Considerations* I demonstrate an inadequate appreciation of the greatness of this last work. This paper is intended partly as a correction or addition to my earlier assessment.

2. *Oeuvres complètes de Madame la Baronne de Staël-Holstein* (Paris: Firmin Didot, 1861) vol. 3, 311. Further references to this work are given in the text by page number.

3. Regarding Staël and England, Robert Escarpit in *L'Angleterre dans l'oeuvre de Madame de Staël* (Paris: Didier, 1954) attempts to reconstruct the *On England* which Staël did not write, despite her admiration of that country.

4. Simone Balayé discusses Staël's attitude toward the Assembly in *Madame de Staël: Lumières et liberté* (Paris: Klincksieck, 1979) 40–41.

5. I am grateful to Professor Tenenbaum, whose remarks can be read at the end of this volume, for pointing out the facts concerning the British constitution which have aided me in reworking and refining the argument presented here.

6. Balayé also points up this depiction of French society, 35.

7. For information on the mutual genesis of these two works, consult Balayé, 230–240.

8. On Staël and conversation see my *The Literary Existence of Germaine de Staël* 122–126; Madelyn Gutwirth, *Madame de Staël, Novelist: The Emergence of the Artist as Woman* (Urbana: University of Illinois Press, 1978) 191; and Carla Peterson, *The Determined Reader: Gender and Culture in the Novel from Napoleon to Victoria* (New Brunswick, N.J.: Rutgers University Press, 1986).

9. *Corinne, ou l'Italie,* 14:1–3.

10. Lucia Omacini notes this same phenomenon in "Pour une typologie du discours Staëlien," in *Benjamin Constant, Madame de Staël et le Groupe de Coppet* (Oxford: Voltaire Foundation; Lausanne: Institut Benjamin Constant, 1982) 378–379.

Delphine and the Principles of 1789: "Freedom, Beloved Freedom"

1. Germaine de Staël, *Essai sur les fictions*, in *Oeuvres complètes* vol. 1 (Geneva: Slatkine Reprints, 1967) 69. Further references in the text will be to this edition.

2. Simone Balayé, *Madame de Staël: Lumières et liberté* (Paris: Klincksieck, 1979) 123. "Mme de Staël could be criticized for not having capitalized on the recent events of an era of paramount importance, and for not having dared to write the great Novel of the Revolution which never saw the light."

3. Ibid.

4. Henri Coulet, "Révolution et roman selon Mme de Staël," *Revue d'Histoire Littéraire de la France* 4 (1987): 655.

5. Germaine de Staël, *Delphine*, 2 vols., ed. Claudine Herrmann (Paris: Editions des Femmes, 1981) 1:7. References to *Delphine* in the text are to this edition. The original quotation was slightly different: "In short, the man who knows how to stand up to opinion and the woman who submits to it and even sacrifices herself to it, both equally display the noble pride of their character." Suzanne Necker, *Mélanges,* 3 vols. (Paris: Charles Pougens, 1798) 3: 386.

6. See Simone Balayé, Preface, *Delphine*, vol. 1 (Geneva: Droz, 1987) 25–30 and 47–50.

7. Albert Soboul, *The French Revolution* (Berkeley: University of California Press, 1977) 72.

8. Alexis de Tocqueville, *De la démocratie en Amérique,* 3 vols. (Paris: Librairie de Médicis, 1951) 2: 316. Further references in the text will be to this edition.

9. Staël, *Considerations on the French Revolution,* in *Oeuvres posthumes* (Geneva: Slatkine Reprints, 1967) 152.

10. Suzanne Necker, *Réflexions sur le divorce* (Lausanne: Durand Ravanel et Comp. Libr., 1794) 29.

11. Claudine Herrmann, Preface to *Delphine,* 1: 12.

12. The author of the line quoted by Mme Necker is still unknown. She wrote in *Mélanges* (1:191): "Someone had engraved on a funerary urn: 'No one answers me, but perhaps someone hears me.'" Staël used this line at the end of the orginal ending of *Delphine* (2:435).

Communication and Power in Germaine de Staël: Transparency and Obstacle

1. *Considérations sur la Révolution française,* ed. Jacques Godechot (Paris: Tallandier, 1983) 427. Hereafter *Considérations.*

2. The problem has of course been discussed, regarding particular texts, by Staël scholars, but never in an overall analysis. Most notable are Madelyn

Gutwirth, "Du silence de Corinne et de la parole," in *Benjamin Constant, Mme de Staël et le Groupe de Coppet* (Oxford: Voltaire Foundation; Lausanne: Institut Benjamin Constant, 1982) 427–434; Simone Balayé, "Les gestes de la dissimulation dans *Delphine,"* *Cahiers de l'Association internationale des études françaises* 26 (1974): 189–202; and Marie-Claire Vallois, *Fictions féminines: Mme de Staël et la voix de la Sibylle* (Stanford: Stanford French Studies, Anma Libri, 1987).

3. Germaine de Staël, *Oeuvres complètes,* vol. 1 (Paris: Treuttel and Würtz, 1844) 83. Hereafter *OC.*

4. Simone Balayé, *"Delphine,* roman des lumières; pour une lecture politique," in *Le Siècle de Voltaire, Hommage à René Pomeau* (ed. Christiane Mervaud and Sylvain Menant) (Oxford: Voltaire Foundation, 1987) 37–45.

5. *Considérations* 427; see 482, 590; *Dix années d'exil,* ed. Simone Balayé (Paris: Bibliothèque 10/18, 1966) 136. Hereafter *Dix années.*

6. *Considérations* 162; *Dix années* 225, 228–229.

7. *Considérations* 72, 74; *Dix années* 201.

8. *Considérations* 76.

9. *Essai sur les fictions,* in *OC* 1: 66; *De la littérature considérée dans ses rapports avec les institutions sociales,* ed. Paul Van Tieghem (Geneva: Droz, 1959) 164. Hereafter *Littérature.*

10. See her criticism of Alfieri's *Octavie* in *Corinne, ou l'Italie,* ed. Simone Balayé (Paris: Gallimard, 1985) 185.

11. *Littérature* 349; see *Des circonstances actuelles qui peuvent terminer la Révolution,* ed. Lucia Omacini (Geneva: Droz, 1979) 288. Hereafter *Circonstances.*

12. *Circonstances* 295.

13. *Littérature* 170; *Circonstances* 294.

14. *Considérations* 340–343, 410.

15. *Considérations* 362.

16. *Considérations* 368.

17. *Considérations* 590.

18. *Littérature* 31; see also 293, 416; *De l'Allemagne,* ed. Simone Balayé (Paris: Garnier Flammarion, 1968) 1:81.

19. *Littérature* 23.

20. *Circonstances* 281.

21. *Littérature* 306.

22. *Essai sur les fictions,* in *OC* 1:63, 65.

23. *Littérature* 28; *Considérations* 79.

24. *Dix années* 213; *Littérature* 161, 213; *De l'Allemagne* 1: 55–56, 174; see 1: 111 concerning interruptions of discourse in French and German.

25. *Littérature* 297, 300; *Dix années* 89.

26. *De l'Allemagne* 2:116; see *Littérature* 382.

27. *De l'Allemagne* 2:197. This debate among the Coppet group has been much studied. See B. Munteano, "Episodes kantiens en Suisse et en France," *Revue de littérature comparée* 15 (1935): 387–459; A. Monchoux, "Mme de

Staël interprète de Kant," *Revue d'histoire littéraire de la France* 66 (1966): 71–84; Ernst Behler, "Kant vu par le Groupe de Coppet," in *Le Groupe de Coppet, Deuxième colloque* (Paris: Champion, 1977) 135–167.

28. *De l'Allemagne* 2:205.

29. *Réflexions sur la paix intérieure* (1798), in OC 1:58; *De l'Allemagne* 2:202.

30. *Essai sur les fictions*, in OC 1:68.

31. *Histoire de Pauline*, in OC 1:100.

32. *Littérature* 232; *De l'Allemagne* 2:18; *Considérations* 531, 556; *Littérature* 242.

33. *Considérations* 556–557.

34. *Littérature* 238.

35. *De l'Allemagne* 1:47.

36. *Delphine*, 5th ed. (1809) 1:11.

37. *Circonstances* 192; *Littérature*, chap. 18.

38. *De l'Allemagne* 1:94, 91, 101.

39. *De l'Allemagne* 1:103, 90.

40. Balayé, "Les gestes de la dissimulation," 193.

41. *Delphine* 1:203; 2:257.

42. *Delphine* 2:257.

43. *Littérature*, 350.

44. *De l'Allemagne* 2:246.

45. *Sophie*, in OC 2:152.

46. *Circonstances* 120.

47. *De l'Allemagne* 1:142; 2:308.

48. *Fictions féminines* 15.

49. "Du silence de Corinne" 433.

Suicide as Self-Construction

This essay will appear in a different form as part of a volume on suicide in eighteenth-century France, co-authored with Patrice Higonnet.

1. Walter Benjamin, *Illuminations*, ed. Hannah Arendt, trans. Harry Zohn (New York: Schocken, 1969) 94.

2. I want to thank Martine de Rougemont and Larry Lipking, who both asked me, while I was working on this paper, what one could say "after Starobinski."

3. Because Starobinski starts from a hunt for the "secret links that unite the life and work of Mme de Staël," he is led to conclude that she failed to let her heroines live their own lives. "Here, the creator did not sacrifice herself to the creature. It is Mme de Staël who solicits our attention, not Delphine or Corinne." Jean Starobinski, "Suicide et mélancholie chez Mme de Staël," *Madame de Staël et l'Europe*, actes du Colloque de Coppet, juillet 1966, ed. Jean Fabre and Simone Balayé (Paris: Klincksieck, 1970) 252. (Further references to Starobinski as JS will be included parenthetically in the text.) One wonders

what a comparison to Constant or Stendhal, rather than Flaubert and Mallarmé, might have produced.

4. The very metaphor recurs in *Sapho,* whose genius feeds cannibalistically on her life, and whose passions devour her genius.

5. The *ad feminam* arguments of Starobinski's closing analysis (JS 249–252) deserve a closer rebuttal than this paper affords. A similar moral judgment is made by Godelieve Mercken-Spaas, who holds, "For Mme de Staël female death is a last attempt to keep intact the stature of the female self narcissistically constructed throughout the novel." "Death and the Romantic Heroine: Chateaubriand and de Staël," in *Pre-text, Text, Context: Essays on Nineteenth-Century French Literature,* ed. Robert L. Mitchell (Columbus: Ohio State University Press, 1980) 85.

6. I shall not be writing here about suicide as a form of social murder, a topic that Simone Balayé has touched on in connection with Staël's analysis of *Werther.* I have developed the links of suicide to civil war and to inner division in *"Delphine*: d'une guerre civile à l'autre," in *Le Groupe de Coppet et la Révolution française,* Actes du quatrième colloque de Coppet 20–23 juillet 1988, eds. Etienne Hofmann and Anne-Lise Delacrétaz (Lausanne: Institut Benjamin Constant, 1988) 211–222.

7. She acknowledges this obsession herself: "I hope not to be accused of having spoken too often in the course of this work about suicide as an act worthy of praise." *De l'influence des passions,* in the *Oeuvres complètes* (Paris: Treuttel & Würtz, 1820) 3: 121n. Further references will be indicated in the text as *Passions.*

8. "A woman in such terrible times as those we have witnessed—a woman condemned to death with the man she loved, who went far beyond the help of courage in her joyful approach to her punishment, took pleasure in escaping the torment of survival, proudly shared the fate of her lover, and perhaps foresaw the moment when she might lose his love—such a woman felt a fierce and tender sentiment that made her cherish death as if it were an eternal reunion" (*Passions* 114–115). In this fierce desire for *liebestod,* Starobinski might find support for his theory of a terrorist love. We should note, however, that it is a motive Staël attributes equally often to men.

9. "Epistle to Sorrow, or Adèle and Edouard" (1795). *Morceaux détaches,* in *Oeuvres complètes* 17: 394.

10. *Jane Grey,* in *Oeuvres complètes* 17: 198.

11. Monika Bosse has offered a political reading of this murder as a rebellion against the socially fetishized male. "*Zulma* ou l'esthétique de la Révolution, à la lumière de l'*Essai sur les fictions,*" in *Le Groupe de Coppet et la Révolution française,* 141–161.

12. *Zulma,* in *Oeuvres complètes* 2: 344. Further references to *Zulma* will be indicated parenthetically in the text.

13. *Delphine,* ed. Claudine Herrmann (Paris: Editions des femmes, 1981) 2: 259. Further references to *Delphine* will be indicated parenthetically in the text.

14. Sigmund Freud, "The Psychogenesis of a Case of Homosexuality in a

Woman," *Collected Papers* (New York: Basic Books, 1959) 2: 221. Similarly, "we have long known that no neurotic harbours thoughts of suicide which are not murderous impulses against others redirected upon himself" (Freud, "Mourning and Melancholia," *Collected Papers* 4: 162).

15. During her nearly fatal illness Corinne hopes " we shall be joined in death as we are in life" (*Corinne, or Italy*, trans. Avriel H. Goldberger [New Brunswick, N.J.: Rutgers University Press, 1987] 284. (All further references to *Corinne* will be included parenthetically in the text.) Oswald invites her to "leap into another life where we would find my father again to welcome us, to bless us! Is that what you want, dear friend?" (289).

16. This is true even of the late *Réflexions sur le suicide, Oeuvres complètes* 3: 336. (Further references to the *Réflexions* will be indicated in the text.) As Simone Balayé has suggested, heroic suicide in Staël's works would be a profitable subject of study.

17. *Oeuvres complètes* I: xxxiv.

18. "Doubtless, if despair always led to the decision to die, the course of the life thus fixed could be organized more boldly" (*Passions* 227). Compare a few pages later: "I have said that he who is willing to make suicide one of his resolutions can enter into the full career of his passions; he can abandon his life to them, if he feels able to end it whenever lightning may strike the goal of all his efforts and desires" (235).

19. "Vous faire passer pour morte" (*Corinne* 382).

20. I develop these points more fully in "Suicide: Representations of the Feminine in the Nineteenth Century," *Poetics Today* 6:1–2 (1985): 103–118.

21. *Oeuvres complètes*, 16: 52.

22. The importance of this theme to Staël may be deduced from the frequency with which she alludes to Voltaire's *Tancrède*, whose hero mistakenly accuses the heroine of infidelity (see *Delphine* 1: 246; *Passions* 112).

23. See Simone Balayé, *Madame de Staël: Lumières et liberté* (Paris: Klincksieck, 1979) 203–205.

24. Virginia Woolf, *A Room of One's Own* (San Diego: Harcourt Brace Jovanovich, 1929) 51.

25. *Sapho*, in *Oeuvres complètes* 16: 320. Further references to *Sapho* will be indicated parenthetically in the text.

26. Writing of Tasso, Staël suggests that his poetic abundance and psychological penetration arose out of his very suffering (*Corinne* 244–245).

27. Charles Baudelaire, "Le Cygne," *Oeuvres complètes*, Pléiade (Paris: Gallimard, 1975) 86.

28. Brooks, *Reading for the Plot: Design and Intention in Narrative*, 1984 (New York: Vintage, 1985) 95.

29. "De la disposition romanesque dans les affections du coeur," *De l'Allemagne* part 3, chapter 18 (Paris: Garnier, n.d.) 2: 215. Further references to *De l'Allemagne* will be indicated parenthetically in the text by part and chapter as well as page.

30. Such a conception was not alien to the eighteenth century, as Roland Mortier has observed. Diderot discovered more strikingly sublime thoughts

among ruins than among monuments preserved entire. Cited by Roland Mortier, *La Poétique des ruines en France* (Geneva: Droz, 1984) 92.

31. Mortier, *Poétique* 196–200; Simone Balayé, "Corinne et Rome, ou le chant du cygne," in Raymond Trousson, ed., *Thèmes et Figures du siècle des Lumières: Mélanges offerts à Roland Mortier* (Geneva: Droz, 1980) 45–58; and Balayé, "Corinne et la Ville Italienne, ou l'espace extérieur et l'impasse intérieure," in *Mélanges à la mémoire de Franco Simone: France et Italie dans la culture européenne* (Geneva: Slatkine, 1984) 3:33–50.

32. As Benjamin Constant would put it, "Les édifices modernes se taisent, mais les ruines parlent." Cited by Mortier, 200.

33. See Bowman in this volume and Balayé, "Corinne et Rome, ou le chant du cygne," *Thèmes et figures du siècle des lumières*, ed. Raymond Trousson (Geneva: Droz, 1980), 52.

34. Marie-Claire Vallois, "Voyage au pays des doubles: Ruines et mélancolie chez Mme de Staël," *L'Esprit créateur* 25, no. 3 (1985): 78.

35. Vallois, 84. Vallois discovers a quest for the absent mother and an archaic expressive space, applying Julia Kristeva's theory of a pre-Oedipal linguistic realm or Chora, in "Noms de lieu," *Polylogue* (Paris: Seuil, 1977) 467–490 and in *La Révolution du langage poétique: l'avantgarde à la fin du dix-neuvième siècle, Lautréamont et Mallarmé* (Paris: Seuil, 1974). My own inclination would be to foreground Freud's theory of the link between a melancholy splitting of the ego and suicide, as laid out in "Mourning and Melancholia."

36. These terms come from Vallois, 76.

37. The verbal fragment may also serve to express the breakdown of the self, as Madelyn Gutwirth has demonstrated in her study of *Delphine*. See "La *Delphine* de Madame de Staël: Femme, révolution, et mode épistolaire," *Cahiers Staëliens*, no. 26–27 (1979): 162–163.

38. Indeed, Corinne's "art" is quintessentially social.

Old Idols, New Subject:
Germaine de Staël and Romanticism

1. An essential reevaluation of Germaine de Staël's works has been provided in Simone Balayé, *Madame de Staël: Lumières et liberté* (Paris: Klincksieck, 1979); Madelyn Gutwirth, *Madame de Staël, Novelist: The Emergence of the Artist as Woman* (Urbana: University of Illinois Press, 1978); and Charlotte Hogsett, *The Literary Existence of Germaine de Staël* (Carbondale: Southern Illinois University Press, 1987). See also my study, *Fictions féminines: Mme de Staël et les voix de la Sibylle* (Stanford French and Italian Series, Sarratoga: Anma Libri, 1987). Joan DeJean's article, "Staël's *Corinne*: The Novel's Other Dilemma" (*Stanford French Review* 11 [Spring 1987]), as well as the chapter of Nancy Miller's recent book, *Subject to Change: Reading Feminist Writing* (New York: Columbia University Press, 1988) entitled "Performances of the Gaze: Staël's *Corinne, or Italy*" (pp. 162–

203), are crucial to a new understanding of Staël's impact on a definition of woman's writing in the context of feminist theories. The various reeditions of Staël's work both in France and in the United States bear witness to Staël's new popularity and importance. For this study I have used Avriel Goldberger's superb translation *Corinne, or Italy* (New Brunswick, N.J.: Rutgers University Press, 1987).

2. The comparison of Staël and Sibyl was made by the Chevalier Guibert, as reported in *Notice sur le caractère et les écrits de Mme de Staël,* by Mme Necker de Saussure, in the *Oeuvres complètes* vol. 3 (Paris: Treuttel et Wurtz, 1836) (my translation).

3. The description of woman as "Pythia" or "Sibyl" was not really original and was more of a timely cultural catchword; Diderot made it one of the most striking arguments in his famous essay "Sur les femmes" (*Oeuvres complètes* [Paris: Garnier, 1875] ed. Assezat, vol. 2, 255). The literary use of the Sibyl figure in Staël's works is, however, totally original and subversive, as I show in *Fictions féminines.*

4. For an analysis of the influence of and reactions to neoclassical style in Staël's writings see Gutwirth, *Madame de Staël, Novelist* 172–182.

5. See P. Grimal, *Dictionnaire de la mythologie grecque et romaine* (Paris: PUF, 1958) and J. Bachofen, *Du règne de la mère au patriarcat* (Lausanne: Ed. de l'Aire, 1980). Marie Delcourt, *L'oracle de Delphes* (Paris: Payot, 1981), Marie Mauxion, "La transmission de la parole oraculaire" in *Le Sexe linguistique,* ed. Luce Irigaray, *Langages* (Paris: Larousse, 1987) and Margaret Homans, *Bearing the Word: Language and Female Experience in Nineteenth-Century Women's Writing* (Chicago: University of Chicago Press, 1986), provide a very pertinent re-reading of the mythological models, such as the one of Athena-Nike and the Sibyl, as they were shaping nineteenth-century female understanding of literary creation.

6. For a more elaborate discussion of the relationship of Staël to Christianity see Frank Bowman's article, "Mme de Staël et l'apologétique romantique," in *Madame de Staël et l'Europe* (Paris: Klincksieck, 1970).

7. Chateaubriand's letter of December 1800 to Louis de Fontanes, in his *Correspondance générale* vol. 1 (Paris: Gallimard, 1977).

8. Roland Mortier, *La Poétique des ruines en France* (Genève: Droz, 1974) 196.

9. Letter to Monti, 7–8 February 1805 quoted in Mortier *La Poétique,* 193.

10. Mortier 196.

11. Letter to Monti, 7 February 1805 quoted in Mortier, 196.

12. *Corinne, or Italy,* translated by Avriel Goldberger, book 15, chap. 4. Subsequent references to this work will be given in the text by book and chapter number.

13. Simone Balayé gives an insightful analysis of the duality "melancholy-enthusiasm" in "A propos du 'préromantisme': continuïté ou rupture chez Madame de Staël," *Le Préromantisme: hypothèque ou hypothèse?,* ed. Paul Viallaneix (Paris: Klincksieck, 1975) 153–168.

14. Letter of 9 April 1805, *Mme de Staël et J.B.A. Suard, Correspondance inédite,* ed. Robert de Luppé (Geneva: Droz, 1970) 25.

15. Ibid.

16. See Simone Balayé, *Les Carnets de voyage de Madame de Staël* (Geneva: Droz, 1971) 16.

17. See T. Todorov, *Introduction à la littérature fantastique* (Paris: Seuil, 1970).

18. I have analyzed the problematical quality of the title and the necessity of a double reading of the novel in *Fictions féminines* 111–112. I am here revising and extending this reading by putting Staël's fiction within the larger context of romantic writing. I extend the notion of the romantic subject reinterpreted in reference to the "aesthetic feeling" that Freud took as particularly relevant to romantic literature in his study *The Uncanny.*

19. Sigmund Freud, *The Uncanny* (New York: Harper Torch Book, 1958) 153.

20. For the figure of the "double" see Freud, *The Uncanny* 140–142.

21. For an analysis of the title as enigma, see my *Fictions féminines* 111–112.

22. See my article, translated by Betsy Wing, "Voice as Fossil; Mme de Staël's *Corinne or Italy*: An Archeology of Feminine Discourse," *Tulsa Studies in Women's Literature* (Spring 1987) 52. See also the analysis of the woman/ novel as sphinx in Naomi Schor, *Breaking the Chain: Women, Theory, and French Realist Fiction* (New York: Columbia University Press, 1985), particularly in the chapter "Smiles of the Sphinx: Zola" 44–46.

23. For an analysis of this novel dealing with the problematic of the "male gaze" see Nancy Miller's brilliant chapter "Performances of the Gaze: Staël's *Corinne, or Italy,*" in *Subject to Change.*

24. See my article "Voice as Fossil" 52. In this analysis I am illustrating the importance of an archeological deciphering which I extend here according to the model implied by the myth of the Sibyl.

25. Sigmund Freud, *Délires et rêves dans la "Gradiva" de Jensen* (Paris: Gallimard, 1949). For a more detailed comparison of Staël's novel and Jensen's *Gradiva* see my article "Voice as Fossil" 53–54.

26. See my *Fictions féminines* 143–147.

27. See "Voice as fossil" ibid. Kaja Silverman analyzes in an insightful way for our thesis the appropriation of the woman's body by the fetishist in her book *The Acoustic Mirror* (Bloomington: Indiana University Press, 1988) 17–22.

28. See the chapter entitled "De l'enthousiasme" in *De l'Allemagne* (*Oeuvres complètes* 2: 251).

29. See *Fictions féminines* 186.

30. See Kaja Silverman's analysis of the passing of "melancholia" according to a reevaluation as well as a criticism of the preeminence of the attachment to the mother (as it is elaborated by Kristeva and Irigaray). It is this

phase that she isolates as "the Negative Oedipus complex" in *The Acoustic Mirror*, 155–162.

31. See Julia Kristeva, "Noms de lieu," in *Polylogue* (Paris: Seuil, 1977) 467–490.

32. See chapters 10, 11, and 12 in *De l'Allemagne*.

33. See Germaine de Staël's article from a review founded by Charles Pougens in 1800, rediscovered by Leo Neppi Modona and reprinted in *Cahiers Staëliens* 7 (1968): 17–31.

Corinne's Shift to Patriarchal Mediation: Rebirth or Regression?

1. *Corinne, or Italy*, trans. Avriel H. Goldberger (1807; New Brunswick, N.J.: Rutgers University Press, 1987) 20:4:413. Subsequent references will appear in the text and will indicate book, chapter, and page numbers. (The page numbers vary in different editions, but the book and chapter numbers do not.)

2. *An Extraordinary Woman: Selected Writings of Germaine de Staël*, trans. Vivian Folkenflik (New York: Columbia University Press, 1987) 25.

3. Madelyn Gutwirth, *Madame de Staël, Novelist: The Emergence of the Artist as Woman* (Urbana: University of Illinois Press, 1978). Those who have read *Corinne* in a way that is to some degree feminist also include Simone Balayé (Simone Balayé, ed., *Corinne ou l'Italie*, by Germaine de Staël [1807; Paris: Gallimard, 1985]); Claudine Herrmann (Claudine Herrmann, ed., *Corinne ou l'Italie*, by Germaine de Staël, 2 vols. [1807; Paris: Editions des femmes, 1979]); Avriel H. Goldberger (in her edition); Enzo Caramaschi ("Le point de vue féministe dans la pensée de Madame de Staël," *Voltaire, Madame de Staël, Balzac* [Padua: Liviana, 1977] 137–198); Marianne Spaulding Michaels ("Feminist Tendencies in the Work of Mme de Staël," diss., University of Connecticut, 1976); Ellen Moers (*Literary Women: The Great Writers* [Garden City, N.Y.: Anchor-Doubleday, 1977] ch. 9); Karen Frank Palmunen ("Mothers and Daughters in the Fiction of Mme de Staël," diss., Brown University, 1979); Ellen Peel ("Contradictions of Form and Feminism in *Corinne ou l'Italie*," *Essays in Literature* 14 [1987]: 281–298); and Marie-Claire Vallois ("Voice as Fossil—Madame de Staël's *Corinne or Italy*: An Archaeology of Feminine Discourse," *Tulsa Studies in Women's Literature* 6 [1987]: 47–60, and "Les Voi[es] de la Sibylle: Aphasie et discours féminin chez Mme de Staël," *Stanford French Review* 6 [1982]: 35–48). It would be reductive to assert that a feminist point of view is the only one from which to regard the novel, and it would be anachronistic to expect the book to fit neatly into a framework of twentieth-century feminism. Nonetheless, much can be learned by employing a feminist perspective, because the text is deeply concerned with women's condition.

4. My translation, 23.

5. Actually, only one of the Edgermond estates is in Northumberland,

whereas the other is near Edinburgh, as is the Nelvil estate. Despite these Scottish elements, Staël generally refers to the northern pole of her symbolic system as England.

6. In fact, in "Contradictions of Form and Feminism" I discuss troubling contradictions that arise even within the novel because it associates feminism with immediacy.

7. Gutwirth discusses Corinne's eloquence in "Du silence de Corinne et de sa parole," *Benjamin Constant, Madame de Staël et le Groupe de Coppet,* ed. Etienne Hofmann (Oxford: Voltaire Foundation, 1982) 427–434. Corinne is skilled in various arts, including writing, but is most known for her improvisations.

8. In this essay I am using "mediation" with the sense of distance and indirectness, in contrast to immediacy. "Mediation" can, however, have another meaning—reconcilement, in contrast to estrangement. In the second sense, Corinne does mediate. At times she acts as "mediatrix to humankind," connecting humanity with nature and heaven, as Gutwirth rightly observes in "Woman as Mediatrix: From Jean-Jacques Rousseau to Germaine de Staël" (*Woman as Mediatrix: Essays on Nineteenth-Century European Women Writers,* ed. Avriel H. Goldberger [Westport, Conn.: Greenwood, 1987] 23). At other times the heroine brings together disparate people or disparate cultures. But such efforts never conflict with her desire for immediacy and presence, for both tendencies work against separation. As practiced by Corinne, mediation has its second meaning: it links previously separate entities rather than separating entities whose relationship was previously close.

9. Vallois considers related issues. In "Voice as Fossil" she tells of critics who hope to hear Staël's voice speaking through her writings (48), and she describes Corinne as a sibyl possessed by others' voices (50). "Les Voi(es) de la Sibylle" similarly deals with *Corinne* as a text in which the mix of voices makes a unified self impossible and in which Italy speaks through the heroine (45).

10. Gutwirth sees Oswald as "mediating" between his father and others (*Madame de Staël, Novelist,* 225).

11. Staël quoted from her own father's writings to produce those of the late Lord Nelvil (8: 1: 427, n. 3; 12: 2: 430, nn. 5–6).

12. Various forms of Corinne's revenge have been noted by critics, including Moers (267) and Palmunen (272 ff.). Citing passages from the last book of the novel, Gutwirth says that Corinne is expressing "wrath of heroic proportions, barely tempered by the language of piety and resignation," but "since the posture of open hate and revulsion is too repellent to our erstwhile Apollonian heroine . . . to be openly assumed, a pose of fate-Erinnye will be the mediating role she adopts instead" (*Madame de Staël, Novelist,* 253). Gutwirth and I differ in emphasis; she stresses the wrath, and I stress the indirectness of its expression. The representation of underground anger recalls the "madwoman in the attic," a character described by Sandra M. Gilbert and Susan Gubar (*The Madwoman in the Attic: The Woman Writer and the Nine-*

teenth-Century Literary Imagination [New Haven: Yale University Press, 1979] 77–80). *Corinne* has no separate madwoman character, but the dying heroine resembles her in the mediated search for revenge.

13. In Goethe's *Wahlverwandtschaften* there appears a similar child named Otto, who resembles not his parents but their lovers. Otto represents the guilt of the parents who, in conceiving the child, thought of their lovers rather than each other.

14. But Gutwirth says of the "complicity" between Corinne and Lucile: "though it is pretended that its aim is Oswald's contentment, [it] seems far more like a pact against him" (*Madame de Staël, Novelist*, 253).

15. *Madame de Staël, Novelist*, 254, 256.

16. I use the term "powers of the weak" more pessimistically than Elizabeth Janeway (*Powers of the Weak* [New York: Knopf, 1980]). Palmunen refers to the "politics of the powerless" (257).

17. In a related way, Nancy K. Miller uses the term "'ricochet' effect" to describe how innocent victims like Mme de Tourvel in *Les Liaisons dangereuses* are appreciated and understood posthumously, making victims in turn of worldly characters like Valmont ("Novels of Innocence: Fictions of Loss," *Eighteenth-Century Studies* 11 [1978]: 333). *Corinne* modifies the pattern of the novels, written by men, that Miller discusses: in its two-woman/one-man triangle the heroine is *both* the innocent victim and the most worldly character. Perhaps feminist sensibilities enable Staël to understand more readily that female innocence can be compatible with knowledge and experience.

18. Jean Starobinski, "Suicide et mélancolie chez Mme de Staël," *Madame de Staël et l'Europe: Colloque de Coppet* (Paris: Klincksieck, 1970) 242.

19. Gutwirth, *Madame de Staël, Novelist*, 307.

20. My translation, *La destinée féminine dans le roman européen du XVIIIe siècle (1713–1807)* (Paris: Colin, 1972) 798. Although Fauchery's tone is sometimes condescending, he is making a helpful observation about how authors responded to the limited options that were available to their heroines. Also see Janet Todd, *Women's Friendships in Literature* (New York: Columbia University Press, 1980) 409–410.

21. Certain acts belong in only one of the two categories, and other acts belong simultaneously in both. The late Lord Nelvil, for instance, performs both kinds when he punishes Oswald indirectly and this punishment takes the form of ventriloquism, which makes the son a spokesman for the father's animus against Corinne.

22. Readers' reactions to *Corinne* are described by Charles Augustin Sainte-Beuve ("Madame de Staël," *Revue des Deux Mondes* 2 [1835]: 434–435), Gutwirth (*Madame de Staël, Novelist*, 256, 259–309), and Moers (263–319).

Narrating the French Revolution: The Example of *Corinne*

1. Simone Balayé, "'Corinne' et la presse parisienne de 1807," *Approches des lumières, mélanges offerts à Jean Fabre* (Paris: Klincksieck, 1974) 11–12.

2. Germaine de Staël, *Oeuvres complètes,* vol. 1 (Geneva: Slatkine Reprints, 1967) 245. All translations from French texts, with the exception of *Corinne,* are my own.

3. Henri Coulet, "Révolution et roman selon Mme de Staël," *Revue d'histoire littéraire de la France* 87 (1987): 638–660.

4. Carla L. Peterson, *The Determined Reader: Gender and Culture in the Novel from Napoleon to Victoria* (New Brunswick, N.J.: Rutgers University Press, 1986) 57–58.

5. Charlotte Hogsett, *The Literary Existence of Germaine de Staël* (Carbondale: Southern Illinois University Press, 1987) 66.

6. Mona Ozouf, *Festivals and the French Revolution,* trans. Alan Sheridan (Cambridge: Harvard University Press, 1988) 212.

7. See Madelyn Gutwirth, *Madame de Staël, Novelist: The Emergence of the Artist as Woman* (Urbana: University of Illinois Press, 1978) 175–181. See also Gutwirth's "Corinne et l'esthétique du camée," *Le Préromantisme: Hypothèque ou Hypothèse,* ed. Paul Viallaneix (Paris: Klincksieck, 1975) 153–168.

8. Nancy Armstrong, *Desire and Domestic Fiction* (New York: Oxford University Press, 1987) 5.

9. Ibid. 10.

10. Marina Warner, *Monuments and Maidens* (New York: Atheneum, 1985) 19, 27.

11. Lynn Hunt, *Politics, Culture, and Class in the French Revolution* (Berkeley: University of California Press, 1984) 13, 26.

12. Gutwirth, *Madame de Staël, Novelist,* 175.

13. Germaine de Staël, *Corinne, or Italy,* trans. Avriel H. Goldberger (New Brunswick, N.J.: Rutgers University Press, 1987) 21. Subsequent references to *Corinne* are from this edition.

14. Warner, *Monuments and Maidens,* 288–289.

15. Anita Brookner, *Jacques-Louis David* (London: Chatto & Windus, 1980) 12. However, although representations of Marat at the time of the revolution may have been artistically redolent of religious themes at a formal level, they did not assume genuine religious or divine meaning, as Frank Bowman has established in "Le 'Sacré-Coeur' de Marat (1793)," *Colloque de Clermont-Ferrand (1974),* ed. Jean Ehrard and Paul Viallaneix (Paris: Société des Etudes Robespierristes, 1977) 155–180.

16. Gutwirth, "Corinne et l'esthétique du camée," 242–243.

17. See also Gérard Gengembre's and Jean Goldzink's discussion of Italy versus England in "L'Opinion dans *Corinne,*" *Europe* 64 (1987): 48–57.

18. Marie-Claire Vallois, "Les Voi(es) de la Sibylle: Aphasie et discours

féminin chez Madame de Staël," *Stanford French Review* 6, no. 1 (1982): 38–52.

19. Peterson, *Determined Reader*, 48.

20. Vallois, "Les Voi(es) de la Sibylle," 45.

21. Monique Wittig, *Les Guérillères* (Paris: Minuit, 1969).

22. Maija Lehtonen, "Le Fleuve du temps et le fleuve de l'enfer: Thèmes et images dans *Corinne* de Madame de Staël," *Neuphilologische Mitteilungen* 69 (1969): 106–107.

Portrait of the Artist as Sappho

1. The following argument is developed at greater length in my *Fictions of Sappho, 1546–1937* (Chicago: University of Chicago Press, 1989).

2. François René, vicomte de Chateaubriand, "Préface," *Mémoires d'outre-tombe*, ed. Levaillant, 2 vols. (Paris: Garnier, 1949) 1: xxxi.

3. Alessandro Verri, *Le Avventure di Saffo*. 1780. *I Romanzi* (Ravenna: Lango, 1975).

4. Verri.

5. Germaine Necker, baronne de Staël, *Corinne ou l'Italie*, ed. Simone Balayé (Paris: Gallimard, 1985) 49. Subsequent references are given in the text by page number.

6. In a preface to Staël's last literary work, the tragedy *Sapho*, her son (who was publishing it posthumously) explains that "it is easy to see that [my mother] drew its original idea from *Corinne.*" Given that the play exploits virtually all that was known about Sappho in France at the turn of the nineteenth century, it is just as "easy to see" that the original idea for Staël's *Sapho*, and for her *Corinne*, was "drawn from" the eighteenth century's fictions of Sappho. Edith Mora was the first recent critic to discuss the resemblances between the plots of *Corinne* and Staël's *Sapho*. See *Sappho: Histoire d'un poète et traduction intégrale de l'oeuvre* (Paris: Flammarion, 1966).

7. Madelyn Gutwirth, *Madame de Staël, Novelist: The Emergence of the Artist as Woman* (Urbana: University of Illinois Press, 1978). Subsequent references are given in the text by page number.

8. Simone Balayé, *Madame de Staël: Lumières et liberté* (Paris: Klincksieck, 1979) 119.

9. A still unpublished letter proves that Staël knew Verri's Sapphic romance.

10. Béatrice d'Andlau, *La Jeunesse de Madame de Staël* (Geneva: Droz, 1970) 130.

11. Théodore Tarczylo, *Sexe et liberté au siècle des lumières* (Paris: Presses de la Renaissance, 1983).

12. Germaine de Staël, *Oeuvres complètes* vol. 16 (Paris: Treuttel & Wurtz, 1820–21) 279–360. Subsequent references are given in the text by page number.

13. As a keystone of its own militaristic, nationalistic project—the effects

of which only become clear on the eve of World War II—philology formulated, most authoritatively in a study published by Friedrich Gottlieb Welcker the year before Staël's death, the theory of Sappho's chastity. Unlikely though this may seem, Welcker and his heirs were familiar with the pulp fiction produced in Napoleonic Italy. I am also convinced that Welcker knew Staël's counterfiction, *Corinne*.

Staël's *Germany* and the Beginnings of an American National Literature

1. Georges Jules Joyaux, "French Thought in American Magazines, 1800–1848"(Ph.D. diss., Michigan State College, 1951). For the entire period Joyaux lists a total of eighty-seven articles.

2. In 1808 alone three editions of *Corinne, or Italy* appeared in America: in Boston (Belcher & Armstrong, in 2 vols.), in New York (D. Longworth, in 2 vols.), and in Philadelphia (Fry & Kammerer, in 2 vols.). In 1813 a Boston reprint of the second London edition of *De la littérature considérée dans ses rapports avec les institutions sociales* appeared as *The Influence of Literature upon Society*. In 1814 when her work *On Germany* appeared in New York (Eastburn, Kirk & Co., 3 vols. in 2), her early *Letters on the Writings and Character of Jean Jacques Rousseau* was published in Boston (Colburn). The *Considerations on the Principal Events of the French Revolution* appeared in New York (J. Eastburn & Co.) in 1818. Up into the second half of the century her major works were reissued repeatedly.

3. "A biographical Notice of Madame de Staël," *Portfolio* 16 (1816): 139–151; "A biographical sketch," *American Monthly Magazine and Critical Review* 2 (Dec. 1817): 146–150; Review article on *Notice sur le caractère et les écrits de Madame de Staël* (Paris, 1819), *The North American Review* 2 (July 1820): 124–140; Review of *Oeuvres inédites de Madame la Baronne de Staël* (Paris, 1821), ibid. 5 (Jan. 1822): 101–129.

4. *The North American Review* 20 July 1820: 125.

5. For Herder's role in the rise of an American concept of national culture and history, see my contribution "Herder and the Formation of an American National Consciousness in the Early Republic," in *Herder Today. Contributions from the International Herder Conference held November 5–8, 1987, Stanford, California* (Berlin and New York: De Gruyter, 1990) 415–430.

6. *The Edinburgh Review* 22 (1814): 198–233. Reprinted in America in the *Analectic Magazine* 3 (April 1814): 284–308.

7. *The Edinburgh Review* 21 (February 1813): 1–50. Reprinted in America in the *Analectic Magazine* 2 (1813): 186–208.

8. Mackintosh, philosopher, historian, lawyer, and politician, published his main work in philosophy, *Dissertation on the Progress of Ethical Philosophy, chiefly during the Seventeenth and Eighteenth Centuries*, only in 1830. Through the marriage of his wife's sister to Sismondi he was in contact with Staël and the Group of Coppet.

9. *The Edinburgh Review* 22 (1814): 201
10. Ibid., 200.
11. Ibid.
12. Ibid., 204
13. On Romantic hermeneutics: *The Hermeneutic Tradition from Ast to Ricoeur*, ed. Gayle L. Ormiston and Alan D. Schrift (Albany: SUNY Press, 1990); and *The Hermeneutics Reader*, ed. Kurt Mueller-Vollmer (New York: Continuum, 1988), especially 8–23, 72–118.
14. *The Edinburgh Review* 22 (1814): 220
15. Ibid., 227
16. Ibid., 221
17. For a well-documented discussion of Kant's reception among the New England Transcendentalists, see René Wellek, "The Minor Transcendentalists and German Philosophy," and "Emerson and German Philosophy," in *Confrontations: Studies in the Intellectual and Literary Relations between Germany, England, and the United States during the Nineteenth Century* (Princeton, N.J.: Princeton University Press, 1965) 153–186 and 187–212.
18. *The Edinburgh Review* 22 (1814): 221
19. Ralph Waldo Emerson, *The Journals and Miscellaneous Notebooks*, ed. Willam H. Gilman and Alfred R. Ferguson (Cambridge: Cambridge University Press, 1960f) vol. 1, 202: "The great warfare in Moral Science is between system (that is deduction from utility) and sentiment; and life between calculation and enthusiasm."
20. On the reception of Staël in England, see Roberta J. Forsberg, *Madame de Staël and the English* (New York: Astra Books, 1967).
21. Russel Blaine Nye, *The Cultural Life of the New Nation, 1776–1830* (New York: Harper, 1960) 235.
22. Mme de Staël, "Des universités allemandes," in *De l'Allemagne*, Première Partie, ch. XVIII, nouvelle édition publiée d'après les manuscrits et les éditions originales par Jean de Pange et Simone Balayé (Paris: Librairie Hachette, 1958–1960). All references are to this definitive edition, from now on quoted as *De l'Allemagne*. For specific testimonies see *The Life, Letters, and Journals of George Ticknor*, ed. George S. Hillard (Boston: James R. Osgood & Company, 1876) vol. 1: 11. On this early group of advocates for an American national culture, see Nye, *The Cultural Life of the New Nation*, 190f., 241ff., as well as the same author's *George Bancroft: Brahmin Rebel* (New York: Knopf, 1947) and *George Bancroft* (New York: Washington Square Press, 1964), Orie William Long's *Literary Pioneers. Early American Explorers of European Culture* (Cambridge: Harvard University Press, 1935) contains much valuable documentation. Harald Jantz in "German Thought and Literature in New England, 1620–1820," *The Journal of English and Germanic Philology*, 41 (1942): 1–45, disputes the importance of Staël's *On Germany* and of the activities of the German-educated American intellectuals for the reception of German culture in America, because there had been previous "intellectual contacts" between American and German culture on which the "available material . . . was not thin and sporadic, but rich, continuous

and significant." The long lists of book titles, names, and dates which Jantz supplies merely document a sometimes respectable interest in pre-Romantic, pre-Kantian German (mostly theological) literature by some equally respectable men in colonial and post-colonial American provincial society. Yet all of this was of no appreciable consequence for the development of an American national culture in the 19th century. The opposite is the case when it comes to the reception of German culture in the wake of Staël's *On Germany* and the activities of the German-educated New England intelligentsia during the 1820s. What happened then was part of a cultural and literary *prise de conscience* of the American nation.

23. Long, *Literary Pioneers* 18.

24. *The Life, Letters, and Journals of George Ticknor*, vol. 1: 98.

25. Ibid., 118f.

26. *The History of the United States from the Discovery of the American Continent*, 10 vols. (Boston: Little, Brown & Company, 1834–1875). Bancroft was the first among the American historians to read backward into the colonial period the concept of an American nationhood (which he and his New England friends helped create during the 1820s) and to reconstruct the beginnings of an "American" history. On Bancroft and the issue of American nationalism see my essay "Herder and the Formation of an American National Consciousness during the Early Republic," in *Herder Today. Contributions from the International Herder Conference, Nov. 5–8, 1987, Stanford California* (Berlin & New York: De Gruyter, 1990) 415–430.

27. Bancroft's *Studies in German Literature*, which first appeared as a series of articles, were published together in his *Literary and Historical Miscellanies* (New York: Harper & Brothers, 1855) 103–246.

28. As quoted in Nye, *The Cultural Life of the New Nation* 241.

29. Paul Revere Frothingham, *Edward Everett: Orator and Statesman* (Boston: Houghton Mifflin, 1925) 67.

30. Scott Holland Goodnight, *German Literature in American Magazines Prior to 1846*, Bulletin of the University of Wisconsin, No. 188, Philology and Literature Series, vol. 4, no. 1 (Madison, Wisconsin, December 1907).

31. Quoted in Nye, *The Cultural Life of the New Nation* 241.

32. Benjamin T. Spencer, *The Quest for Nationality. An American Literary Campaign* (Syracuse, N.Y.: Syracuse University Press, 1957), 160.

33. *Encyclopaedia Americana*, 13 vols. ed. Francis Lieber, assisted by E. Wigglesworth and T. G. Bradford (Philadelphia: Carey & Lea, 1829–1833). On Francis Lieber, see Frank B. Freidel, *Francis Lieber, Nineteenth-Century Liberal* (Baton Rouge: Louisiana State University Press, 1947).

34. On the reception of Staël among the New England Transcendentalists, see Emma G. Jaeck, *Madame de Staël and the Spread of German Literature* (New York: Oxford University Press, 1915) pt. 2, 251–342 (offers a helpful compilation of facts and names without much perspective); Benjamin T. Spencer, *The Quest for Nationality: An American Literary Campaign* (New York: Syracuse University Press, 1957) 91f, 293; Frederick Augustus Braun, *Margaret Fuller and Goethe* (New York: Henry Holt & Co., 1910) 31ff; Stan-

ley M. Vogel, *German Literary Influences on the American Transcendentalists* (New Haven: Yale University Press, 1957) 63–64; Henry A. Pochmann, *German Culture in America: Philosophical and Literary Influences, 1600–1900* (Madison: University of Wisconsin Press, 1957) 101–102, 552 n313, n314; René Wellek, *Confrontations* 187 n17. An excellent bibliographical overview is provided by Danielle Johnson-Cousin in her article, "The Reception of Madame de Staël's *De l'Allemagne* in America," *Actes du VIIè Congrès de l'Association Internationale de Littérature Comparée, Montréal-Ottawa, 1973* (Budapest: Publishing House of the Hungarian Academy of Sciences, 1973) 151–157.

35. *The North American Review,* 5 (January 1822): 102.

36. A turning point seems to be the recent German edition by Monika Bosse, *Madame de Staël: Über Deutschland* (Frankfurt a.M.: Insel Verlag, 1985) with its exemplary commentary and documentation.

37. Though enjoying a "tremendous vogue" in America at the time, according to Pochmann, what Staël had to tell the American public about "the new German culture" was "neither profound nor accurate," her discussions of German literature were often "vague and superficially facile," and the same supposedly holds true for her "feeble attempts to explain German metaphysics" (*German Culture in America* 101). The quotation is from Pochmann, *German Culture in America* 552, n314.

38. Ralph Waldo Emerson, W. H. Channing, J. F. Clarke, *Memoirs of Margaret Fuller Ossoli* vol. 2 (Boston: Roberts Brothers, 1874) 12–13: "Transcendentalism was an assertion of the inalienable integrity of man, of the immanence of Divinity in instinct. . . . On the somewhat stunted stock of Unitarianism had been grafted German Idealism, as taught by masters of most various schools,—by Kant and Jacobi, Fichte and Novalis, Schelling and Hegel, Schleiermacher and De Wette, by Madame de Staël, Cousin, Coleridge and Carlyle."

39. Ralph Waldo Emerson, *Essays and Lectures,* ed. Joel Porte (New York: Library of America, 1983) 1158–1159; *The Journals and Miscellaneous Notebooks,* vol. 7, 317 (Entry for Nov. 28, 1839), and vol. 8, 524, n18.

40. Braun, *Margaret Fuller and Goethe* 31.

41. Allen Margaret Vanderbaer, *The Achievements of Margaret Fuller* (University Park: The Pennsylvania State University Press, 1979) merely summarizes what had been known. The association of Margaret Fuller with Staël seems to have been something of a common place in the nineteenth century. See, for example, Thomas Wentworth Higginson's biography *Margaret Fuller Ossoli* (Boston: Houghton Mifflin & Co., 1887) 30, 37, 45, 109.

42. Quoted in Braun, *Margaret Fuller and Goethe* 19.

43. So Pochmann, *German Culture in America* 607, n418. Wellek, *Confrontations* 187, sees in Emerson "a remarkable artist who assimilated all foreign ideas" into his own way of expression. The point is, however, that such alleged "foreign ideas" are at the heart of romantic literary discourse, in Emerson as well as in Novalis or Coleridge.

44. Pochmann, *German Culture in America* 607, n418.

45. Thomas Carlyle, *Critical and Miscellaneous Essays,* vol. 1 (vol. 15 of Thomas Carlyle's *Works*) (London: The Ashburton Edition, 1887) 633.

46. Ibid. 443, 444.

47. "Kant voulut rétablir les vérités primitives et l'activité spontanée de l'âme, la conscience dans la morale, et l'idéal dans les arts" *De l'Allemagne* 4: 113. This means that Staël did not wish to describe Kant's philosophy in any technical sense, but only insofar as it concerned these three transcendentalist beliefs. (This and all other translations are my own.)

48. It seems significant that Emerson's usage of these terms should occur in his definition of Transcendentalism in his lecture, "The Transcendentalist," in 1842: "Idealism of the present day acquired the name of Transcendental, from the use of that term by Immanuel Kant of Königsberg, who replied to the sceptical philosophy of Locke . . . that there was a very important class of idea, or imperative forms, which did not come by experience" (*Essays and Lectures* 198).

49. *The Journals and Miscellanous Notebooks* 202. He calls the Leibnizean phrase "the great improvement of modern philosophy." But it had already been quoted by Mackintosh in his review of *On Germany* in *The Edinburgh Review* 22 (Oct. 1813): 237. It occurs in *De l'Allemagne* 4: 108, where the original Latin formulation is given.

50. *De l'Allemagne* 4: 187.

51. Ibid. 136.

52. Ibid. 187f. "l'enthousiasme se rallie à l'harmonie universelle: c'est l'amour du beau, l'élévation de l'âme, la jouissance du dévouement, réunis dans un même sentiment qui a de la grandeur et du calme."

53. A promising beginning was made over twenty-five years ago by Kenneth Walter Cameron, *A Commentary on Emerson's Early Lectures (1833–1836), with an Index Concordance* (Hartford, Conn.: Transcendental Books, 1961) which even bears the dedication: "To Madame de Staël whose *Germany* awakened young Emerson at Harvard in 1820–1821 and whose voice pleads in these lectures for a brave new world." But besides providing a superfluous synopsis of *On Germany* (based strangely enough only on part 3 of the book), Cameron's commentary never succeeds in thematizing the Emerson/Staël relation in any consequential way.

54. Ralph Waldo Emerson, *Nature, The Conduct of Life and Other Essays,* introduction by Sherman Paul (London: Dutton, 1970) 21. Cf.: *The Journals and Miscellaneous Notebooks,* vol. 4 (Nov. 16–18, 1834) 337.

55. "Presque tous les axiomes de physique correspondent à des maximes de morale" *De l'Allemagne* 4: 246.

56. Another formulation in chap. 10 (note 59) of the correspondence theory which is also echoed in Emerson's *Nature* reads: "C'est une belle conception que celle qui tend à trouver la ressemblance des lois de l'entendement humain avec celle de la nature, et considérer le monde physique comme le relief du monde moral" (Ibid. 245).

57. *Nature* 15.

58. *De l'Allemagne,* 2: 118.

59. *Nature* 15.

60. *De l'Allemagne* 5: 166–167.

61. In the final version the forty lines of alleged excerpts from Novalis represent a segment of exactly 131 lines of the original German text: *De l'Allemagne* 5: 164, ll. 8–13; 165, ll. 1–16; 166, ll. 1–13; 167, ll.1–4; *Novalis: Schriften*, ed. P. Kluckhohn and R. Samuel, rev. R. Samuel (Darmstadt: Wissenschaftliche Buchgesellschaft, 1971) 1: 85, ll.1–88, 23.

62. The Novalis passage from which Staël's concluding statement has been developed reads: "Keiner irrt gewiss weiter ab vom Ziele, als wer sich selbst einbildet, er kenne schon das seltsame Reich, und wisse mit wenig Worten seine Verfassung zu ergründen und überall den rechten Weg zu finden. Von selbst geht keinem, der los sich riss und sich zur Insel machte, das Verständnis auf, auch ohne Mühe nicht. Nur Kindern, oder kindlichen Menschen, die nicht wissen, was sie thun, kann dies begegnen. Langer, unablässiger Umgang, freie und künstliche Betrachtung, Aufmerksamkeit auf leise Winke und Züge, ein inneres Dichterleben, geübte Sinne, ein einfaches und gottesfürchtiges Gemüth, das sind die wesentlichen Erfordernisse eines ächten Naturfreundes, ohne welche keinem sein Wunsch gedeihen wird" (*Novalis Schriften,* 87, ll. 13–24). The version in Ms. A already reflects a process of condensation and semantic transformation of the original: "Nul n'est plus éloigné de la connaissance de la nature que celui qui se persuade qu'il connaît déjà son inconcevable empire et qu'il peut ⟨l'embrasser⟩ l'expliquer en quelques mots, ou trouver un chemin direct ⟨qui va droit⟩ pour arriver au but. Celui qui veut l'observer comme ⟨s'il en étoit séparé⟩ s'il ne faisoit pas un avec elle n'en aura jamais la moindre idée." Here a positive term ("s'il ne faisoit pas un avec elle") has replaced Novalis's negative one ("der sich losriss"). In other words, it is Staël's own Transcendentalist conception of the correspondence theory that surfaces in her reworking of the text and culminates in the final (published) formulation: "Il faut, pour connoître la nature, devenir un avec elle" (*De l'Allemagne* 5: 166).

63. Ibid. 186.

64. Melville's personal copy of *On Germany* with his markings and annotations is preserved in the Houghton Library at Harvard University.

Staël: Liberal Political Thinker

1. On this topic, see Susan Tenenbaum, "Liberal Heroines: Mme de Staël on the 'Woman Question' and the Modern State," *Annales Benjamin Constant* 5 (1985): 37–52.

2. Edmund Burke, *Reflections on the Revolution in France* (Indianapolis: Bobbs-Merrill Co., 1955) 109.

3. Joseph de Maistre, *On God and Society* (Chicago: Henry Regenry, 1959) 29.

4. Germaine de Staël, *Des circonstances actuelles qui peuvent terminer la Révolution française* (Paris: Fischbacker, 1904) 137. (Translation is mine.)

Two Views of the *Considerations on the French Revolution*

1. The specifics of Revolutionary language and eloquence have been brought out in recent studies, for instance in *La Carmagnole des muses* (Paris: Armand Colin, 1988). See the contributions of Jean-Claude Bonnet and Philippe Roger.

2. Aurelio Principato, "La tradition rhétorique et la crise révolutionnaire: l'attitude de Mme de Staël," *Annales Benjamin Constant* 8–9 (1988) 107–120.

3. Michel Delon, "La métaphore théâtrale dans les *Considérations sur la Révolution française*," *Annales Benjamin Constant* 8–9 (1988) 163–173.

Staël and the Fascination of Suicide: The Eighteenth-Century Background

1. John McManners, *Death and the Enlightenment* (Oxford: Oxford University Press, 1981) 409.

2. See Montaigne, *Essais*, book 2, chap. 3; Charron, *De la sagesse*, book 2, chap. 11. Also see Lester G. Crocker, "The Discussion of Suicide in the Eighteenth Century," *Journal of the History of Ideas* 13 (1952): 47–72.

3. Montesquieu, *Persian letters*, trans. J. Robert Loy (New York: Meridian Books, 1961) 156–157. All other translations in this article are my own.

4. Ibid. 279.

5. Roland Mortier, *La Poétique des ruines* (Geneva: Droz, 1974).

6. Diderot, *Salons, Salon de 1767* (Oxford: Oxford University Press, 1963) 228–229. My translation. For an analysis of this new aesthetic of the sublime, see Gita May, "Diderot and Burke: A Study in Aesthetic Affinity," *Publications of the Modern Language Association of America* 75 (December 1960): 527–539.

7. Rousseau, *La Nouvelle Héloïse* (Paris: Garnier Flammarion, 1963) 278–291. See also Jean-Albert Bédé, "Mme de Staël, Rousseau, et le suicide," *Revue d'Histoire Littéraire de la France* 66 (January–March 1966): 52–70.

8. Ibid. 356.

9. Ibid. 357.

10. Ibid. 373.

11. *Lettres sur les écrits et le caractère de J.-J. Rousseau* (Paris: H. Nicolle, 1814) 189.

12. Ibid. 262–263.

13. *Réflexions sur le suicide* (Paris: H. Nicolle, 1814) 2.

14. Ibid. 38.

15. Ibid. 40–41.

16. On Corinne's self-willed death, see Jean Starobinski, "Suicide et mélancolie chez Mme de Staël," *Madame de Staël et l'Europe: Colloque de Coppet*

(Paris: Editions Klincksieck, 1970) 242–253. Also see Gita May, "Le Staëlisme de Corinne," *Symposium* 12 (Spring–Fall 1958): 168–177.

17. See Gita May, *Madame Roland and the Age of Revolution* (New York: Columbia University Press, 1970).

18. See Madelyn Gutwirth, "Madame de Staël, Rousseau, and the Woman Question," *Publications of the Modern Language Association of America* 86 (January 1971): 100–109. Also see her important study, *Madame de Staël, Novelist: The Emergence of the Artist as Woman* (Urbana: University of Illinois Press, 1966).

Germaine de Staël among the Romantics

1. J. Christopher Herold, *Mistress to an Age, a Life of Madame de Staël* (Indianapolis: Bobbs-Merrill, 1958).

2. Chateaubriand, *Mémoires d'outre-tombe*, IV, xii, chap. 9. Emphasis mine.

3. "Cet examen nous conduira . . . à juger l'action d'immoler sa vie sous deux points de vue absolument contraires, le sacrifice inspiré par la vertu, ou le dégoût qui résulte des passions trompées" (*Réflexions sur le suicide, Oeuvres complètes* [Paris: Firmin-Didot, 1838] 1: 186.) Further references are given in the text by page number.

4. Bédé, "Madame de Staël, Rousseau et le suicide," *RHLF* 66, no. 1 (January–March 1966): 66.

5. Staël, *Oeuvres complètes* 1: 130.

6. See Joan DeJean, "Portrait of the Artist as Sappho," in this volume.

7. George Sand, *Lélia*, ed. B. Didier (Meylan: Editions de l'Aurore, 1987) 2: 25. Further references are given in the text by volume and page number.

8. There was also a copy of *Corinne* in its original 1807 edition in Sand's library at Nohant. But when she actually read it is not precisely known.

9. Sainte-Beuve, "Madame de Staël," *Portraits de femmes, Oeuvres complètes* (Paris: Pléiade, 1960) 2: 1107.

10. George Sand, *Correspondance*, ed. Georges Lubin (Paris: Garnier, 1967) 3: 434.

11. "Est-ce un homme, une femme, est-ce un ange, un démon? De quel genre te faire, équivoque sublime? Sand, es-tu fils des cieux ou fille de l'abyme? Es-tu Sapho, de Staël, ou Jean-Jacques ou Byron?" Cited by Georges Lubin, ed., in George Sand, *Correspondance* (Paris: Garnier, 1966) 2: 722 note.

12. Marie-Jacques Hoog, "George Sand and the Romantic Sibyl," *Proceedings of the Seventh George Sand Conference* (New York: University Press of America, forthcoming).

13. Germaine de Staël, *Corinne*, ed. Simone Balayé (Paris: Folio, 1985) 353. Further references will be given in the text by page number.

14. George Sand, *Histoire de ma vie, Oeuvres autobiographiques*, ed. Georges Lubin (Paris: Pléiade, 1971) 2: 159.

15. Staël, *Sapho, Oeuvres complètes* (Paris: Treuttel and Würtz, 1821) 16: 281.

16. I am using here Avriel Golberger's translation of *Corinne* (New Brunswick, N.J.: Rutgers University Press, 1987) 245.

17. Béatrice Didier, in her introduction to *Lélia*, expresses it this way: "Sand a trouvé dans le roman de Mme de Staël [*Corinne*] la confirmation de ce qu'elle avait vécu dans sa propre vie: la difficulté pour une femme de concilier la supériorité de l'intelligence, la volonté de créer, avec le bonheur, avec l'existence à deux" (*Lélia* 1: 22).

18. Sainte-Beuve, "Mme de Staël," in *Portraits de femmes, Oeuvres complètes*, 2: 1133. Emphasis mine.

Corinne as an Autonomous Heroine

1. Paramount, 1987; directed by Adrian Lyne.

2. Ellen Moers, *Literary Women: The Great Writers* (Garden City, N.Y.: Doubleday, 1976) 173, 174.

3. Folio edition (Paris: Gallimard, 1985) 214–215, 219–220.

4. *Memoirs of a Dutiful Daughter*, trans. James Kirkup (Harmondsworth: Penguin Books, 1977), 89–91, 110–111, 140.

5. Marie-Claire Vallois, *Fictions féminines: Mme de Staël et les voix de la Sibylle*. Stanford French and Italian Studies (Stanford: Anma Libri, 1987) ix. Staël, *De l'Allemagne*, chap. 18, "De la disposition romanesque dans les affections du coeur,"in *Oeuvres complètes* (Paris: Treuttel and Würtz, 1836) 3: 217, "Les femmes cherchent à s'arranger comme un roman, et les hommes comme une histoire." Translating this line illustrates the difficulty in making the distinction and the standard translation appears to contradict what I am saying. In eighteenth-century French usage, *roman* commonly meant a far-fetched idealistic fiction, or "romance"; since the nineteenth century, it has more often meant a realistic fiction, or "novel." *Histoire* was often used in the titles of fictions intended to be true to life, believable, or "realistic" in a loose sense; still today it can be translated into English as either "history" or "story." My point is that the line might equally well be translated as "Women try to present themselves as romances, and men as novels."

6. *Corinne*, book 16 chap. 4. Quoted from the "édition féministe" by Claudine Herrmann (Paris: Editions des Femmes, 1979) 2: 168. Translation by Avriel H. Goldberger, *Corinne, or Italy* (New Brunswick, N.J.: Rutgers University Press, 1987) 315.

Politics, Feminism, and Patriarchy: Rereading *Corinne*

1. My remarks on *Corinne* are adapted from the discussion of the novel in my book *Subject to Change: Reading Feminist Writing* (New York: Columbia University Press, 1988).

2. For further discussion of Staël and Sand, see Isabelle Naginski's essay in the present volume.

3. Carla Peterson makes this point in her book, *The Determined Reader: Gender and Culture in the Novel from Napoleon to Victoria* (New Brunswick, N.J.: Rutgers University Press, 1986).

4. Joan DeJean has addressed the question of generations in "Staël's Corinne: The Novel's Other Dilemma," *Stanford Literature Review* (Spring 1987).

5. *Fictions féminines: Mme de Staël et les voix de la Sibylle* (Stanford: Anma Libri, 1987).

BIBLIOGRAPHY

The decline in the literary reputation of Germaine de Staël in the course of the nineteenth century and during the first part of the twentieth is in inverse proportion to its extraordinary strength while she was alive. Retained in the manuals of literature as an important transitional figure and as a force in the delineation of romantic doctrine in the preromantic period, she was ejected from the canon of authors to be read. Yet her genius was readily acknowledged by such of her celebrated contemporaries as Goethe, Schlegel, Sismondi, Schiller, and, though less enthusiastically, by Chateaubriand, and echoed by Lamartine and even Sainte-Beuve. Her women readers, who followed her avidly, some of them trying even to be Corinne, numbered George Sand, George Eliot, Jane Austen, Mary Godwin Shelley, Charlotte Brontë, Fanny Kemble, and Elizabeth Barrett Browning. It has been known for some time that in the United States, Margaret Fuller, Lydia Maria Child, Willa Cather, and others strongly felt her influence, but it is only in the present volume that Kurt Mueller-Vollmer shows her central importance for the American Transcendentalists.

Until the new era in Staël studies of recent years, Staël has been obliged to pay in her literary reputation what has never been accepted or forgiven her private reputation. That is, she is still paying for a sexual freedom in her private life that is overlooked or cheerfully admitted in male writers. She is still penalized for her efforts to play a political role in the events of her day. For example, Christopher Herold's carefully researched and tendentiously titled *Mistress to an Age* (1958) denigrates the author, as does Ghislain de Diesbach's *Madame de Staël* (1983). Even feminist writers like Ellen Moers in *Literary Women* (1976) and Julia Kristeva in her article on Staël in *Romantisme* (1988) suffer from such an approach.

The modern era of Staël studies, begun in the 1920s, was given lasting impetus by the founding of the Société des études staëliennes in Paris by the Comtesse de Pange in 1929 and its continuation after her death by her·son Victor. Since the 1960s, long-held attitudes about Staël have been revised in the light of new insights. Under the guidance of Simone Balayé, dean of Staël studies, the scope and activities of the Society and of Staël studies generally have increasingly broadened. Under Balayé's presidency, there have been four major conferences, eleven one-day seminars at Coppet, and two meetings per year in Paris. Thanks to her tireless efforts, a body of authoritative texts is being established and previously unpublished material is being made available. Her own writing on Staël gives new and invaluable perspective on the writer and her period. Not only has Balayé thus provided a framework for renewed exploration, but she has encouraged it the world over by her example and personal generosity. Enlightened by her groundbreaking *Lumières et Liberté* (1979), we await publication of the definitive biography now under preparation.

On this side of the Atlantic, Madelyn Gutwirth has been the moving force behind the creation of vigorously pursued research into Staël's work, writing extensively on the author since the 1960s, giving precious time and encouragement to all those who come to her for discussion and aid. With the publication of her revolutionary book on Staël subtitled *The Emergence of the Artist as Woman* (1978), she has provided a baseline for study of the author in the light of developing feminist theory.

Despite the mocking tone of Ellen Moers's chapter on Staël in *Literary Women* (1975), the American critic did launch a productive search for filiations in the English-speaking world, and by extension for filiations in France. Recent studies, articles, and books have focused on the writer's literary voice.

Concurrent with the renewed interest in Staël as a political thinker, and necessary to an exhaustive pursuit of the subject, is the establishment of authoritative editions of all of her work. A great deal has been done already, and we now await the *Considerations on the French Revolution*. This is the major remaining work as yet available only in the modified form Auguste de Staël found advisable to publish after his mother's death in 1817, when the political climate was hostile to her ideas.

As the list below suggests, there is strong interest in study of Staël's literary voice, often subversively and indirectly asserted in a world dominated by patriarchal discourse. In this area, critics such as Charlotte Hogsett, Marie-Claire Vallois, Joan DeJean and Nancy K. Miller have made important contributions.

The bibliography appended is of course only a partial one, designed to answer the desires of American readers who wish to pursue an interest in Staël's work. One area in which a great deal of work needs to be done is that of translation, where, as the listing below reveals, the English-speaking public has but limited access to Staël's writing. Vivian Folkenflik has provided a much-needed anthology, while Avriel Goldberger has published *Corinne* and is currently working on *Delphine*. Given the breadth and volume of the Staëlian production, these are clearly only a beginning.

Works by Germaine de Staël

FIRST EDITIONS

Oeuvres complètes, 17 vols. (Paris: Treuttel and Würtz, 1820–1821; Geneva: Slatkine Reprints 1836 and 1967).

MODERN EDITIONS

De la littérature considérée dans ses rapports avec les institutions sociales. Edition critique par Paul Van Tieghem. (Geneva: Droz; Paris: Minard, 1959).

De l'Allemagne. Edition critique par Jean de Pange avec le concours de Simone Balayé. 5 vols. (Paris: Hachette, 1958–1960).

Delphine. Une édition féministe de Claudine Herrmann. (Paris: Editions des Femmes, 1981). Edition continue de Simone Balayé et Lucia Omacini. (Geneva: Droz, 1987).

Corinne ou l'Italie. Une édition féministe de Claudine Herrmann. (Paris: Editions des Femmes, 1979). Edition présentée, établie et annotée par Simone Balayé. (Paris: Gallimard, 1985).

Considérations sur la Révolution française. Introduction, bibliographie, chronologie, et notes par Jacques Godechot. (Paris: Tallandier, 1983).

Dix années d'exil. Introduction et notes par Simone Balayé. (Paris: Bibliothèque 10/18, 1966).

Correspondance générale. Texte établi et présenté par Béatrice W. Jasinski. (Paris: Pauvert, 1960–1978; Hachette, 1982–1985).

Mon Journal. Publié par Simone Balayé, in *Cahiers Staëliens* 28 (1980): 55–79.

Des circonstances actuelles qui peuvent terminer la Révolution et des principes qui doivent fonder la république en France. Edition critique de Lucia Omacini. (Geneva: Droz, 1979).

MODERN TRANSLATIONS

Madame de Staël on Politics, Literature, and National Character, trans., ed., and with an introduction by Morroe Berger (Garden City, N.Y.: Doubleday, 1964).

Ten Years of Exile, trans. Doris Beik, with an introduction by Peter Gay (New York: Saturday Review Press, 1972).

Corinne, or Italy, trans. and ed. Avriel H. Goldberger (New Brunswick, N.J.: Rutgers University Press, 1987).

An Extraordinary Woman. Selected Writings of Germaine de Staël, trans. and with an introduction by Vivian Folkenflik (New York: Columbia University Press, 1987).

Congress Proceedings

Madame de Staël et l'Europe. Actes du Colloque de Coppet, 18–24 juillet 1966, organisé pour la célébration du deuxième centenaire de la naissance de Madame de Staël. Préface par Jean Fabre et Simone Balayé. (Paris: Klincksieck, 1970).

Le Préromantisme: hypothèque ou hypothèse. Colloque organisé à Clermont Ferrand les 29 et 30 juin 1972 par le Centre de Recherches Révolutionnaires et Romantiques de l'Université. Paul Viallaneix, ed. (Paris: Klincksieck, 1975).

Le Groupe de Coppet. Actes et documents du deuxième Colloque de Coppet, 10–13 juillet 1974 (Geneva: Slatkine; Paris: Champion, 1977).

Le Groupe de Coppet et l'Allemagne. Actes du Colloque au Goethe Institut, 10–11 mai 1985. Préface par Simone Balayé et Erika Tunner. *Cahiers staëliens* 37 (1985–1986).

Benjamin Constant, Madame de Staël et le Groupe de Coppet. Actes du 2e Congrès de Lausanne à l'occasion du 150e anniversaire de la mort de Benjamin Constant et du 3e Colloque de Coppet, 15–19 juillet, 1980. Etienne Hofmann, ed. (Oxford: Voltaire Foundation; Lausanne: Institut Benjamin Constant, 1982).

Le Groupe de Coppet et la Révolution française. Actes du quatrième Colloque de Coppet, 20–23 juillet 1988 (Lausanne: Institut Benjamin Constant, 1988).

Critical Studies

Balayé, Simone. "Absence, exil, voyage," in *Madame de Staël et l'Europe* (Paris: Klincksieck, 1970) 289–300.

———. *Les Carnets de voyage de Madame de Staël: Contribution à la genèse de ses oeuvres* (Geneva: Droz, 1971).

———. "Fonction romanesque de la musique et des sons dans *Corinne,*" *Romantisme* 3 (1972): 17–32.

———. "A propos du 'préromantisme': continuité ou rupture chez Madame de Staël," in *Le Préromantisme: hypothèque ou hypothèse.* Paul Viallaneix, ed. (Paris: Klincksieck, 1975) 153–168.

———. *Madame de Staël: Lumières et liberté* (Paris: Klincksieck, 1979).

———. "Du sens romanesque de quelques oeuvres d'art dans *Corinne* de

Mme de Staël," in *Littératures. Mélanges offerts à André Monchoux* (Toulouse: Le Mirail, 1979) 345–364.

Blanchard, Paula. "*Corinne* and the 'Yankee Corinna': Madame de Staël and Margaret Fuller." In *Woman as Mediatrix: Nineteenth-Century Women Writers*, ed. Avriel Goldberger (Westport, Conn.: Greenwood Press, 1987).

Bowman, Frank. "Mme de Staël et l'apologétique romantique," in *Madame de Staël et l'Europe* (Paris: Klincksieck, 1970) 157–170.

Borowitz, Helen. "The Unconfessed Précieuse: Madame de Staël's Debt to Mademoiselle Scudéry." *Nineteenth-Century French Studies* 1–2 (Fall–Winter 1982): 32–59.

Bosse, Monika. "*Corinne ou l'Italie*: Diagnostic d'un dilemme historique," in *Il Gruppo di Coppet et l'Italia* (Pisa: Pacini, 1988) 83–107.

———. "*Zulma* ou l'esthétique de la Révolution, à la lumière de l'*Essai sur les fictions*," in *Le Groupe de Coppet et la Révolution française* (Lausanne: Institut Benjamin Constant, 1988) 141–161.

DeJean, Joan. "Staël's *Corinne*: The Novel's Other Dilemma." *Stanford French Review* 11 (Spring 1987): 77–87.

———. *Fictions of Sappho 1546–1937* (Chicago: University of Chicago Press, 1989).

Delon, Michel. "La métaphore théâtrale dans *Les Considérations*" in *Le Groupe de Coppet et la Révolution française* (Lausanne: Institut Benjamin Constant, 1988) 163–173.

———. "La Saint-Barthélemy et la Terreur chez Mme de Staël et les historiens de la Révolution au XIXème siècle." *Romantisme* 31 (1981): 49–62.

Diesbach, Ghislain de, *Madame de Staël* (Paris: Librairie Académique Perrin, 1984).

Goldberger, Avriel H. "Germaine de Staël's *Corinne*: Challenges to the Translator in the 80s." *French Review* 63/5 (Spring 1990): 800–809.

Gutwirth, Madelyn. "Madame de Staël's Debt to *Phèdre: Corinne*." *Studies in Romanticism* 3 (1964): 161–176.

———. "Madame de Staël, Rousseau, and the Woman Question." *PMLA* 86 (January 1971): 100–109.

———. *Madame de Staël, Novelist: The Emergence of the Artist as Woman* (Urbana: University of Illinois Press, 1978).

———. "La *Delphine* de Madame de Staël: femme, révolution, et mode épistolaire." *Cahiers Staëliens* 26–27 (1979): 151–165.

———. "Forging a Vocation: Germaine de Staël on Fiction, Power, and Passion." *Bulletin of Research in the Humanities* 86 (1983–1985): 242–254.

———. "Women as Mediatrix: From Jean-Jacques Rousseau to Germaine de Staël." In *Woman as Mediatrix: Nineteenth-Century Women Writers*, ed. Avriel H. Goldberger (Westport, Conn.: Greenwood Press, 1987) 13–29.

Gwynne, G. E. *Mme de Staël: femme, la Révolution Française, politique, philosophie, littérature* (Paris: Nizet, 1969).

Herold, Christopher. *Mistress to an Age: A Life of Madame de Staël* (Indianapolis: Bobbs-Merrill, 1958).

Higonnet, Margaret R. "*Delphine*: d'une guerre civile à l'autre," in *Le*

Groupe de Coppet et la Révolution française (Lausanne: Institut Benjamin Constant, 1988) 211–222.

Hogsett, Charlotte. *The Literary Existence of Germaine de Staël* (Carbondale: Southern Illinois University Press, 1987).

Kitchin, Joanna. "La littérature et les femmes selon Madame de Staël." In *Benjamin Constant, Madame de Staël, et le Groupe de Coppet,* ed. Etienne Hofmann (Oxford: The Voltaire Foundation and Lausanne: Institut Benjamin Constant, 1980) 401–425.

Kristeva, Julia. "Gloire, deuil et écriture. Lettre à un 'romantique' sur Mme de Staël." *Romantisme* 62 (1988): 7–14.

Man, Paul de. "Madame de Staël et Jean-Jacques Rousseau." *Preuves* 190 (1966): 35–40.

Mercken-Spaas, Godelieve. "Death and the Romantic Heroine: Chateaubriand and de Staël." In *Pre-Text, Text, Context. Essays on Nineteenth-Century French Literature,* ed. Robert L. Mitchell (Columbus: Ohio State University Press, 1980) 79–86.

Miller, Nancy K. "Performances of the Gaze: Staël's *Corinne, or Italy.*" In *Subject to Change: Reading Feminist Writing* (New York: Columbia University Press, 1988) 162–203.

Moers, Ellen. "Performing Heroism: The Myth of Corinne." In *Literary Women: The Great Writers* (Garden City, N.Y.: Doubleday, 1976) 173–210.

Peel, Ellen. "Contradictions of Form and Feminism in *Corinne ou l'Italie.*" *Essays in Literature* 14 (1987): 281–298.

Peterson, Carla L. "*Corinne* and *Louis Lambert:* Romantic Myth Making." In *The Determined Reader: Gender and Culture in the Novel from Napoleon to Victoria* (New Brunswick, N.J.: Rutgers University Press, 1986) 37–81.

Posgate, Helen B. *Madame de Staël* (New York: Twayne, 1969).

Poulet, George, "La pensée critique de Madame de Staël." *Preuves* 190 (December 1966): 27–35.

Sourian, Eve. *Madame de Staël et Henri Heine: les deux Allemagnes* (Paris: Didier, 1974).

Starobinski, Jean. "Suicide et mélancolie chez Mme de Staël." In *Madame de Staël et l'Europe: Colloque de Coppet,* ed. Jean Fabre and Simone Balayé (Paris: Klincksieck, 1970) 242–252.

Swallow, Noreen J. "The Weapon of Personality: A Review of Sexist Criticism of Madame de Staël." *Atlantis* 8/1 (Fall 1982): 79–82.

Szmurlo, Karyna. "Le jeu et le discours féminin: la danse de l'héroïne staëlienne." *Nineteenth-Century French Studies* 15 (Fall–Winter, 1986/87): 1–13.

Tenenbaum, Susan. "Literary Criticism as Political Discourse." *History of Political Thought* 1/3 (1980): 453–473.

———. "Liberal Heroines. Staël on the 'Women Question' and the Modern State." *Annales Benjamin Constant* 5 (1985): 37–52.

Vallois, Marie-Claire. *Fictions féminines: Mme de Staël et les voix de la Sibylle* (Stanford: Anma Libri, 1987).

NOTES ON THE CONTRIBUTORS

SIMONE BALAYÉ, Conservateur at the Bibliothèque Nationale in Paris, is the foremost Staël scholar of this era. Editor with Mme Jean de Pange of the Hachette edition of *De l'Allemagne* (1958–1960), she has also been sole editor of Staël's *Lettres à Ribbing* (Gallimard, 1960) and her *Carnets de voyage* (Droz, 1971). Author of numerous articles, historical and interpretive, on all facets of Staël's work, her *Madame de Staël, lumières et liberté* was published by Klincksieck in 1979. Simone Balayé presides over the Société des études staëliennes, which publishes the *Cahiers staëliens*, a review on the works and careers of Staël and the Groupe de Coppet, her circle of scholar-authors.

FRANK PAUL BOWMAN is Professor of Romance Languages at the University of Pennsylvania. His recent publications include *Le Christ des barricades, 1789–1848* (Editions de Cerf, 1987) and *French Romanticism, Intertextual and Interdisciplinary Readings* (The Johns Hopkins University Press, 1990).

JOAN DEJEAN is Trustee Professor at the University of Pennsylvania. She is the author of *Fictions of Sappho, 1546–1937* and co-editor (with Nancy K. Miller) of *Displacements: Women, Tradition, Literatures in French*.

MICHEL DELON, before becoming Professor of French literature at the University of Paris-Nanterre, taught at the Universities of Caen and

Orléans. He is the author of *L'Idée d'énergie au tournant des Lumières* (P.U.F., 1988), *Les Liaisons dangereuses de Laclos* (P.U.F., 1986), and coauthor (with R. Mauzi and S. Menant) of *De l'Encyclopédie aux Méditations* (Arthaud, 1984). He is currently editing Sade's works at the Bibliothèque de la Pléiade.

BEATRICE FINK, Professor of French at the University of Maryland, served as Secretary-General of the International Society for 18th-Century Studies (1979–1987). She is the author of numerous articles in American and European journals and the editor of special issues of *Dix-huitième siècle, Eighteenth-Century Life, Annales Benjamin Constant* (forthcoming).

AVRIEL GOLDBERGER is Professor and Chair of French at Hofstra University. Her translation of Staël's *Corinne* with introduction and notes was published by Rutgers University Press in 1987. In April 1991, the same press brought out her translation of Emilie Carles's autobiography, *A Life of Her Own: A Country Woman in Twentieth-Century France*. She is currently working on a new English version of Staël's *Delphine*.

MADELYN GUTWIRTH, Professor of French and Women's Studies at West Chester University of Pennsylvania, is the author of *Madame de Staël, Novelist: The Emergence of the Artist as Woman* (University of Illinois Press, 1978) and of other studies on Staël and Laclos. She is preparing a book for Rutgers University Press entitled, "The Twilight of the Goddesses: Representations of Women in the French Revolutionary Era."

MARGARET R. HIGONNET, Professor of English and Comparative Literature at the University of Connecticut, has edited *The Representation of Women in Fiction, Behind the Lines: Gender and the Two World Wars,* and the journal *Children's Literature*. She has published articles on Mme de Staël, literary theory, the German romantics, women's suicide, and children's literature in journals such as *Critical Inquiry, Comparative Literature,* and *Poetics Today*.

CHARLOTTE HOGSETT teaches Latin and French at Richland Northeast High School in Columbia, South Carolina. She is the author of *The Literary Existence of Germaine de Staël* (Southern Illinois University Press, 1987).

DORIS Y. KADISH, Professor of French and Chair of Romance Languages at Kent State University, has written papers on nineteenth- and twentieth-century French novelists, notably Balzac, Flaubert, and Gide. She is also the author of books on Nobel writer Claude Simon (*Practices of the New Novel*) and nineteenth-century description of landscape (*The Literature of Images*). Her study of narrative and artistic representations of women in the aftermath of the French Revolution, entitled *Politicizing Gender*, will be published by Rutgers University Press.

GITA MAY, Professor and Chair of French at Columbia University, is the author of *Diderot et Baudelaire, critiques d'art; De Jean-Jacques Rousseau à Madame Roland, Essai sur la sensibilité préromantique et révolutionnaire; Madame Roland and the Age of Revolution* (winner of Columbia University's Van Amringe Distinguished Book Award); *Stendhal and the Age of Napoleon*. She has written numerous articles and reviews, and has edited Diderot's *Essais sur la peinture* for the complete critical edition of Diderot's works, and co-edited *Diderot Studies III*.

NANCY K. MILLER is Distinguished Professor of English at Lehman College and the Graduate Center, CUNY. She is the author of *The Heroine's Text: Readings in the French and English Novel, 1722–1782* and *Subject to Change: Reading Feminist Writing*. She is the editor of *The Poetics of Gender*, and co-editor with Joan DeJean of *Displacements: Women, Tradition, Literatures in French*.

KURT MUELLER-VOLLMER is Professor of German Studies and Humanities at Stanford University. He studied in Germany, France, and the United States. He has written books on Dilthey, Herder, Humboldt, Goethe, and hermeneutics, as well as numerous articles on European Romanticism, Staël, Vico, language theory and German-French and German-American literary relations.

ISABELLE NAGINSKI is Associate Professor of French at Tufts University and the author of *George Sand: Writing for Her Life*, published by Rutgers University Press in 1991. She has written extensively on romanticism and the nineteenth-century novel.

ELLEN PEEL is Assistant Professor in the Departments of World and Comparative Literature and of English at San Francisco State University. Her major interests are the novel, literary theory, and feminist criticism and theory. Her work on Staël is part of a book in progress: "Beyond Utopia: Persuasion, Narrative, and Skeptical Feminism."

ENGLISH SHOWALTER, JR., is Professor of French at Rutgers, Camden. He has written frequently on eighteenth-century fiction and is currently part of a team editing the correspondence of Françoise de Graffigny.

EVE SOURIAN, Professor of French at the City College and Graduate Center of CUNY, is the author of *Madame de Staël et Henri Heine: Les Deux Allemagnes* (Marcel Didier, 1974) and the editor of *Nouvelles: La Marquise, Lavinia, Metella, Pauline* by George Sand (Les Editions des Femmes, 1986). She has written many articles on Staël and Sand. Her critical introduction to Sand's *Isidora* was published in 1990 by Les Editions des Femmes.

KARYNA SZMURLO, Assistant Professor of French at Clemson University, taught previously at Rutgers University where she organized the first international conference on Staël in the United States (1988). She has written on both eighteenth- and nineteenth-century women writers, performing arts, and language theory. Currently, she is preparing a book called "Performative Discourses: Germaine de Staël."

SUSAN TENENBAUM is Assistant Professor of Political Science at Baruch College, CUNY. Her areas of specialization are public policy, public finance, and political theory. She is the author of numerous articles on Staël and the Coppet Circle. Presently she is working on a book entitled "The Political Thought of Germaine de Staël."

MARIE-CLAIRE VALLOIS, Associate Professor at Miami University, is the author of *Fictions féminines: Mme de Staël et les voix de la Sibylle*. She has written on both eighteenth- and nineteenth-century authors (Montesquieu, Diderot, Chateaubriand, and Hugo). She is currently completing a study to be called "Changing Places: Women, Fiction, Revolution (1735–1848)."

INDEX

abuse of language, 57–58
accrual of literary texts, 156–158.
  See also intertextuality; "reworking" pattern
Aeschylus, *The Eumenides*, 84
aesthetics, 87–88, 116
Alders, Etta Palm d', 176
Alexander I (czar), 30
Alfieri, Vittorio, *Octavie*, 57n10
alienation, 185
allegory, 8, 18, 75, 77, 81, 108,
  114–116, 195
American: culture, 142, 147n22,
  149, 151; history, 148n26; literature, 141–158; Revolution, 14
anagnorisis, 64
ancien régime, 43–45, 115, 116,
  117, 168
Ancillon, Frédéric, *Tableau of the
  Revolutions* . . . , 25
Andlau, Béatrice d', 133n10
anger, female, 107–110, 107n12,
  111, 127
Anglophilia, 61, 162. *See also* England
anthropomorphism in fiction, 86–
  87, 90–91
antifeminism, x, 2, 2n5, 14–15, 227

antithetical tensions: in discourse
  formation, 2, 9–10; in history, 4,
  165, 167; in philosophy, 3–4
"anxiety of influence," 35. *See also*
  father
aphasia, 5–6. *See also* silence
Apollo, 50, 83, 84, 116
archeological quest, 91–93
aristocracy, 44, 46, 120; values of,
  115, 117, 120
Aristotle, 30, 32
Armida, 128
Armstrong, Nancy, *Desire and Domestic Fiction*, 114–115
Astorg, Bertrand d', 31n13
Austen, Jane, 227
authenticity, 79
authority, feminine, 8
authorship metaphor, 34–35, 161–
  162
autonomy, through suicide, 71–72

Bachelard, Gaston, 1n1, 2
Bachofen, J., *Du règne de la mère au
  patriarcat*, 84, 84n5
Balayé, Simone, 3n9, 13–21, 35n4,
  36n6, 37n7, 42n2, 44n6, 51,
  55n2, 56, 56n4, 65, 71n6, 74n16,

Balayé Simone (*continued*)
76n23, 80n31, 80n33, 82n1,
86n13, 87, 102, 102n3, 113, 131,
164, 228, 233
Balzac, Honoré de, 186
Bancroft, George, 142, 147–
149; *The History of the United
States . . .* , 148, 148n26; *Studies
in German Literature*, 149n27
Barthélemy, abbé Jean-Jacques, *Voy-
age du jeune Anacharsis en Grèce*,
8, 123, 132
Baudelaire, Charles, 77
Beauvoir, Simone de, 189; *The Sec-
ond Sex*, 189, 193–194
Becq, Annie, 3n9
Bédé, Jean-Albert, 172n7, 179
Behler, Ernst, 60n27
Belgioioso, Cristina Trivulzio,
princess, 9
Bender, Karlheinz, 24n5
Benjamin, Walter, 69, 78; *Origins of
the German Trauerspiel*, 79
Bernadotte, Jean, 20
Bloom, Harold, 35
body: female (metaphoric), 6; male,
124–125, 127–128
Boehme, Jakob, 157
Bonaparte, Caroline, 124–125
Bonaparte, Napoleon. *See* Napoleon
I
Bonnet, Jean-Claude, 165n1
Bosse, Monika, 72n11, 151n36
Bouineau, Jacques, 25n7
bourgeoisie, values of, 115–117,
120
Bowman, Frank Paul, 6, 55–68, 80,
80n33, 84n6, 116n15, 165–166,
233
Braun, Frederick Augustus, 150n34
Broglie, Victor de, 164
Brontë, Charlotte, 227; *Jane Eyre*,
189
Brookner, Anita, 116n15
Brooks, Charles Timothy, 150
Brooks, Peter, 78
Browning, Elizabeth Barrett, 9, 227
Burke, Edmund, 161
Byron, George Gordon, Lord, 82,
152

Calderón de la Barca, Pedro, *La
Vida es sueño*, 79
calumny, 57
Calvert, George H., 150
Cameron, Kenneth Walter, 155n53
canon, literary, 2, 2n5, 82, 114–
115, 227
Caramaschi, Enzo, 102n3
Carlyle, Thomas, 152–154, 152n38;
"Novalis" [essay], 153–154
Carmagnole des muses, La, 165n1
Casanova de Seingalt, Giovanni Gia-
como, *Story of My Life*, 31
categorical imperative, 60
Cather, Willa, 227
Catholic Church, values of, 169
Cato the Younger, 73–74, 170
censorship, 17, 58, 65
Channing, Edward T., 148–149
Channing, William H., 151, 152n38
Charles I [of England], 27
Charrière, Mme de, 67
Charron, Pierre, 168
Chateaubriand, François René,
vicomte de, 6, 32n16, 84–87,
114, 197, 227; *Le Génie du chris-
tianisme*, 96; *La lettre . . . sur la
campagne romaine*, 86, 171;
Mémoires d'outre-tombe, 32, 122,
177
Chaussard, J.-B., *Fêtes et courtisanes
de la Grèce*, 125
Child, Lydia Maria, 227
chora, 80n35, 94, 94n31
Christianity, 49, 84n6, 183
Christian morality, 169, 172–173
Cixous, Hélène, 2, 2n8
Clarke, James Freeman, 150,
152n38
class, in the Republic, 115–117
classicism, 178, 183
Coleridge, Samuel Taylor, 152–153,
152n38
communication, 5–6, 55–56, 75,
80, 103; flattery and, 57; hypocrisy and, 63–66; impeded, 62–67;
irony and, 59–60; non-verbal, 62.
See also abuse of language; eloquence; inauthentic discourse;
silence; "white lies"

conditional tense, 4–5, 30, 39–40, 165, 167
Condorcet, Marie Jean Antoine Caritat, marquis de, 26
conscience, 106
considération, 4, 23
Constant, Benjamin, 42, 58, 67, 80n32, 167, 188, 197
Constituent Assembly [France 1789], 16, 34–35, 35n34, 38, 44, 161, 165
constitution, English, 35, 35n5, 38–39, 162
constitutional system, 28, 44
control through suicide, 71, 74
conversation, 36, 38, 38n8, 67; inauthentic, 64–65
Coppet, Group of, 3, 55, 60n27, 143n8
Corneille, Pierre, *Le Cid*, 45
correspondence theory, 156n56, 158, 158n62
cosmopolitanism, 3, 17–18
Coulet, Henri, 43, 113
counter-Revolution, 22–23, 50
Cousin, Victor, 152n38
Couthon, Georges, 57
creativity, 2, 80–81, 162, 195. *See also* conversation; improvisation; voice
crisis scenes, 65
Crocker, Lester G., 169n2
cultural: identity, 147–149; values, and women, 195
Cumean Sibyl, 83, 88
Curchod, Suzanne. *See* Necker, Suzanne
Cybèle, 94

Dante Alighieri, 194
David, Jacques-Louis, 116
death, 75–78; in *Corinne*, 92, 108–110; and rebirth, 87, 92, 103–104; and romantics, 87. *See also* suicide
death wish, in *Corinne*, 110
dechristianization, 49
deciphering, 90–91, 90n24, 93
Declaration of the Rights of Man . . . , 43
dédoublement, 75

Degérando, Joseph M., 62; *Des signes et de l'art de penser* . . . , 96
DeJean, Joan, 8–9, 9n14, 82n1, 122–137, 122n1, 178–179, 181, 194, 196n4, 228, 233
Delcourt, Marie, 84n5
delegation of discourse, 90–91
Delon, Michel, 3–4, 3n9, 22–33, 24n3, 25n8, 32n15, 164–167, 233; "La Métaphore théâtrale dans les *Considérations*" [essay], 167
Delphic Sibyl, 83–84, 88, 90, 94
Delphyné, 84
de Man, Paul, 4
democracy, 47
"dénarré," 167
depopulation, 134–135
despotism, 56–59; oriental, 29n12
destiny, 192; women's, 180, 186, 189–190
Dial, The, 152, 156
Diderot, Denis, 79n30; *Jacques the Fatalist*, 171; *Salons*, 170–171, 171n6; "Sur les femmes," 83n3
Didier, Béatrice, 186n17
Diesbach, Ghislain de, 227
Directorate, 28
disguised revenge, 108–111
displacement, 4–5, 62, 80, 87, 110–111, 114, 165–167
dissident role, of women, 161
divinity, in Transcendentalism, 155, 157
divorce, 47–48
domestic: issues, and history, 115; virtues, 160
double, in *Corinne*, 87–92, 87n18, 87n20, 95, 106, 133–134
dramatic irony, 64
Dwight, John S., 150

Edinburgh Review, 143–44
Eichendorf, Joseph, baron von, 152
eighteenth-century writing, 170, 189. *See also* classicism; philosophes; romanticism
Eliot, George, 188–189, 227
eloquence, 57–59, 103n7, 166; revolutionary, 57, 165n1

Emerson, Ralph Waldo, 146, 146n19, 149–158, 152n38, 152n39, 153n43, 155n48, 155n49; diaries, 156; *Nature* [essay], 9, 141–142, 152–158, 156n56
Empire (First), 29
enchantment, 128
Encyclopaedia Americana, 150
Encyclopédie, 68
England, 14, 34–35, 35n3, 146, 146n20; in *Considerations* . . . , 25, 37; in *Corinne*, 18, 61, 102–103, 102n5, 117–118, 117n17, 132, 191; in *Delphine*, 18; and patriarchy, 191
English: constitution, 35, 35n5, 38–39, 162; literature, 61; philosophy, 146; Revolution, 25
enigmatic language, 88–90
Enlightenment, xi, 14, 23, 25–29, 144, 168; ironic wit of, 59–60
enthusiasm, 92, 96, 96n32, 145–146, 155; and melancholy, 92
epistolary novel, 43, 63, 171
Escarpit, Robert, 35n3
Estates General, 24
ethics, 60. *See also* morality
Everett, Edward, 142, 147, 149

faith, in *Delphine*, 49
fame vs. happiness, for women, 180
family romance, 130
fantasies, 189
fantastic, 87–88
fatalism, 26–27
fate-Erinnye, Corinne as, 107n12
father, 106, 118–120, 130, 134, 166; and king, 118–119; replacement of, 119–120; scriptural affiliation with daughter, 37–40, 161–162, 165
Fauchery, Pierre, 110, 110n20
feeling, 62, 154
female: anger, 8, 9, 107–110, 107n12; counter-discourse, 4–5, 7, 36; epics, 114–115; genius, 195; heritage, 9, 104; imagery, 107–108, 115; and improvisation, 117; scriptural strategies, 5–9, 102–

103, 129; sexuality, 137; suicide, 5, 178. *See also* women
feminine: authority, 8; mystery, 89–90; Other, 91; voice, literary, 2, 38, 94
feminism, 102–103, 102n3, 103n6, 193–197
feminist: criticism, xi, 2, 82n1, 114–115, 227–228; legacy, 196; reading of *Corinne*, 82, 82n1, 114; role of *Corinne*, 120–121
Fénélon, François de Salignac de la Mothe, *Télémaque*, 87
fetishism, 91, 91n27
Fichte, Johann Gottlieb, 152–153, 152n38
fiction. *See* novel; romance
Fink, Beatrice, 164–167, 234
"first mimesis," 194
Flaubert, Gustave, 57, 77
Folkenflik, Vivian, 101, 103, 228
Forsberg, Roberta J., 146n20
Foucault, Michel, 5, 115
France, 14, 30, 36, 40–41, 43, 49–50, 59, 115–117, 152
freedom, 43, 47–48, 50–51, 116–117, 169–170; through divorce, 47; of the press, 58; of speech, 17; through suicide, 71, 74, 170; for women, 47, 75, 189. *See also* liberty
Freidel, Frank B., 150n33
French: language, 129; novel, 197; romanticism, 181; society, during Revolution, 36
French Republican Army, 46
French Revolution. *See* Revolution
Freud, Sigmund, 72–73, 73n14, 80n35, 87n20, 90; *The Uncanny*, 87n18, 88
Frothingham, Paul Revere, 149n29
Fuller, Margaret, 9, 150–152, 152n41, 227

Gaïa, 84, 94
gender, 166, 179; and genre, 190; and language, x, xii, 2, 4–6, 7, 35, 36, 38, 39, 61, 166
generations, in *Corinne*, 196n4
Genette, Gérard, *Figures II*, 1n1